THE RISE OF THE MERCHANT CLASS
IN TOKUGAWA JAPAN, 1600–1868
AN INTRODUCTORY SURVEY

CHARLES DAVID SHELDON

THE RISE
OF THE MERCHANT CLASS
IN TOKUGAWA JAPAN,

1600—1868

AN INTRODUCTORY SURVEY

NEW YORK / RUSSELL & RUSSELL

MONOGRAPHS OF THE ASSOCIATION
FOR ASIAN STUDIES

V

FIRST PUBLISHED, 1958, BY
THE ASSOCIATION FOR ASIAN STUDIES
REISSUED, 1973, BY RUSSELL & RUSSELL
A DIVISION OF ATHENEUM PUBLISHERS, INC.
BY ARRANGEMENT WITH
THE ASSOCIATION FOR ASIAN STUDIES, INC.
L. C. CATALOG CARD NO: 72-97536
ISBN: 0-8462-1725-2
PRINTED IN THE UNITED STATES OF AMERICA

TO

MY WIFE, JACQUELINE

For her patience and understanding during the long student years.

TABLE OF CONTENTS

PREFACE

THERE IS little in the history of the Tokugawa period which is not relevant to the phenomenon of the rise of the merchant class. The present study is an introduction to this vast subject. It is also an introduction and survey of the very large literature of secondary studies by Japanese scholars. There are several rival schools of Japanese economic historians, some of whose work is marred by ideological commitments. I have drawn more from the Kyoto school (especially Honjō, Horie, Miyamoto and Kanno) than any other, as I found it the most lucid and objective, and the least affected by ideological considerations. All material from Japanese sources, whether primary or secondary, has been translated by the author unless otherwise indicated.

This study was written first as a Ph.D. dissertation at the University of California. The chairman of my dissertation committee, Dr. Delmer M. Brown, interested me in Japanese economic history in my undergraduate days, and patiently guided my first studies in this field. I should like to express my warmest appreciation to him. I wish to thank the two other members of the committee, Drs. Toshio George Tsukahira and Denzel Carr, for their many helpful criticisms, suggestions and corrections.

Also, I wish to express my gratitude to the administrators of the Educational Exchange Service, U.S. Department of State, who awarded me a Fulbright scholarship to do research in Japan during the academic year 1953–1954, to the officers of the Ford Foundation who very kindly granted me a supplemental award in the form of a Ford Foundation fellowship, and to the Association for Asian Studies for undertaking the publication of this monograph. My work in Japan was under the guidance of Professor Horie Yasuzō, then Chairman of the Faculty of Economics in Kyoto University, one of the foremost Japanese economic historians.

Professor Horie gave me a desk in his private study and free access to his excellent library. I am deeply indebted to him also for his kind counsel both in seminars and in private discussions, and I am glad to take this opportunity to acknowledge this indebtedness. I wish to thank Mr. Daniel Meloy of the Department of State for proof-reading and helpful suggestions. While acknowledging the assistance of the persons and organizations mentioned here, I take full responsibility for all interpretations and conclusions, as well as for any inadequacies and errors which may remain uncorrected.

NOTE ON JAPANESE NAMES

Japanese personal names are given in the Japanese order, with family name first, and with macrons to indicate long vowels. However, in citing English works by Japanese authors, I have not attempted to add macrons where they do not appear in such works. Also, I have omitted the macrons in the names of the well-known cities of Tokyo, Osaka, and Kyoto, except when they are part of the transliterated title of a book or article.

ABBREVIATIONS

KSK   =   *Keizai Shi Kenkyū*

KUER =   *Kyoto University Economic Review*

NKSJ =   *Nihon Keizai Shi Jiten*

TASJ =   *Transactions of the Asiatic Society of Japan*

INTRODUCTION TO THE SECOND PRINTING

Since this monograph was published at the end of 1958, much work has been done touching on the history of the merchants in the Tokugawa period and since. It has served to modify some of the emphases and conclusions of this book and to add important details to the general picture. My book, as an introductory study, was meant to stimulate such further work. I wrote the book originally not as an economist, although I had had a modicum of training in economics, but as a historian, in an effort to see how the history of the merchants could clarify the larger picture of Japan's historical development. I tried to make use of the best scholarship available at the time.[1] Since the book was first published, my interests have shifted toward general and political history, although I have maintained a certain proprietary interest in the still controversial field of Tokugawa economic history.

Ideally, a new edition would be a revised and expanded one incorporating these new points. Also, some quite justified criticisms have been made in reviews of the book since its first appearance. A new edition should attempt to meet these criticisms, to the extent that the author considers them just. Unfortunately, the economics of the publication of scholarly books have ruled out that possibility.

But fortunately, not long before I was informed by the Association for Asian Studies that this study was to be reissued, I had published a short article in *Modern Asian Studies*, "'Pre-modern' Merchants and Modernization in Japan." This was precisely intended to reconsider the subject in the light of criticisms and more recent scholarship, and to project the chronology of the study into the Meiji period, summarizing briefly some of the more recent scholarship in English bearing on Meiji entrepreneurship and modernization.

Crucial problems of Tokugawa and Meiji economic history which we are now in a slightly better position to understand include the follow-

1 For skilled readers of Japanese, there is now available a book by Naramoto Tatsuya, rather misleadingly entitled *Chōnin no jitsuryoku* (The real power of the townsmen), recently recommended in the *Journal of Asian Studies* as the best study of Tokugawa merchants. I am doubtful. It is an interesting but rambling, undocumented discussion of general Tokugawa history rather than a study of merchants *per se*. It is more impressionistic than analytical, and was not intended as a scholarly study. Those sections concerning the merchants, mostly on their lives and cultural activities, are, however, very interesting and useful.

ing: After the century of remarkable economic expansion, what were the causes of the slowdown which resulted in the "Tokugawa plateau"? How are evidences of increasing productivity after that time compatible with the impoverishment and economic troubles of the non-commercial classes, or, more accurately, those who failed to adjust to the new money economy? Was there an "inevitable contradiction" between the feudal system based on land and the burgeoning commercial economy, with its incipient capitalism? What were the results of the shift of farm land to cash crops in the more developed areas around the cities? To what extent did government policies, especially the *sankin kōtai*, create both the early economic expansion and the later financial and economic troubles? Was a solution to those troubles possible without a major political change? If this new economy really did erode away the feudal system, why was it that perhaps the most feudalistic of domains, Chōshū and Satsuma, combined to bring down the Tokugawa regime? Why did the resulting Imperial government, largely led by samurai from Chōshū and Satsuma, proceed to the surgical removal of the feudal system from the body politic? What role, exactly, did the various types of merchants play in the economic modernization of Meiji times? We have learned something about the great variations in types of provincial merchants, but not a great deal about the social and economic reasons for their emergence. Nor have we learned, or are we likely to learn very much more, about how far the "cash nexus" replaced feudal relationships. My article in *Modern Asian Studies* was intended to summarize the general lines suggested by more recent work. The gaps in our knowledge are still great, and we can hope for progress. But inherent inadequacies in basic data, especially the lack of reliable Tokugawa period statistics, will probably prevent ultimate solutions to these questions.

I am very grateful that the publishers of this reissue have agreed to reprint the article as an appendix to this book. I hope it will serve as a useful summary of my more recent thoughts on the subject, in the context of Japan's historical development, and that it will go some way towards meeting justified criticisms and towards bringing the study up to date in terms of recent scholarship.

CHARLES D. SHELDON

January 1973, University of Cambridge, Cambridge, England

INTRODUCTION

AMONG STUDENTS of Japan, it is a truism that the unprecedented rise of the money economy and the merchants who controlled it signalled the decline of the feudal society and made an important contribution to the fall of the Tokugawa regime. It is also generally accepted that in the development of the modern state, the weakness of the merchant class as compared to European counterparts meant that the merchant class did not lead, but rather was led by circumstances into a compromise with feudal elements in the Meiji Restoration, enabling the "former feudal leaders and the feudal outlook to exercise far greater influence than in most other modern societies."[1]

A study of the process and an analysis of the extent to which the merchants, the lowest in the class structure, gradually achieved power in a restrictive feudal society has yet to be done in a Western language. Even in Japanese, it has not received a treatment which could be called definitive,[2] although literally thousands of treatises and studies have been written by Japanese scholars during the last three hundred years touching on this phenomenon and the problems arising from it. The question of what to do with the upstart merchant class which was disturbing the feudal relationships was a problem which exercised economic thinkers of the period, and was one which defied solution in practice.

The main points which we have selected for an attack on the problem of the rise of the merchant class can be expressed in the following questions. The present study proposes to answer them, in each of nine chapters:

[1] E. Herbert Norman, *Japan's Emergence as a Modern State* (New York: 1940), 5.

[2] The closest to a full study is the small volume, unfortunately only partially documented, by Sakata Yoshio 坂田吉雄, *Chōnin* 町人 [The Townsmen] (Tokyo: 1939). It is a descriptive essay rather than a historical treatment.

1

1. How was the rise of the merchant class possible ?
2. What was the merchants' social and political position ?
3. How did the merchants organize themselves in their search for security ?
4. How and to what extent did they gain financial power ?
5. When did they achieve a degree of security, and what effect did this have on Japanese culture and society ?
6. What was the historical development of the merchants after this time ?
7. What did contemporary scholars (including merchant scholars) have to say about this force which was proving subversive to feudal interests ?
8. What was the new competitive mercantile force of the last years of the Tokugawa period and what effect did it have ?
9. What significance did the rise of the merchant class have for Japanese culture, society and economy ?

By dealing with these questions, it is our intention to outline the history of the merchant class in the period. Economic and social changes, usually gradual, do not lend themselves easily to chronological treatment. We have therefore selected an essentially topical approach within a roughly chronological framework, attempting to maintain a historical perspective throughout.

The Tokugawa period was one of transition from a feudal political structure, with feudal economic relations, towards a capitalistic economic structure largely within the feudal system. It is therefore filled with paradoxes and conflicts. The post-Restoration period is by no means unique in Japan for its conflicts between the old and the new. To understand the changes which took place in Tokugawa Japan, it is essential to understand the role of the merchant class which was, as a class, the most important factor in these changes.

Modern Japan is a complex amalgam of the materials of traditional Japan combined with, and greatly changed by, the multifarious influences of the modern West. In the present Japanese economic system, with its close political ties, "feudal remains" — a term often used but seldom clearly understood — are still very much in evidence. A study of the pre-modern economy is of importance to an understanding of present problems, as well as for its contribution to a more complete insight into the history of Tokugawa times.

CHAPTER I

THE HISTORICAL BACKGROUND AND DEVELOPMENT TO THE EXCLUSION EDICTS OF 1638

THE FIRST Europeans to reach Japan in 1542 found her in the throes of an internal conflict, a time of trouble known as the *sengoku jidai* 戰國時代 (the age of the country at war). War which had been frequent before had become endemic since the outbreak of the Ōnin war in 1467. The feudal lords were eager to establish commercial relations with the Europeans, and an important new foreign trade sprang up. Moreover, domestic commerce began to change in organization and to take the first significant steps towards a nation-wide commercial economy with the breakdown of old feudal barriers by Nobunaga, whose policy of incorporation of large conquered territories included the freeing of commerce from some of the existing restraints. The unification of the country was carried further by Hideyoshi and established on a stable basis by Tokugawa Ieyasu by his victory in the battle of Sekigahara in 1600. The ensuing "pax Tokugawa" which lasted for 267 years, appropriately called "the Great Peace,"[1] was of vast importance to the development of commerce and to the rise of the merchant class.

In economic terms, commerce functions as a mediator to bring producers and consumers together. The development of commerce, then, requires a separation both in space and time of producer and consumer. For commerce to exist as a separate activity, it is necessary that there be a continuous excess in the production of goods. It is very clear that this situation existed in both agriculture and industry from the first years of the Tokugawa period, and there was a close inter-relationship between the increase in production and the rapid development of commerce. Different from the earlier self-sufficiency

---

[1] *Tenka Taihei* 天下太平, a common expression of the time. Akabori Mata-jirō 赤堀又次郎, "Tokugawa Jidai no Shōnin 德川時代の商人" [The Merchants of the Tokugawa Period], *Nihon Shōnin Shi* 日本商人史 [A History of Japanese Merchants] (Tokyo: 1935), 188.

of the feudal economy, where the bulk of the production not con-
sumed by the producers was bartered or sold directly to the consumers, the Tokugawa period was one in which the bulk of production went through the hands of merchants as intermediaries. This
development of "merchant commerce"[2] reached its height in the
famous Genroku era (1688–1703) and from then on maintained itself
on a high level throughout the rest of the period.

The so-called "unification" of the country under the Tokugawa
which was of such great significance to commerce requires some
definition. It was by no means the political and economic integration
seen in a modern national state. In a sense it was a military truce with
elaborate safeguards, under an alliance between two powerful groups
of feudal lords (daimyō 大 名), those who fought with Ieyasu at
Sekigahara and those who fought against him. The Tokugawa domains (tenryō 天 領) covered about one-fourth the area of the
country and were distributed in 47 out of 68 provinces. The rest of
the area was a checkerboard with squares assigned to the fudai
("inner") lords who had fought with Ieyasu and who were in hereditary vassalage to the Tokugawa house, and with the other squares
assigned to the tozama ("outer") lords whose loyalty was somewhat
questionable.[3] The feudal lords all enjoyed a considerable degree of
autonomy. In many aspects, the economy of the Tokugawa period
was not a single one, but two: that of the Tokugawa bureaucracy
(the Bakufu 幕 府) and that of the feudal lords. However, the

[2] A term commonly used by Japanese economic historians to differentiate the
Tokugawa type of commerce from earlier commerce. Cf. Kanno Watarō
菅 野 和 太 郎, Nihon Shōgyō Shi 日 本 商 業 史 [Commercial History of
Japan] (Tokyo: 1930), 74, and the volume under the same title by Miyamoto
Mataji 宮 本 又 次 (Tokyo: 1943), 137.

[3] See James Murdoch, A History of Japan (London: 1926), I, 1–61 for a detailed analysis of the Tokugawa political system. In 1602, there were 119
fudai and 72 tozama lords, as well as 4 collateral members of the Tokugawa
family. There were numerous changes, and in 1866, there were 145 fudai,
97 tozama, and 23 collateral houses. See Toshio George Tsukahira, The Sankin
Kōtai System of Tokugawa Japan (Unpublished Ph. D. Dissertation, Harvard University: June, 1951) 27–8. For a list of daimyō with classifications,
see Honjō Eijirō, 本 庄 榮 治 郎 ed., Nihon Keizai Shi Jiten 日 本 經 濟
史 辭 典 [Dictionary of Japanese Economic History] (Tokyo: 1940),
975–991.

unification was without doubt the most effective in Japanese history, and herein lies perhaps the most basic difference between the Tokugawa period and earlier times.

The stabilization of economic life which resulted from the establishment of peace permitted an increase in population and a greater increase in the amount of land under cultivation,[4] as well as a rise in agricultural productivity. It is generally accepted that there was more variation in crops and that there were important improvements in agricultural techniques at this time, notably the increased use of iron implements[5] and the use of tread-mills which "in the early Tokugawa Period ... were generally popularized."[6] These factors combine to supply an economic explanation for the migration from the country to the city which occurred in the years before and during the Tokugawa period, and the resulting increase in agricultural production over population created excess goods for commerce and an increase in the standard of living.

Paralleling the increase in agricultural efficiency which freed peasants from the land in the economic sense was an unprecedented development of towns and cities. They existed on a comparatively small scale during the early *sengoku* period, but expanded greatly in the late sixteenth century in part due to the use of firearms which necessitated the building of large castles and in part due to the larger concentrations of fighting men around the fewer and more powerful feudal lords who emerged in the sixteenth century. Previously,

[4] The area of land under cultivation was almost doubled in the period 1600 to 1730. Matsuyoshi Sadao 松好貞夫, "Tokugawa Bakufu no Kaikon Seisaku Kanken 徳川幕府の開墾政策管見 [A Personal Interpretation of the Policy for the Increase of Arable Land of the Tokugawa *Bakufu*], *Keizai Shi Kenkyū* 經濟史研究 [Studies in Economic History] (henceforth cited as *KSK*), XIII, 3 (Mar. 1935), 13–14. As for population, no census figures are available for the years before 1721, but Ryoichi Ishii, in *Population Pressure and Economic Life in Japan* (London, 1937), 3, 8, quotes an estimate of the population in the period 1573–1591 at 18 million, and for the Genroku period (1688–1703) at 26 million.

[5] Yosoburo (sic) Takekoshi, *The Economic Aspects of the Civilization of Japan* (New York: 1930), I, 370.

[6] Takao Tsuchiya, *An Economic History of Japan*, Transactions of the Asiatic Society of Japan (hereafter cited as *TASJ*), 2nd Series, XV (Dec. 1937), 155.

castles were generally built on mountains or hilltops, for purely military reasons. Now, they began to be built on the plains where transportation facilities were good. Commercial centers grew up around these castles.[7] The expansion of castle towns was accelerated in the Tokugawa period by the migration of peasants, merchants and artisans to the towns to provide the samurai with all the necessities of life as well as military supplies. This separation of the samurai from the small agricultural community brought the merchant into prominence as a mediator in trade and ushered in the period of merchant commerce. The samurai crowded into the castle towns found it difficult to barter their stipend rice for other goods. Moreover, "not only was the exchange value of rice extremely unstable, but its use as money raised the problem of storage. Therefore, it became necessary for them to exchange it for specie."[8] Ogyū Sorai (1666–1728) described the samurai as living a "hotel existence." Sorai deplored this situation: "As in hotel life one must needs buy all things necessary for living, money is the most important thing for travellers. Never in any age since the foundation of the country has money been so indispensable to life as during the last hundred years."[9]

The ranks of the merchants and artisans in the castle towns were swollen in large part by peasants, but also by samurai. Merchants' of samurai descent were particularly numerous and successful during the last years of the *sengoku* period and the first years of the Tokugawa. Some examples are the houses of Suminokura 角倉 and Chaya 茶屋, who made their money in foreign trade. The Chaya were once drapers and purveyors of silks for Tokugawa Ieyasu.[10] Other families

---

[7] For a standard study of castle towns but written in a difficult style, see Ono Kin 小野均, *Kinsei Jōka-machi no Kenkyū* 近世城下町の研究 [A Study of Castle Towns in the Early Modern Period] (Tokyo: 1928). For an excellent and suggestive study in English, see the article by John W. Hall, "The Castle Town and Japan's Modern Urbanization," *Far Eastern Quarterly* XV, 1 (Nov. 1955), 37–56.

[8] Kanno, *Nihon Shōgyō Shi*, op. cit., 84.

[9] *Taiheisaku* 太平策, in *Nihon Keizai Sōsho* 日本經濟叢書 [Japanese Economic Series] (Tokyo: 1914–17), III, 554–5, as translated in Eijiro Honjo, *The Social and Economic History of Japan* (Kyoto: 1935), 123.

[10] Honjō Eijirō, ed., *Nihon Keizai Shi Jiten*, op. cit., 1055. Henceforth, *NKSJ*. For the Suminokura, see *ibid.*, 893–4.

who have continued to flourish are the Mitsui 三井, Sumitomo 住友 and Kōnoike 鴻池.[11] Many of the merchants of Ōmi 近江 province who played such a leading role in the commerce of the Tokugawa period were descended from samurai.[12]

People settled in the new castle towns not merely under the natural stimulus of commercial opportunities. It was common for the feudal lords to encourage this settlement actively. This was a notable feature of Nobunaga's policy which was motivated by the military necessity of providing food, shelter and a continuing supply of arms for large concentrations of troops. It has been pointed out[13] that the usual assumption that Nobunaga was the protector of commerce should not be accepted without asking the reason. It appears that from the first, he compromised with new economic forces already fairly well entrenched in order to use them in forwarding his overriding ambition to consolidate his military power. When he entered Kyoto in 1568, he was offered territories by the Shogun, but he rejected them for direct control of Ōtsu and Kusatsu, both markets on the road to Kyoto. Ōtsu was an important port on Lake Biwa, in Ōmi, in the fief of the Sasaki family, who were the first to break down the established monopolies and establish a free market (*rakuichi* 樂市) in 1539.[14]

Besides the Buddhist organizations which proved formidable enemies for Nobunaga, there were several commercial towns which had gained a considerable degree of autonomy during the Ashikaga period and which had proved their fighting ability. The most striking examples were those which combined foreign with domestic trade and commissariat functions for the armies engaged in the wars of the *sengoku* period. The most famous was Sakai, a port south of Osaka,

---

[11] *NKSJ*, 1559–61; 892–3; 523–4. The first two are prominent zaibatsu families, the third, a lesser zaibatsu, operates one of the major banks, the Sanwa Ginkō.

[12] Kanno, *Nihon Shōgyō Shi*, op. cit., 131. There is some doubt as to the validity of Mitsui's claims to samurai extraction.

[13] Yoshimura Miyao 吉村宮男, "Edo Jidai ni okeru Shōgyō no Seishitsu 江戸時代に於ける商業の性質" [The Nature of Commerce in the Edo Period], *Rekishi Kyōiku* 歴史教育 [History and Education], XI, 3 (1936), 196–7.

[14] *Ibid.*, 195. For *rakuichi-rakuza* 樂市樂座, free markets and guilds, see *NKSJ*, 1669–71. Kusatsu was at the junction of two important roads, the Tōkaidō and the Nakasendō.

whose citizens opposed the feudal lords successfully, building bamboo palisades and surrounding themselves with huge moats.[15] The artisans of Sakai were the most famed makers of weapons, especially guns, in Japan.[16] Hakata in Kyūshū and Ōminato on Ise Bay were largely self-governed. For a time, Nagasaki was also self-governed.[17] Kuwana, a port in Ise Bay, showed the desire to be self-governing when it disregarded feudal commands, only to be forcefully subjugated.[18] Lending large sums to feudal lords in return for privileges was one source of strength. Also, the phenomenon of payment of taxes in money and the contracting for taxes by established merchants and residents of market cities became the powerful means by which merchants liberated themselves from the lords. In addition, constant changes of port towns from one feudal lord to another during the *sengoku* period gave opportunity for the development of merchant-controlled administration, a necessity for order and continuity of government, as in the case of Muro (near present Tatsuno, in Hyōgo Prefecture) whose power in the sixteenth century forced other ports to admit Muro boats tax-free.[19]

Self-governing commercial towns began to flourish just at the time when decentralized feudalism was being centralized. The centralizers, Nobunaga, Hideyoshi and Ieyasu, all understood the importance of economic power, and their encouragement of commerce and merchants, although effective in promoting their mutual interests, was not ultimately a policy to add to the merchants' freedom of action. They encouraged merchants to settle in their cities and treated them generously, but did not permit them to gain a political position comparable to the merchants of Sakai. Osaka and Edo furnish the most important examples of this policy.

The so-called "three cities" of the Tokugawa period were Edo, Osaka, and Kyoto. They were the chief cities controlled directly by

[15] Miyamoto, *Nihon Shōgyō Shi, op. cit.*, 117.
[16] Takekoshi Yosaburō 竹越與三郎, *Nihon Keizai Shi* 日本經濟史 [The Economic History of Japan] (Tokyo: 3rd ed., 1936), III, 274.
[17] Takekoshi, *Economic Aspects* . ., I, 327.
[18] Miyamoto, 177.
[19] Takekoshi, *Economic Aspects* . ., I, 359.

the *Bakufu*. Others included Sakai, Nagasaki, Ōtsu, and Sumpu. Kyoto, the Imperial city, had been important for centuries, but Edo and Osaka were both new. Much of the economic history of the Tokugawa period could be written about these two cities.[20]

At the beginning of the *sengoku* period, the town of Osaka consisted of only a small branch temple with its commercial district (*monzen machi*). In 1533 it became the headquarters of the Shin Sect, and grew rapidly in size and power to 1580. It was in a strategic situation with the Inland Sea on the west, and the Yodogawa, a most important waterway to Kyoto, winding about in marshy fields on the other three sides.[21] For ten years (1570–80), Osaka repelled various attacks by Nobunaga, but finally capitulated. When Hideyoshi took over power at Nobunaga's death in 1582, he built (1583–6) the largest castle in Japan in Osaka and made it his capital, having selected it primarily for its strategic position. Hideyoshi did not want nearby Sakai as a military rival. However, he did not attack it, but was successful in having its wide moats filled in. Then he encouraged its merchants to move to Osaka, many of whom did.[22] There were ample opportunities for merchants in Osaka, and many made fortunes. For example, Yodoya Keian, a war contractor for Hideyoshi, became a land speculator in Osaka, and founded one of the most famous of Osaka merchant houses.[23]

Osaka under Hideyoshi became the major collection point for troops and supplies for the Korean campaigns. After 1615, when the fall of Osaka eliminated the last rivals of Ieyasu, Osaka was no longer an important political center, but an important system of canals was built, a number of merchants were brought from Fushimi, near Kyoto,

---

[20] Cf. Kōda Shigetomo 幸田成友, *Edo to Ōsaka* 江戸と大阪 [Edo and Osaka] (Tokyo: 1934). Portions of this work are translated in Neal Skene Smith, ed., "Materials on Japanese Social and Economic History: Tokugawa Japan," *TASJ*, 2nd Series, XIV (June 1937), 35, 51–75; 79–116; 123–6; 137–47; 164–7. Sumpu is the present Shizuoka.

[21] Osaka Municipal Council (大阪市参事會), comp., *Ōsaka Shi Shi* 大阪市史 [History of the City of Osaka], I, 93.

[22] Royal Wald, *The Development of Osaka during the 16th Century* (Unpublished M.A. thesis, Univ. of Calif., 1947), 57–8. The writer has relied mainly upon this study for the summary of Osaka's early development given here.

[23] Takekoshi, *Economic Aspects*.., II, 242, 246–7.

and it became the commercial center of Japan. The *daimyō* of the Kantō and Ōu districts built warehouses (*kurayashiki*) in Edo, but others built in Osaka. Temples and shrines did likewise, so that there were five or six hundred such warehouses in Osaka, mostly built in the early years of the Tokugawa.[24] Industry as well as commerce flourished there, and as vast amounts of goods, including food, were collected and processed for consumers all over the country, Osaka came to be called the "kitchen" of Japan.[25]

Edo was a village of not more than a hundred houses of farmers and townsmen when Ieyasu first saw it in 1590, but after the battle of Sekigahara he made it his capital and began work on the castle and on large scale land reclamation and canal projects.[26] He invited merchants to Edo, offering free business sites.[27] The traditional tax on houses and lots upon which houses were built (*chishi-sen* 地子錢) was not levied in Edo until 1696.[28] The townsmen of Osaka were excused indefinitely from paying these taxes, and from time to time residents of Kyoto, Nara and other towns were similarly favored.[29] In addition, money gifts were even distributed by the Shogun among the townspeople of the "three cities," on festive occasions.[30]

With this favorable combination of policies and natural economic forces, the cities grew rapidly. Osaka's population (excluding samurai) was 279,610, according to a census taken in 1625.[31] In 1634, the first

[24] Yoshimura, *op. cit.*, 198.

[25] *NKSJ*, 141.

[26] *Ibid.*, 119.

[27] Takekoshi, *Economic Aspects..*, I, 523.

[28] *Ibid.*, 538. For *chishi-sen* (also called *jishi-sen*), see *NKSJ*, 1043. The concessions and encouragements to Edo and Osaka townspeople before 1615 suggest a certain competition between Ieyasu and the remnants of the Hideyoshi adherents.

[29] Sakata, *Chōnin*, 5-6. Nobunaga and Hideyoshi adopted this policy on several occasions. Ono, in his study of castle towns, *op. cit.*, 54, has found examples of exemption from *chishi-sen* before 1555, but early examples were usually due to the fact that emergency exactions had been made.

[30] Sakata, 5.

[31] The method of census-taking seems to have been to count houses and to ask the people how many lived in each house, a method which, according to contemporary accounts, left out large numbers. Matsuyo Takizawa, *The Penetration of Money Economy in Japan* (New York: 1927), 52. The purpose of the census was tax collecting. The samurai population were not included

figures available for Kyoto show a town population of 410,089. However, by 1721, when the first census was taken in Edo, the population of townsmen had surpassed that of both Osaka and Kyoto, with a recorded 501,394.[32] Considering the fact that the samurai population was far greater in Edo, its total population may well have reached over 800,000.[33] The economic needs of these large population concentrations spurred the development of transportation, the money economy and commerce, as well as commercial credit among merchants of the "three cities." It put the cities in a position of dependence upon the merchants who controlled this new commercial economy. It was a degree of dependence totally unknown in earlier times.

In the field of commodity circulation as well as in the establishment and control of cities, the policy developed first to break up the old system, and then to reform it into a new system. This was the function of the *rakuichi-rakuza* (free markets and guilds).[34] Nobunaga, no doubt learning from feudal lords like the Sasaki of Ōtsu, carried out a thoroughgoing program in his territories of denying the special privileges of the existing trading and market guilds (*za*) and decreeing open access to all types of markets and trading activities. This policy, continued by Hideyoshi, created free fairs and markets which were exempted from all taxes, and the merchants were permitted to deal with any disorders in the markets without interference from the feudal lords.[35] Merchants from other districts were permitted to engage freely in business with free guilds (*rakuza*) and in free ports (*rakushin* 樂 津) where vessels could enter taxfree. Although peasants

---

because they were not taxed, and also because their numbers were military secrets. Ono Takeo 小 野 武 夫, *Nōson Shakai Shi Ronkō* 農 村 社 會 史 論 講 [Discussions on the Social History of Peasant Villages] (Tokyo: 3rd ed., 1935), 110.

[32] Honjō Eijirō, *Jinkō oyobi Jinkō Mondai* 人 口 及 び 人 口 問 題 [Population and Population Problems] (Tokyo: 1930), 91.

[33] Smith, *op. cit.*, 35, estimates the samurai population of Edo at the time of the Restoration at something over 400,000, since the nation-wide total of samurai and their families in 1872 reached about two million.

[34] Miyamoto, *Nihon Shōgyō Shi*, op. cit., 177.

[35] Yokoi Tokifuyu 横 井 時 冬 *Nihon Shōgyō Shi* 日 本 商 業 史 [Commercial History of Japan] (Tokyo: 1926), 182.

were prohibited from leaving their native provinces, merchants were allowed to engage freely in commerce in other districts. It was common for *daimyō* to compete with one another in attracting trading ships, domestic as well as foreign, to their ports.[36] Towns where merchants were predominant, like Nagasaki, Sakai, and Hirano offered free access to merchants, and their number was swelled greatly by the *rakuichi-rakuza* policy of Nobunaga and other feudal lords. Under the Tokugawa, *Bakufu* commercial centers afforded free access to merchants, as did many of the castle towns of the *daimyō*. However, this policy of commercial freedom was far from complete from the first. Both Nobunaga and Hideyoshi granted monopoly rights to certain new guilds, under their protection.[37] The major change was the elimination of old type guilds (*za*) under the protection of temples, shrines and ancient noble families (*kuge* 公家), and this was a definite contribution to the freedom of commerce. At the same time, the tendency from the first was for the feudal lords to incorporate new types of commercial organizations under their control either by granting them special rights or merely by silent assent.[38] Their desire for economic autonomy in their own domains (*han* 藩) led them to restrict the number of towns and ports to which merchants of other *han* were permitted free access.[39]

Barriers (*sekisho* 關所, or merely *seki*), erected as early as Nara times, multiplied during the Ashikaga period along the roads, rivers and in harbors. There were three hundred and eighty along the Yodo River and thirty along the coast of Ise.[40] *Sekisho* were established for military and economic reasons, and persons as well as goods which

---

[36] Yokoi, *Nihon Shōgyō Shi*, 182.

[37] *NKSJ*, 1670–1. These new guilds were still called *za*, but the new type of guilds which evolved in the early Tokugawa had different names.

[38] *Ibid.*

[39] In the same way that the *Bakufu* limited foreign trade to one port — Nagasaki — the *daimyō* fixed the number of ports in their territories (often designating only one) where boats from other *han* were permitted entrance. Horie Yasuzō 堀江保藏, "Tokugawa Jidai no Suijō Kōtsū 德川時代の水上交通 "[Water Transportation of the Tokugawa Period], *KSK*, xiv, 1 (July, 1935), 83.

[40] *NKSJ*, 908. The Yodo River, which flows into the Inland Sea at Osaka from the junction of the Katsura and the Uji, is only about 49 miles long.

passed through were taxed. They were important obstacles to commerce, and Nobunaga began in 1568 to abolish them in territories under his control. Hideyoshi continued the process.[41] This policy was essential to the unification of the country, and was continued in the Tokugawa period, when the private construction of *sekisho* was prohibited, and the function of existing *sekisho* specifically limited to policing.[42]

The policy of abolishing *sekisho* and the change in their function did much to clear the way for commercial goods to pass from one part of the country to another. This did not mean, however, that there were no more obstacles. Barriers were still maintained in many of the feudal domains (*han*), where, in the final analysis, the *daimyō* could do as they wished. The movement of commerce was really free only over *Bakufu* territories and between *Bakufu* ports, as the feudal lords restrained trade in various ways within their own domains while pursuing their policies of maintaining a self-sufficient economy and preventing the outflow of money.[43]

Provincial economy arose in the middle ages with the establishment of territories by the feudal lords. This was made possible by the fact that the domains comprised a natural economic zone, as they were generally centralized in one area, not scattered about as were the *shōen* ("manors") of the nobility and of the temples. During the

---

[41] Kanno, *Nihon Shōgyō Shi*, 75–79. Cf. Curtis A. Manchester, *The Development and Distribution of Sekisho in Japan* (Unpub. Ph.D. dissertation, Univ. of Michigan, 1946).

[42] Horie Yasuzō, *Kinsei Nihon no Keizai Seisaku* 近世日本の經濟政策 [Economic Policies of Japan in the Early Modern Period] (Tokyo: 1942), 113. By *Kinsei* Professor Horie means the Tokugawa period, but some writers define it as beginning with the first coming of the Portuguese in 1542 or 1543, or with 1568, when Nobunaga established himself in Kyoto as *de facto* Shogun. Since the term is used to differentiate it from *kindai* 近代, also translated "modern," these terms seem best translated as "early modern" and "recent modern."

[43] Horie, ..*Keizai Seisaku*, 60. Methods of preventing the movement of food and other goods included: by sea (*tsu-dome* 津留), over county boundaries (*gun-kiri* 郡切), over village boundaries (*mura-kiri* 村切). Stoppage of the transport of grain whenever discovered was called *koku-dome* 穀留. *NKSJ*, 1090. See also E. Herbert Norman, "Ando Shōeki and the Anatomy of Japanese Feudalism," *TASJ*, 3rd Series II (Dec. 1949), 63.

Edo period, although the territories under direct Tokugawa control were scattered, the domains of the various separate feudal lords were generally centralized in one place. Among these feudal lords, the domains of the *fudai* ("inner") *daimyō* often included some small parcels of territory separate from their main domains, called *tobi-chi* 飛地.[44] The "outside" (*tozama*) fiefs, on the other hand, were strongly centralized, and were generally more successful in their mercantilistic policies.[45]

Improvement of transportation and communication facilities was another factor of great importance to the development of commerce and the rise of the merchant class. In order to make its rule effective, it was necessary for the *Bakufu* to improve existing roads,[46] and to build and maintain new roads and harbor facilities to provide a network of roads and sea routes leading to Edo, where they had formerly converged on Kyoto.[47] Politically, the immediate need for roads was to provide better means for official travel (*e.g.*, for tax collectors), the despatch of messages, etc. Economically, the immediate necessity was to facilitate the transport of food, especially tax rice from the scattered *Bakufu* territories, and other essentials to Edo. Also, it became increasingly necessary for the various *daimyō* to use the roads for travel and to ship their excess tax rice and specialty goods to the central markets.[48]

Five main highways were maintained during the Tokugawa period, all leading to Nihonbashi in Edo.[49] The most important was the Tōkaidō from Edo to Kyoto, soon extended to Osaka, which became

---

[44] *Tobi-chi* were formed through the enlarging or the diminishing of the fiefs, changing and incorporating them into others, etc., after they were granted in the first place as feudal benefices. Horie, . . *Keizai Seisaku*, 60. See also *NKSJ*, 1190.

[45] Horie, . .*Keizai Seisaku*, 60–1. Horie writes, "It is clear that the feudal lord was the only master within the fief."

[46] Nobunaga had been "a pioneer in road construction in Japan, where there had been nothing but narrow paths or lanes." Takekoshi, *Economic Aspects*. ., I, 352.

[47] Horie, "Tokugawa Jidai no Rikujō Kōtsū 徳川時代の陸上交通 [Overland Transportation of the Tokugawa Period], *KSK*, XI, 2 (Feb. 1934), 74.

[48] *Ibid*. "Excess" rice was that which was left over after all local payments and exchanges were made.

[49] Smith, "Materials. .," *op. cit.*, 51.

the scene of the bustling and colorful life immortalized in the color prints of Hiroshige and Hokusai. Relaying stations (*shukueki* 宿 驛) were built at intervals of several miles each, and, as part of the *Bakufu* police control through barriers, travel at night was prohibited. Fear of highwaymen was practically eliminated. The police examinations at the barriers were primarily for political control rather than control of crime, but they served also to slow down traffic. Perhaps the most important deterrent to efficient transport and travel was the lack of technological development. There were some minor improvements in palanquins and carts, but power was mainly manpower, and carts were used only for short hauls,[50] evidently due to the difficulties of fording the innumerable swift rivers.[51] In the rainy season, travellers often had to wait days for the Ōi River floodwaters to recede.[52] Horses were used more for travel, mainly by the samurai, and for the carrying of mail, than for transport. Bridge building seems to have been limited by military considerations. There were only two permanent bridges on the Tōkaidō, built in Ieyasu's time, and Iemitsu, the third Shogun, seems to have been particularly opposed to bridge building, thinking, no doubt, that bridges would facilitate an attack on Edo.[53] But the natural difficulties of bridge construction over rivers which often changed course and whose volume of flow had great seasonal variations may well have made the building of bridges with the means at hand purely an academic question.[54]

The improvements in overland communications facilitated mainly travel and itinerant trade, but not the transport of goods.[55] For bulky

[50] Horie, "..Rikujō Kōtsū..," 76; Kanno, *Nihon Shōgyō Shi*, 165. Inns at the relaying stations became almost indistinguishable from houses of prostitution, until a chain of inns was organized into a group called the Naniwa Kō 浪花講, advertising that member inns did not provide prostitutes, so tired travellers could get some sleep. *NKSJ*, 1234-5.

[51] Horie, "..Rikujō Kōtsū..," 76.

[52] *Ibid*. Even with optimum conditions, delays could be caused by porters and palanquin-bearers who "would not budge without being offered a tip" above the official rates for carrying travellers over the rushing waters. *Ibid*. The word for tip, *sakate* 洒 手, "*sake* money," reminds one of the French *pourboire*.   [53] Smith, "Materials..," *op. cit.*, 55.

[54] *Ibid*. Horie, in his article on overland transportation, *op. cit.*, 76, stresses natural obstructions to bridge building, and does not mention any military considerations.   [55] Kanno, *Nihon Shōgyō Shi*, 165.

staples such as rice and textiles, it was far less expensive to ship by sea, and the waterways were used as much as possible.[56]

An attempt, not entirely successful, was made by the Tokugawa regime to standardize weights and measures. Standard weights and measures were fixed by law and bureaus set up which, under authorized merchants in Edo and Kyoto, sold scales and measuring equipment. This equipment was pronounced official and the use of unauthorized equipment prohibited. Despite these measures, at least eighteen different *shaku* 尺, a linear measure, and ten different *shō* 升, a measure of capacity, persisted in use in the provinces. More success seems to have been experienced in the standardization of weights, perhaps because of their relationship to coins.[57]

The establishment of a standard currency system was another policy of much importance in the stimulation of commerce and the money economy. The currency situation was particularly chaotic at the beginning of the Tokugawa period. Chinese copper coins had been used since early times for commercial transactions, but importation was not sufficient for the greatly increased need for money accompanying the unprecedented commercial expansion in the late sixteenth century.[58] Fortunately, however, a number of gold and silver mines were discovered at this time, and methods for more efficient exploitation were learned from the Portuguese.[59] Feudal lords coined various types of copper coins, mostly of poor quality, and silver and gold coins as well, which began to be used as media of exchange for the first time in Japanese history.[60] All coins had to be

---

[56] John Henry Wigmore, ed., "Materials for the Study of Private Law in Old Japan," *TASJ* XX (1892), Supplement I, Introduction, 160. See also Horie, ". .Suijō Kōtsū. .," *op. cit.* Japanese pirates, for centuries the scourge of the sea lanes, were eliminated after Hideyoshi's conquest of Kyūshū in 1587. *NKSJ*, 210.

[57] *NKSJ*, 1206–08; 1307. The official bureaus were called *hakari-za* 秤 座. They were established in Ieyasu's time.

[58] Delmer M. Brown, *Money Economy in Medieval Japan: A Study in the Use of Coins* (New Haven: 1951), 96.

[59] Sawada Sho, "Financial Difficulties of the Edo Bakufu" (trans. by H. Borton), *Harvard Journal of Asiatic Studies*, I, 3–4 (Nov. 1936), 311; Takekoshi, *Economic Aspects. .*, I, 546.

[60] T. Tsukamoto, *The Old and New Coins of Japan* (Osaka: 1930), 4.

scrutinized for quality and carefully weighed to determine their value, a great inconvenience to commercial transactions.

As a logical part of his efforts to establish and stabilize the Tokugawa hegemony, Ieyasu soon turned to this monetary problem. In 1601, both gold and silver coins were being minted by the *Bakufu* as standard coins, to establish an official monetary system. However, the predominance of Chinese copper coins posed a difficult problem for the establishment of a standard Japanese copper coin. The first step was to ban the use of the most important Chinese copper coins, in 1608.[61] After several experimental mintings, a standard coin was finally produced in large quantities from 1636, a coin which was most used in small everyday transactions and which was a force stimulating the development of money economy, whether in the cities or in the agricultural communities.[62]

The establishment of a standard Japanese copper coin and the abolishment of competing coins which became effective in time, meant the removal of the inconvenience of determining their value. However, this success was not extended to the entire currency system. Gold coins functioned as a currency of numerical calculation. Silver, on the other hand, was generally calculated by weight. Each of the three coins was a currency with a fixed legal ratio to one another. However, the legal ratios were seldom adhered to in practice, and values were actually fixed in markets. In time, the values for the country were established in Osaka for silver and in Edo for copper (in terms of gold).[63]

In Europe, where polymetallic standards existed and were effectively enforced, there was an evolution toward a single gold standard when world silver prices declined. In Japan, where unification was not complete, parities were not enforced. This failure to enforce the currency ratios, paradoxically, made the monetary system workable,

---

[61] *Koji Ruien* 古事類苑 [An Encyclopedic Collection of Historical Materials] (60 vols., Tokyo: 1935–38 ed.), XXVI, 125. See also Hamamura Shōzaburō 濱村正三郎 "Eiraku-sen no Kinshi wo Ronzu 永樂錢の禁止を 論ず" [Comments on the Prohibition of Eiraku-sen], *KSK*, XXVII (1942), 362–78.

[62] Horie, . .*Keizai Seisaku*, 72–3.

[63] *NKSJ*, 367.

but at the same time, it slowed the evolution towards a single standard, with auxiliary coins.[64]

In the fields of domestic policy discussed here, both positive and negative aspects can be discerned. The policy of attracting merchants (and artisans) to the castle towns and the related establishment of free markets and guilds contributed to the stimulation of commerce and the economic importance of the merchant, but not to his independence of action. Improvements in transportation did much to foster the developing nation-wide economy, but were inhibited by the limitations of technology as well as military considerations. The abolition of the barriers as deterrents to commerce was an important forward step, but the lack of complete unification left many significant islands of economic self-sufficiency. Even the attempted standardization of weights and measures, and of the currency system, which did much to further the development of commerce, was equally limited by the incomplete nature of the national unification.

The *sankin kōtai* system was a positive factor in the development of the commercial economy. It was a unique and essential part of the Tokugawa system as a political control which the *Bakufu* could wield on a nation-wide basis. It required all feudal lords to attend the Shogun's court at periodical intervals, and to leave their wives and children in Edo as hostages while they were in their own territories. It existed to some extent in Ieyasu's time, but was regularized and made entirely compulsory in 1634.

Forced thus to live a double life, the *daimyō* had to pay for their residence in Edo and the expenses of travel for themselves and large numbers of retainers in specie which they themselves had no right to coin. Further, with an increased standard of living, ultimately they came to require credit from the wealthy merchants of the "three cities." For security and to pay these loans, they had to ship their excess rice and other products out to a central market.[65] Although the feudal lords did their best to maintain economic autonomy, "complete independence from nation-wide economic intercourse was

---

[64] Cf. Takimoto, Seiichi 瀧本誠一, *Nihon Kahei Shi* 日本貨幣史 [A Monetary History of Japan] (Tokyo: 1929), 73–4.

[65] Horie, ..*Keizai Seisaku*, 65.

but a wished-for ideal."[66] The *sankin kōtai* system drew the feudal lords into the nation-wide economy. It was a political measure which had vast significance for the economy. In the words of Professor Honjō, "It contributed to the prosperity of Edo and made for its great expansion; it impoverished the feudal lords; it stimulated the development of commerce and industry, and did much to further the spread of the money economy and to form the basis for a nation-wide economy."[67]

An element in the economic history of the time which was of special importance in the early years of the Tokugawa period was foreign trade. Hideyoshi granted licenses to the ships of the great merchants of Kyoto, Nagasaki and Sakai to push an aggressive trade in the commercial centers of south China and the South Seas.[68] Ieyasu continued this policy of encouragement to foreign trade, giving licenses to merchants of Osaka and Edo as well, and to some of the feudal lords, as well as to some individual samurai retainers. Since both risks and profits were great, this overseas trade gave rise to a type of bottomry called "nagegane" 投銀, literally "throwing silver," arranged among capitalists and trading merchants.[69]

Ieyasu also continued to welcome foreign ships to Japanese ports. No duties were imposed on the foreign trade at Nagasaki.[70] However,

[66] *Ibid.*, 62.

[67] *NKSJ*, 660. The impoverishment of the *daimyō* was in line with the policy of weakening them financially to prevent their rising against the Tokugawa. See also Honjō's article, "Sankin Kōtai Seido no Keizaikan 参覲交代制度の經濟觀" [An Economic View of the Sankin Kōtai System] *Keizai Ronsō* 經濟論叢 [Essays in Economics] III, 6 (Dec. 1916), 828–841; IV, 4 (Oct. 1917), 55–74. See also Toshio George Tsukahira, *The Sankin Kōtai System of Tokugawa Japan (1600–1868)*, *op. cit.*

[68] These ships in the official trade were the well-known *Shuin-sen* 朱印船. See *NKSJ*, 765–8. Four interesting pictures of Japanese ships of Western design can be seen on page 767.

[69] Shiba Kentarō 柴謙太郎, "Nagegane to wa nani, Kaijō Kashitsuke ka, Kommenda Tōshi ka? 投銀とは何、海上貸付かコンメンダ投資か [What was "Nagegane"? A Marine Loan, or Commenda Investment?], *KSK* 45–7 (July–Sept., 1933), 617–634; 14–27; 123–145. Also, *NKSJ* 1228. Bottomry is a contract by which a ship is hypothecated as security for repayment for the financing of a voyage. Commenda was an early type of bottomry.

[70] Takekoshi, *Economic Aspects.* ., I, 378.

he became increasingly suspicious that the Europeans were looking for an opportunity to gratify their territorial ambitions, using religious propagation as a device, and he attempted, as had Hideyoshi, to separate trade from religion. This proved unfeasible except with the Dutch, and from 1633 restrictions were placed both upon the number of foreign ships entering Japanese ports and the number of Japanese ships going out. In the most definitive of the exclusion edicts, the Portuguese were expelled in 1638 and the death penalty provided for Japanese who left the country or, having left, should return. To prevent ocean voyages, the building of vessels of more than 500 *koku* (roughly 2,500 bushels) capacity was forbidden. By 1641, the system of exclusion under which Japan was to live for more than two hundred years was completed, with a limited trade with the Dutch at Deshima in Nagasaki harbor and with Chinese traders who were permitted in Nagasaki itself.[71]

The motivations for the closing of the country were mainly political, and no doubt based primarily on the fear of a coalition of powerful outside clans (particularly Mōri and Shimazu) aided by Europeans who were trading with them and who could supply guns and ships against the Tokugawa.[72] Economic factors appear to have played a part. As Professor Horie concludes, "No doubt an important reason was the desire to restrict the free economic activities of wealthy merchants by bringing commerce entirely under feudal control, and to halt the increase in the power gained through trade by the western feudal lords. This point is little more than conjecture, but the fact remains that commercial policy found itself placed in this position, mainly by political considerations."[73]

It remains to assess the effects of the policy of the closed country on commerce and the merchant class. It should first be pointed out, as is well known, that the exclusion was not complete. A restricted trade, which tended to become more restricted towards the end of the seventeenth century, continued to exist under *Bakufu* supervision

---

[71] Horie, . . *Keizai Seisaku*, 116; George B. Sansom, *The Western World and Japan* (New York: 1950), 177–8.

[72] Cf. Sansom, *The Western World* . ., 178–9.

[73] Horie, . . *Keizai Seisaku*, 116.

with the Dutch and Chinese at Nagasaki.[74] Trade was carried on in Tsushima with the Koreans, and by Shimazu in the Ryūkyū Islands, but due to its very small scale, it had the "silent assent" of the *Bakufu*.[75] In addition, there seems to have been a certain amount of smuggling, despite *Bakufu* attempts to eliminate it.[76]

Besides the fact that foreign trade, although restricted, continued after the exclusion, another reason why the exclusion was not a major blow to the economy of the time was the one-sided nature of the Nagasaki trade. The main imports were Chinese raw silk, piece goods and medicines, and the major exports were copper and other precious metals, especially silver.[77] Other exports paid for only 25% of the imports in the Chinese and only 29% in the Dutch trade in the period from 1657 to 1662, a situation apparently not greatly different from the pre-exclusion period.[78] A beneficial by-product of the limitation of imports which accompanied the exclusion was a "great stimulation of domestic production of formerly imported goods, particularly raw silk and woven silk goods."[79]

The implications of the "closed country" for the present were not nearly as great as for the future. Professor Nomura summarizes its immediate significance as follows:[80]

How was it possible to close the country? An important reason was that European capitalism had not matured and had not reached the stage where it could exploit the markets of the Far East. On the other side, Japanese merchants had no organized power to oppose the

---

[74] See Takekoshi, *Economic Aspects*.., II, 378–392, for fragmentary estimates of the amount of trade, taken mainly from the researches of the German historian, Nachod.

[75] Horie, ..*Keizai Seisaku*, 118.

[76] *Bakufu* officials themselves were sometimes implicated in this smuggling. Takekoshi II, 158–185.

[77] Takekoshi, *Economic Aspects*.., II, 148, 411, 414–5. For the export of copper, see John W. Hall, "Notes on the Early Ch'ing Copper Trade with Japan," *Harvard Journal of Asiatic Studies* 12 (1949), 444–61.

[78] Takekoshi, II, 377, 380.

[79] Miyamoto, *Nihon Shōgyō Shi*, 139.

[80] Nomura Kanetarō 野村兼太郎, "Tokugawa Hōken Sei to Shōgyō 徳川封建制と商業" [The Tokugawa Feudal System and Commerce] *Shakai Keizai Shi Gaku* 社會經濟史學 [Studies in Social and Economic History], VI, 10 (Jan. 1937), 120.

militaristic policy of the Tokugawa. Also, the foreign trade of the time had no close connection with basic domestic production, and from this it can be concluded that local domestic markets were the main object of commerce. The spirit of bold enterprise which arose in the late Ashikaga period found a partial outlet in secret trade and on the other hand shifted towards domestic commercial development accompanying the political stability.

The exclusion had wide and important implications for the future. It denied Japan a source of food in times of famine, and to a large extent put her farther outside the stream of world events and world progress. From the standpoint of the development of commerce and the rise of the merchant class as well, there is much to be said on the debit side. First, the Nagasaki trade, although one-sided, might well have continued to develop, especially with Europeans of different nationalities competing for the trade. However, not only was the trade limited, but it was placed under feudal (*Bakufu*) control, with monopoly privileges granted to special merchants. Second, prohibition against Japanese going overseas was perhaps more important in limiting commercial development in a field where there was more scope for independence on the part of merchants.[81] It closed the door to an active development overseas. In a general sense, the exclusion policy limited industrial development to the narrow scope of domestic demand.

[81] It appears to have been more important because, judging from trade conditions from the middle sixteenth century on, the expansibility of the trade in Japanese ports was limited. It was limited by the volume of goods and money which the Japanese could provide for foreign goods. Merchandise played a small part in Japanese exports, and the copper and other precious metals which the Japanese could mine, and which found their way to China, whether by Chinese or European vessels, also had limits. Moreover, the limits were felt more and more in the seventeenth century with the marked decrease in the production of Japanese mines. Horie, ..*Keizai Seisaku*, 101–2; Takekoshi, *Economic Aspects*.., II, 230, 305. The Japanese who went overseas, on the other hand, were learning from the Europeans not only how to make money in the carrying trade, but how to build more efficient ships and guns. Sansom permits himself to conjecture on this point: "Japan would no doubt have suffered from further civil war, and it is just possible that after an interval she herself would have followed the European example and, with a rapid development of shipbuilding and the manufacture or ordnance, taken a part in the struggle between trading powers that began to develop in the Pacific after 1600." *The Western World and Japan*, 179.

The exclusion policy and the foreign trade policy under the exclusion served to maintain peace and to prolong the feudal control of the Tokugawa regime.[82] This was an important achievement in itself, but it was made at a sacrifice. Although in the short run there appeared some stimulation of domestic industry and commerce, the result ultimately was the restraint of future industrial and commercial development.[83] It also meant the decline of the type of independent merchants of Hakata and Sakai, as well as the new foreign trade capitalists of Nagasaki.[84] Professor Miyamoto concludes, "Having lost the seas and unable to stride freely about the earth, a spirit of retrogression and conservatism set in ... the merchants inevitably reflected this spirit. They came to lack competitive spirit and progressiveness, and were quite content to keep their customers and a fixed share of the distribution system, repeating over and over the same kind of transactions."[85]

From the exclusion of 1638 onwards, the remarkable changes of the late *sengoku* and early Tokugawa periods were brought to a halt. The "refeudalization" process was being completed and the Tokugawa political system had taken its unique shape. The rise of the merchant class before 1638 was given impetus first by the natural consequences of the unification of the country and the ensuing peace: increased population, land under cultivation and agricultural productivity, and the freeing of peasants to go to the fast-growing cities and towns.

[82] Tsuchiya Takao 土屋喬雄 argues that the *Bakufu*, "by restricting the inflow of foreign, particularly European, goods, retarded the development of commercial and industrial capital, the factors leading the feudal society towards disintegration." *Nihon Keizai Shi Gaiyō* 日本經濟史概要 [An Outline of Japanese Economic History] (Tokyo: 1934), I, 167. Endō Masao 遠藤正男 believes this is only a partial explanation. He suggests that usury would have served as a strong competitor for foreign trade capital, retarding the development of foreign trade. *Nihon Kinsei Shōgyō Shihon Hattatsu Shi Ron* 日本近世商業資本發達史論 [An Essay on the History of the Development of Commercial Capital in Japan in the Early Modern Period] (Tokyo: 1936), 25.

[83] Horie, . .*Keizai Seisaku*, 119.

[84] Miyamoto, *Nihon Shōgyō Shi*, 138–9, points out that when trade was forced into the narrower channels of domestic trade, there was a marked decline of such towns as Hakata and Sakai.

[85] *Ibid.*, 139.

Then, government policies contributed to conditions favorable to the merchant class: the encouragement of merchants and artisans to settle in the castle towns; the establishment of free markets and guilds; the breaking down of the barriers (*sekisho*); the improvements in transportation, and the standardization of weights and measures, and of the currency system. On the other hand, none of these policies could be complete due to the incomplete nature of the unification itself. There were three factors in particular which militated against an increase in merchant influence and independence: the tendency for the feudal ruling classes to bring commercial activities under their control so far as they could; the existence of provincial economies which opposed the development of a nation-wide economy, and the exclusion policy which barred the path to economic power through foreign trade—a path which in Europe by 1600 had already proved of such importance in the rise of the merchant class.

CHAPTER II

THE SOCIAL AND POLITICAL POSITION OF THE MERCHANT CLASS IN THE EARLY TOKUGAWA PERIOD

IN THE FIRST years of the Tokugawa period, the merchants felt the restrictions accompanying the "refeudalization" process which was completed with the stabilization of the regime. Then, as a response, they gradually achieved, in the next century or century and a quarter, a degree of security and *de facto* economic power, although despised as the lowest in the social structure, and still in a weak position, with no real legal or political powers or rights. Since the rise of the merchant took place within the unusual feudal society of Tokugawa Japan, we must first look at the development of the social structure, in order to understand the merchant's position in it. Sociologically, it was a status society based on occupation. The class distinctions which had evolved during the late middle ages had been placed into a rigid form by Hideyoshi, who, as a means of stabilization and control, defined the classes as samurai, peasants, artisans and merchants (*shinōkōshō* 士農工商), with samurai at the top, merchants at the bottom.[1] This social hierarchy, generally accepted by Confucian scholars and statesmen, was adopted as a basic ingredient of the Tokugawa feudal system and was insisted upon as the correct arrangement of society.[2] It was based upon a physiocratic

---

[1] Sakata, *Chōnin*, 2. Also see Honjo's article, *Shinōkōshō*, in *NKSJ*, 727–9. The court nobles (*kuge* 公家), Buddhist and Shinto priests, as well as outcasts (*eta* 穢多 and *hinin* 非人) were comparatively small in number and not included.

[2] A representative Confucian point of view was expressed by Yamaga Sokō (1622–1685), who justified the existence of the four classes by pointing out the necessary division of labor among farmers, artisans and merchants, and the necessity for a fourth class, the ruling class, to prevent the covetousness of the other classes from finding expression in banditry and war. *Yamaga Gorui* 山鹿語類, in *Yamaga Sokō Shū* 山鹿素行集 [Collection of the Writings of Yamaga Sokō], *Kinsei Shakai Keizai Gakusetsu Taikei* (Tokyo: 1935), 171–2. Professor Horie comments, "In a feudal society which has such a structure, the unchanging is thought of as the ideal. Therefore the com-

view of society common to the agrarian states of Asia. Agriculture was considered the only source of production. The peasant, whose occupation was the only truly productive one, was the pillar of the state. Artisans merely changed the form of goods already produced by the peasants. Merchants were ranked below the artisans because artisans did provide goods for the samurai class, especially weapons and military supplies. Merchants, on the other hand, were entirely unproductive and therefore dispensable.

Tokugawa legislation and policies were based on the felt necessity of maintaining the social structure intact and class lines rigid. However, the four-class arrangement was part of a military organization of society better adapted to times of war than to peace, and from the first was more of an ideal than a reality. In actual practice, there were three types of deviation from the norm. In the first place, the occupational functions of the people did not fall into strict specialization. Second, there was a considerable degree of social mobility, especially in the early years, and third, the actual treatment of the various classes was not in accord with the theory but tended to be in terms of immediate interest.

There was a considerable overlapping in occupational functions. For example, there were two types of artisans: those retained by the *Bakufu* or feudal lords, and those who manufactured commercial goods for sale. The latter were commonly called "artisan-merchants" (*shoku-akindo* 職商人), since their occupation placed them into both categories.[3]

It was quite common for peasants to supplement their meager incomes by handicraft work done in their homes. Although the authorities did their best to see that this domestic industry did not interfere with the peasant's primary task of cultivation of the fields,[4] this type of cottage industry eventually surpassed the output of artisans in the castle towns and cities.[5] Some peasants even engaged in

mon basic viewpoint was concern for the maintenance of stability. How was this to be done ? First, by guarding rigidly the distinctions of social status and function of the four classes." . .*Keizai Seisaku*, 173.

[3] Horie, . .*Keizai Seisaku*, 47–8.   [4] *Ibid.*, 46.

[5] Horie Yasuzō, *Nihon Shihon Shugi no Seiritsu* 日本資本主義の成立 [The Formation of Capitalism in Japan] (Tokyo: 2nd ed., 1948), 32. Samurai

trade in the countryside. Prohibitions of both commercial and manufacturing activities in agricultural villages were common, and merchants were often specifically forbidden to reside in the countryside
as "useless and harmful persons."[6] But despite regulations, peasants
sometimes engaged in trade in their villages, and merchants came
from the towns to sell commercial goods. As legal restraints proved
most difficult to enforce, there were cases where trade in specific
commercial commodities such as candy and tobacco-pipes (*kiseru*)
was legally permitted. In some domains (*han*) the authorities merely
looked the other way, or justified the existence of merchants in the
villages by calling them peasants. It is true that in many cases they
were part-time peasants.[7]

Actual changes of status were quite common among the lower
three classes during the first hundred years of the Tokugawa period.
Cases of commoners attaining samurai status, on the other hand, were
rather exceptional until the later years of the period. The movement
downward of samurai to merchant, already referred to, tended to
become rarer after the closing of the country.[8] Artisan-merchant
changes were quite frequent, and were hardly noticed by the authorities. Changes of peasants to *chōnin* constituted the major factor in
the increased population of the towns and cities, and apparently
were not actively opposed by the feudal authorities until later in the
seventeenth century. Attempts to bind the peasants to the land are
often cited, such as the law of 1643 preventing alienation of land and
the series of laws beginning from 1673 specifically restricting peasants
to their land. It should be noted that these laws were conspicuously
ineffective.[9] Also, it is rather surprising to find evidence that the *Baku-*

families also carried on handicraft work in their homes, but this is a development characteristic of the later years of the period.

[6] Miyamoto Mataji, "Kinsei no Sonraku to Shōgyō 近世の村落と商業"
[Villages and Commerce in the Early Modern Period], *Hikone Kōshō Ronsō*
彦根高商論叢 [Journal of Hikone Higher Commercial School], 29 (June,
1941), 171. This article is reprinted, with a few changes, in Miyamoto's
Kinsei Shōgyō Keiei no Kenkyū 近世商業經營の研究 [Studies in Commercial Operations in the Early Modern Period] (Kyoto: 1948), 173–208.

[7] Miyamoto, "Kinsei no Sonraku to Shōgyō", 160–2.

[8] Miyamoto, *Nihon Shōgyō Shi*, op. cit., 177–8.

[9] Nomura, "Tokugawa Hōken Sei to Shōgyō," 116, 118; Sakata, *Chōnin*, 2.

fu at one time actually gave legal assent, although probably no encouragement, to peasants to leave their villages and change their occupations. In a regulation of 1637, there is an item which reads as follows: "Any person who leaves his native place to go into service (*hōkō* 奉公) or commerce must give prior notice to the local courts (*rakuchaku-sho* 落着所) through the office of the local headman (*Shōya* 庄屋) and the five-family associations (*gonin-gumi* 五人組)."[10] After about 1735 the influx of peasants into the cities came to a virtual halt, and the population of cities became generally quite stable. This was apparently due not to the prohibitions against peasants' leaving their native places, but to the lack of employment in the cities.[11]

The official policy towards the lower classes was not consistent with the four-class theory. It must be taken up here in some detail, in order to show what type of restraints were applied to the three lower classes. We have already discussed attempts to bind the peasants to their land. The economic burdens piled on the peasants were extremely heavy. The very high rate of land tax[12] of 40% or 50% of yield which was generally levied during the *sengoku* period to pay the high costs of war was maintained during the Tokugawa period, and farmers continued to be pressed down to a very low level of livelihood.[13] The usual "four to the lord, six to the people" was formally

---

[10] *Tokugawa Kinrei Kō* 徳川禁令考 [A Commentary on Tokugawa Prohibitory Regulations] (Tokyo: 1932 ed.), V, 231. Persons in "service" (*hōkō*) included unskilled day laborers, persons entering apprenticeships, and retainers of samurai. *NKSJ*, 1498.

[11] Horie, ..*Shihon Shugi*.., 47. Horie points out that during the first century of the Tokugawa period, there were many large construction enterprises in the cities which supplied work for peasants who had left their villages, but after that time it became increasingly difficult to find work, and "this explains why the only alternatives left to these poor peasants were to rise in rebellion or to resort to limitation of the population." *Ibid.*

[12] *Nengu* 年貢, literally, "yearly tribute". It was not a land tax in the modern sense, but was more of a land rent levied as a tax in kind, usually paid in rice. Horie, ..*Shihon Shugi*.., 3. For the various uses of the term, see *NKSJ*, 1273.

[13] Sakata Yoshio, "Meiji Ishin to Tempō Kaikaku 明治維新と天保改革" [The Meiji Restoration and the Tempō Reform] *Jimbun Gakuhō* 人文學報 [Journal of Humanistic Science], II (1952), 3. Nomura, *op. cit.*, 118, writes, "It seems that almost everyone who treats the economic and social history of this period cites the words attributed to Ieyasu that peasants should be taxed to the point where they will neither die nor live." Nomura feels this

changed to five and five during the administration of Yoshimune (1716–1745), but local practices continued to vary considerably.[14] Considering the very small land holdings of each peasant family, this left only a bare subsistence even in the best years.[15]

should not be represented as a typical attitude of the feudal ruling classes. *Ibid.*

The scholar-statesman Kumazawa Banzan 熊澤蕃山 (1619–1692) states the position this way: "If you take too small an amount in land tax, then the people will neglect the cultivation of their fields in their love of pleasure and comfort. If you take too much, then they will lack strength in the misery of famine and cold. There is no limit to their production of the five grains when they are neither neglectful nor hungry." *Shūgi Washo* 集義和書, in *Nihon Rinri Ihen* 日本倫理彙編 [Collection of Japanese Works of Moral Philosophy] (Tokyo: 1901), I, 427.

[14] Horie, ..*Shihon Shugi*.., 35. According to Prof. Horie, official statistics are misleading in this regard because peasants were usually successful in hiding some 10% or more of their crops from the officials. Officials could also be bribed to overlook some of the yield. Apparently it was rather rare that the land tax was as much as half. For the method of crop measuring by sample and determination of land tax, usually haphazard and unfair, see *NKSJ*, 471-4.

[15] There is a difference of opinion among social and economic historians as to the exact position of the peasants. Some describe them as serfs, as do Endō, ..*Shōgyō Shihon*.., op. cit., 30, and Tsuchiya, *An Economic History of Japan*, op. cit., 145–6. Sansom follows Honjō very closely in painting a rather dark picture of the restraints put on the peasants. On the other hand, Nomura (for example, in his article cited above, p. 118) has reservations in regard to this interpretation. Asakawa, the noted authority on Japanese feudalism, stresses the degree of self.government enjoyed by the peasants and their rights of tenure, protected by the feudal authorities. The evidence already given in the present study showing a degree of legal assent to peasant changes of occupation serves to rule out the use of the term "serf" in the legal sense, and restrictions on social mobility were ineffective in practice. Professor Horie clarifies the position in this way: "The social status of the peasants was actually rising during the Edo period, as seen in the change of their relationship to the land and in the nature of peasant *corvée*. However, this improvement in status was not accompanied by any economic improvements; on the contrary, their burdens became heavier." Horie, ..*Shihon Shugi*.., 43. It should perhaps be added that the "peasants" actually comprised two distinct groups: (1) landholders, many well-to-do, of higher social status, often tracing back to warrior ancestors, and (2) poor tenants and servants (*genin* 下人). See Thomas C. Smith, "The Japanese Village in the Seventeenth Century," *Journal of Economic History*, 12, 1 (Winter 1952), 1–20.

Peasants were often called "stupid people" in Tokugawa edicts which strove to regulate their lives in the most minute matters. They were exhorted to rise early in the morning, not to buy *sake* or tea, not to use tobacco, not to eat rice but to eat coarse grains, and to divorce any wife who drank tea.[16] These provisions, embodied in a proclamation of 1649, and often repeated, reveal an extraordinary contempt and lack of sympathy for the peasant.

The rationalization for this treatment was that the peasants were economically secure. They were guaranteed their source of income, the land. Another argument often advanced but of little relevance in peacetime was that the peasants should pay well for their freedom from military duties.[17] However, it is obvious that their own economic interests led the samurai overlords to oppress the peasants and to despise them in practice, although maintaining that their status in society was second only to the samurai themselves.

Real treatment of the merchants and artisans was vastly better than that of the peasants, although in theory the merchants were scorned as beneath notice. In the colorful words of Professor Honjō's translators, merchants were viewed "as a class of people who indulged in the despicable enjoyment of life; who were shamelessly devoted to a life of profit-making through exchange of goods; and who would resort to any dubious method in order to coax others to buy high-priced goods, thereby stimulating a habit of luxury."[18] There was no real distinction made between artisans and merchants, in practice. They were popularly lumped together in the term *"chōnin"* (townspeople), a word often found in sumptuary legislation, and peasants certainly had no privileges which *chōnin* did not share.[19] Actually,

---

[16] *NKSJ*, 1068, an article on *chōnin* by Prof. Honjō which brings together in concise form some of the scattered remarks that can be found in his *Social and Economic History of Japan*. George B. Sansom, in *Japan, a Short Cultural History* (New York: 1943), 466, cites the proclamation of 1649 ordering peasants to "abstain from tea and tobacco." However, in regard to tea, the wording of this proclamation was, "Sake, cha wo kai nomi mōsu majiki sōrō," literally, "It is forbidden to buy and drink *sake* and tea," with emphasis on the buying. Apparently no efforts were made to prevent peasants from consuming products produced by themselves.

[17] Nomura, "Tokugawa Hōken Sei to Shōgyō," 116.

[18] *Social and Economic History of Japan*, 253.   [19] Sakata, *Chōnin*, 2.

Bakufu attitudes towards the *chōnin* appear almost magnanimous, when compared to the attitudes towards the peasants, and even towards the *daimyō* whom they kept in a state of impoverishment and controlled with the ingenious set of complicated and despotic controls which were the work of the political genius of Ieyasu. Interference in the lives of the *chōnin* did not constitute a heavy burden. They were prohibited, for example, from wearing silk, using parasols, hair ornaments, house furnishings of raised lacquerware; from selling vegetables out of season, and taking advantage of current fads to make unusual profits. However, they were not regularly taxed, and were required to make regular monetary contributions only after the time of Yoshimune (1716–1745).[20]

The explanation for this difference in treatment can be found in immediate economic interest rather than in the principles of proper social relations avowed by the authorities. In the early days of the Tokugawa period, the *chōnin* were not considered as producers of wealth but rather as essential servants of the economic needs of the samurai in the castle towns and cities. Moreover, *chōnin* were thought to be in a very insecure position due to their dependence upon the fluctuating conditions of trade and production. The insecurity of the samurai arose from the fact that "any morning" he might be called upon to sacrifice his life for his lord. It was only the peasant who could enjoy security, safe from military service and confirmed in his landholding, "so long as he paid his taxes." The higher these taxes, the larger the number of merchants and artisans to fulfill the economic demands of the samurai, and the more abundant the materials of life for the samurai. Conversely, it was only the samurai who could increase and maintain the maximum in tax yield, and therefore he was in a controlling position. With the merchants generally brought under feudal political control in the cities and towns, the feudal ruling classes were confident that they would never be in a position to become a problem to them.[21]

The samurai's contempt for commercial activities was part of his boast of separateness and moral superiority. Besides, this attitude

[20] Sakata, *Chōnin*, 10; NKSJ, 1068.
[21] Sakata, *Chōnin*, 10.

was legally reinforced. Samurai were absolutely forbidden to engage in any kind of commerce.[22] The actual result of this was to give to the merchants a special and exclusive right to manage commercial enterprises. Although despised by the samurai, the merchant had a far freer and wider area for his activities than the samurai himself. The social relations of townspeople were tied together by money and commerce which had no direct relation to land. The principles of prerogative and obedience and of feudal obligations and service were as meaningless between samurai and merchant as among merchants. Moreover, the activities of merchants were free in that they were not necessarily tied to the economy of a single feudal territorial unit. Another advantage enjoyed by the merchants was that in a society where the distinction between master and servant was rigidly maintained, and where the blood inheritance system was equated with social order, the merchant and artisan classes alone were able to select men of ability and put them in charge of their family and their family enterprises. This gave them a flexibility and a protection against ruin by a worthless or dissolute heir not enjoyed by the samurai class, and it was one of their sources of strength.[23]

Despite these obvious advantages, it must be remembered that the merchants were in a position of political impotence. They had to operate within a feudal society in which the old military spirit was still strong. We have already discussed the process by which the feudal lords brought the merchants under their political control. One further example may be cited to show how the merchants gained certain economic advantages while losing elements of independence which they may have enjoyed in the political realm. It will also serve to introduce the subject of the role of merchants in town administration during the Tokugawa period. Ōtsu was a point of key economic importance. Located on Lake Biwa only one stop from Kyoto on the Tōkaidō, it was the main market as well as the collection and distribution point for the province of Ōmi.[24] Ōtsu itself had a long history of an enterprising and independent merchant class, and was

---

[22] Sakata, *Chōnin*, 10.   [23] *Ibid.* 12, 69; Horie, *..Shihon Shugi..*, 43.
[24] 江 近. As a province, it was perhaps the most economically advanced, well known for its industries and itinerant traders.

the location of a free market as early as 1539.[25] After his victory at Sekigahara (1600), Ieyasu left the town administration in the hands of a wealthy Ōtsu merchant, but placed a *Bakufu* official[26] in Ōtsu to oversee the mechanics of administration. This continued until 1602, when Ōtsu was brought under a council of five *Bakufu* deputies and two city elders (*machi doshiyori* 町年寄), and five-family associations were organized throughout the town as a means of control. Simultaneously with this action, the payment of augmented town property taxes[27] was waived, a clear example of giving something with one hand while taking away something with the other. In 1617, Ōtsu was brought under direct *Bakufu* control and the administration was reorganized to make it conform more or less to other *Bakufu* city administrations.[28]

Not only in the towns and cities controlled directly by the *Bakufu*, but in the towns of the various *han*, it was common practice to exercise control over townsmen through councils of important merchants. Practices differed according to local custom. Edo and Osaka give good examples of this. In all *Bakufu*-controlled cities and towns, the official who held the real power was the town magistrate (*machi bugyō*). This *Bakufu*-appointed official of samurai class held administrative, judicial and police powers.[29] Under his jurisdiction were councils of *chōnin*, variously named. In Edo, the highest body of *chōnin* was a hereditary council of city elders (*machi doshiyori*) who were the heads of three families (Taru 樽, Naraya 奈良屋, and Kitamura 喜多村) first appointed in 1590, when Edo, still a small village, was selected by Ieyasu as his future capital. They were permitted to wear swords, and in times of stress exhibited a feudal loyalty to the Shogun.[30] Under them were the *nanushi* (名主, headmen), also hereditary, of whom there were 263 in 1722.[31]

[25] See above, page 7.

[26] *Bugyō* 奉行, an elastic term for various types of functionaries which could be translated "commissioner" or "magistrate."

[27] Augmented to pay special temple and shrine expenses. *NKSJ*, 236.

[28] *NKSJ*, 152.

[29] *Ibid.*, 1537. *Machi Bugyō* were often of *hatamoto* rank, "banner knights" below *daimyō* rank.

[30] *NKSJ*, 124–5. At one time (1693) the privilege of sword-wearing was revoked.

[31] *Nanushi* had charge of from one to more than ten *machi* (streets or dis-

In Osaka, the council which corresponded to the Edo *machi doshiyori* was called the *sō toshiyori* 惣年寄, or "supervisory town elders." They were also hereditary, and were twenty-two in number at first, but gradually dwindled to twelve. Under them were the *machi doshiyori* who corresponded in function to the *nanushi* of Edo, but their positions were neither fully paid nor were supposed to be hereditary. House owners in each *machi* elected one candidate from their group. One third of these candidates were selected for the council.[32] Even this elective office, however, tended to become hereditary.[33] The *machi doshiyori* of Osaka, different from any other city or town, were permitted to continue managing their own businesses, and were paid only a nominal fee (literally, money for *hakama*, a skirt worn over the kimono). As they had little time to go to the town office and meeting place (*machi kaisho* 町會所), they deputized clerks to handle the day-to-day business. Osaka townsmen do not seem to have welcomed the position, although it did carry some honor with it.[34]

In order to have some idea of the political importance of the merchants, we should look at the functions of these semi-official merchant functionaries. It appears that their major duty, both in Edo and Osaka, was to transmit *Bakufu* orders and regulations down to the next lower echelon. In Edo, for example, the "chain of command" was *machi doshiyori-nanushi-gonin gumi*. The *machi doshiyori* in Edo, besides overseeing the *nanushi*, had special responsibilities. These changed somewhat with time, but the most important appears

---

tricts). Until 1668 they were all permitted to have surnames and to wear swords, but after that date they could wear swords only when on duty as official purveyors (*yōtatsu*) in cases where they were engaged as such. *Ibid.*, 124–5.

[32] It is interesting to note that they were selected on a point system "so that there would be no complaint." The point system was based on age, years of residence, amount of wealth, etc. Those selected on this basis were then subjected to a "hitogara-mi 人柄見", or determination of character by the *sō toshiyori* before their names were submitted to the *machi bugyō* for appointment. *NKSJ*, 1536.

[33] Sakata, *Chōnin*, 4.

[34] *NKSJ*, 1536; Takigawa Masajirō 瀧川正次郎, *Nihon Shakai Shi* 日本社會史 [A Social History of Japan] (Tokyo: 3rd ed., 1948), 311.

to have been supervision of the water supply. The responsibilities of the *nanushi* were: (1) transmission of orders downward; (2) prevention and extinction of fires, and (3) census taking. In Osaka, the *sō toshiyori* had several additional responsibilities, including: (1) collection of certain fees on behalf of the *machi bugyō*; (2) appointing of lesser town functionaries; (3) before the granting of official approval, the *sō toshiyori* approved new literary works before printing, and all petitions made by women.[35] Osaka was excepted from the payment of *chishi-sen*, a tax on houses and city lots. However, house owners paid a city tax whose amount was fixed by the *machi doshiyori* and disbursed by them under the supervision of the *sō toshiyori*. This tax was meant to make the city administration entirely self-supporting, and all city officers, even the *machi bugyō*, were paid from these funds.[36]

In Osaka, the city of *chōnin*, it might be imagined that these fiscal functions, together with the much larger number of duties performed by the Osaka merchant councils, would have given them a share of political power. But if their duties are closely examined, it will be seen that they were all in the nature of services for the *Bakufu* officials. Although they looked in some ways like self-governing bodies, there apparently was very little room for initiative. As a general principle, no matter how despotic and authoritarian a government may be, there must be a degree of social assent and feeling of participation or representation on the part of the ruled if the regime is to achieve any real stability. It is no doubt true that such councils of townspeople, like the corresponding councils in the agricultural villages, by the mere fact of their existence acted as a check on absolutism. However, it can be stated as a historical fact that the town councils were subservient to their feudal masters. Even in Osaka, where the merchant officials were the most important of their type in Japan, their positions were considered honorary, were not particularly welcomed, and, as one authority puts it, "Their positions existed only as a convenience to the *Bakufu*, and this fact greatly limited their independence."[37]

[35] *NKSJ*, 124–125; 938.   [36] *NKSJ*, 1538.
[37] Sakata, *Chōnin*, 61. It would appear that well-to-do peasants who were

It is clear that the merchant class enjoyed no real political influence, and this lack of political power played an important role in turning their rise to economic power into almost an underground movement, a contrast with the development of the merchant class in Europe which has colored all subsequent Japanese history and has no doubt played a role in the formation of the Japanese character. The merchants' political impotence was in marked contrast to their economic potential. They enjoyed a monopoly in commercial activities and money transactions at a time when the commercial and money economy had entered a period of unprecedented expansion. The feudal political power based on the land was separate from the power based on the new commercial and money economy. This separation was to grow to such vast proportions that it eventually threatened the whole feudal structure.

In the first years of the Tokugawa period, however, the only threat to the power of the Shogun was from potential feudal rivals, a threat which was most skillfully met and eliminated. In the economic realm, the feudal lords were kept in an impoverished condition which ruled out the possibility of rebellion. The economic position of the *Bakufu* was strong. The Tokugawa domains covered about one fourth the entire land surface producing more than one fourth of the rice of the country, and the *Bakufu* treasury was filled with gold and silver as no Japanese treasury had ever been before.[38] Control of all mines and

appointed as *toshiyori* and headmen (*ōshōya*) 大庄屋, *shōya*, *nanushi*, etc.) in the villages attained more real power in their role of assistants to the feudal rulers than did the merchant councils in the cities. Village headmen, for example, were consulted in some cases about policy. Sword-wearing *ōshōya* even functioned as *daikan*, an office usually monopolized by samurai. However, the village headmen do not seem to have used their influence on behalf of ordinary peasants. On the contrary, they often had to be disciplined for using their privileges to oppress their fellow peasants. *NKSJ*, 831–2.

[38] Even after gaining Hideyoshi's huge stores of gold and silver, Ieyasu had economized in order to store up more riches, and in 1605 when he retired and transferred the office of Shogun to his son, Hidetada, there was enough in the treasury to buy five million *koku* 石 of rice, with a purchasing power of one *ryō* 兩 of gold equal to two *koku* of rice at the time. Takekoshi, *Economic Aspects..*, I, 550. Ieyasu retained a large amount in his personal treasury, and after his death in 1616, a large store of foreign goods, in ad-

minting operations was another significant source of revenue for the *Bakufu* during the first years of the period while the mines were still very productive.[39]

With its economic position secure, with no precedent either in Japanese or in Chinese history of economic power based on commerce undermining a government,[40] and with the merchant class apparently well under control, there was no reason to fear that commerce would ever break down the feudal system. Indicative of this confidence was the continuation by the *Bakufu* of the policy of freedom of commerce begun by Nobunaga, Hideyoshi and Ieyasu as part of their unification of the country. The cities in which the merchants lived were enveloped in the feudalistic government and social organization, and did not develop into self-governing cities as in Europe. Accordingly, fixed boundaries were drawn about the free development of commerce. However, within these boundaries, the policy and attitude of the *Bakufu* was one of commercial freedom from the first.[41]

dition to 50,000 *kan* 貫 of silver and 940,000 *ryō* of gold, was found there and added to the *Bakufu* treasury. Sawada, *op. cit.*, 313. According to the market quotations for 1616, 50,000 *kan* of silver was equivalent to 925,000 *ryō*. *NKSJ* 367. The *ryō* of the time has been estimated to have corresponded roughly to $10 in 1938 (William A. Spurr, "Business Cycles in Japan before 1853," *Journal of Political Economy*, XLVI, 5 (Oct. 1938), 653), or about $20 in 1958. Therefore, if we are to accept these figures, the *Bakufu* treasury must have held something like the equivalent of $87,300,000 in gold and silver.

[39] There was a sharp decrease in output of gold and silver after 1627, while copper continued to be mined in quantities for some time. Takekoshi, *Economic Aspects..*, II, 230, 305. For methods of operation and reasons for decrease in productivity, see Horie, *..Keizai Seisaku..*, 100–2; *NKSJ*, 179, 502. The *Bakufu* monopoly of mining and minting was not entirely effective. For secret mines in the provinces, see *NKSJ*, 1090, and secret minting, *ibid.*, 464.

[40] Chinese history was considered a handbook for statesmen. In China, the Confucian bureaucracy had been remarkably successful in controlling the merchant class. Cf. Karl Wittfogel, "The Foundations and Stages of Chinese Economic History," *Zeitschrift für Sozialforschung* IV (1935), 26–60, and my article, "Some Economic Reasons for the Marked Contrast in Japanese and Chinese Modernization, as Seen in Examples from 'Pre-modern' Shipping and Trading by Water," *Kyoto University Economic Review* (hereafter cited as *KUER*), XXIII, 2 (Oct. 1953), esp. pp. 57–60.

[41] Cf. Horie, *..Keizai Seisaku*, 114.

The principle of freedom of commerce was consistent with Confucian teaching. The Confucian ideal was not a feudal, but a bureaucratic state. However, there is no doubt that Confucian teachings were useful for the maintenance of the feudal society, and provided a theory for feudal differentiation of status. In addition, the Confucian argument which gave emphasis to the productive power of land was useful as a philosophy to maintain the feudal society. Especially, the Confucian spirit of government made control from above its fundamental basis, professing this control to be both benevolent and virtuous. It made the people dependent upon it while keeping them in ignorance. It was for these reasons that the Tokugawa made Confucianism the official orthodoxy. However, on the other hand, Confucianism contains anti-feudal elements, for example, the "Kingly way" 王道 thesis of Chu Hsi, its equalitarian doctrine, as well as the argument for facilitating commerce. This last was to become a particular problem. In the first years of the Tokugawa period, trade was free. Restrictions were applied by degrees, not as a denial of commerce itself, but due to policy considerations in internal control.[42]

The official policy of freedom of commerce of the early Tokugawa period was a great advantage to the merchants. However, it should not be concluded from this that the *Bakufu* policy towards merchants was a benign one. Sir George Sansom's well-known formula, "Statesmen thought highly of agriculture, but not of agriculturalists,"[43] could, in quite another context, apply to commerce and merchants. Not only could an unfortunate merchant be cut down with impunity for some imagined offense,[44] but merchants had virtually no political rights, and in addition, their property was denied any semblance of legal protection.[45] The insecure position of the merchant in the

---

[42] Nomura, "Tokugawa Hōken Sei to Shōgyō," 117. Nomura explains that closing the country did not imply a denial of the advantages of trade itself. The two chief economic justifications put forward were both *ex post facto* by almost a hundred years: They argued (1) self sufficiency, no need for foreign trade; (2) a loss to the country to export gold, silver and copper. *Ibid.*, 117–8.   [43] *Japan, a Short Cultural History*, 465.

[44] *Ibid.*, 462–3. This was the notorious *kirisute-gomen* 切捨御免, permission for samurai to cut down and leave without further ado.

[45] John W. Hall, "The Tokugawa Bakufu and the Merchant Class," *Occasional Papers*, Center for Japanese Studies, University of Michigan, No. 1 (1951), 27.

early Tokugawa period is interestingly revealed in an incident which occurred in 1608, at the time the use of the Chinese coins, *Eiraku-sen*, was prohibited.[46] *Eiraku-sen* were the most highly prized of copper coins, and they were held in large amounts by prosperous merchants, especially in Edo, while coins of poor quality were held mainly by less prosperous people. The prohibition, which relegated the *Eiraku-sen* to "mere pieces of metal"[47] was disastrous to these merchants, but was applauded by the day laborers and other poor people. Officials of the *Bakufu* (even including the *metsuke* 目 附, censors and spies in the provinces) quickly paid their bills in *Eiraku-sen* before the order was issued, taking advantage of foreknowledge. When this happened, some of the merchants guessed that there would be a prohibition, and feverishly tried to unload their *Eiraku-sen*, but too late, and many were forced into bankruptcy.[48]

The insecurity of the merchants' position in Tokugawa society led them into a search for security. Enmeshed in the feudal society and denied the means of achieving a degree of political power, they naturally turned to economic means. As individuals they could try to ingratiate themselves with officials and *daimyō* in order to gain special privileges. They could also form themselves into new types of organizations which were protective in nature, and in which they could lose themselves in anonymity. It is to this development which we shall now turn.

---

[46] Cf. above, page 17, and Hamamura, "Eiraku-sen no Kinshi wo Ronzu," *op. cit.*, 370-1.

[47] Hamamura, "Eiraku-sen no Kinshi wo Ronzu," 367.

[48] *Tōdaiki* 當 代 記 [Contemporary Record] (covering the period 1565-1615), in *Dai Nihon Shiryō* 大 日 本 史 料 [Materials of Japanese History] (Tokyo: 1902-43), Series 12, V, 972.

CHAPTER III

THE QUEST FOR SECURITY

DESPITE THEIR initial legal and political disabilities, the merchants found a number of roads to security in the peculiar conditions of the first century of Tokugawa rule, while the new economy was developing and expanding. They elaborated complex systems of transportation, commerce and finance, and monopolized economic life through organizations which prevented competition, cemented merchant class solidarity and furnished needed protection. But this was not done all at once, and from the first, the merchants relied on borrowed strength. In return for protection and privileges granted by the ruling classes, the merchants furnished essential economic services. There were innumerable ways in which the merchants could be of service to the samurai class. Their economic lives came to be closely intertwined. Rice as a medium of exchange was being replaced by coins and becoming a commercial commodity. In the cities and towns, this change had already taken place in the early years of the period. Most excess rice was tax rice and reached the market, together with other agricultural products in increasing amounts, through the hands of the samurai class, where it was converted into money.[1] Under such conditions, the merchants did not function merely as providers of commercial goods, which is their usual role. As an additional function, they performed the important service of converting tax rice and other commodities collected as taxes into the money which the samurai class needed to buy the commodities required for everyday life, and also the luxuries to which this huge non-productive class was becoming more and more accustomed.[2] As a third function,

[1] Takizawa, *The Penetration of Money Economy in Japan*, op. cit., 7, emphasizes the importance of this change: "No period in the whole economic history of Japan is more significant than the period of transition from natural economy to money economy."

[2] One might be tempted to use the term "leisure class" to describe the samurai, but many samurai were salaried administrators, all ordinary samurai were

merchants engaged in these services made advances on the security of the tax rice and became the creditors of the samurai class.

It was common for merchants to ingratiate themselves, sometimes with gifts and bribes, with the *daimyō* and *Bakufu* officials, receiving protection and special privileges from them. Permission to participate in the foreign trade at Nagasaki was generally obtained in this manner, and merchants later often bid for the privilege of joining this favored group.[3] It is interesting to note that it was privileged (or protected) merchants (*goyō shōnin* 御用商人)[4] rather than samurai functionaries or professional artisans who managed the many huge construction projects which characterized the early Tokugawa period, when many castles, temples, warehouses (*kurayashiki*), and *daimyō*'s residences with samurai quarters (*yashiki*) were built.[5]

There were a number of different types of merchants who achieved privileges from the *Bakufu* and the *daimyō*. Merchant dishonesty was common, and almost expected, when transactions were not on a regular basis,[6] and people preferred to do continuous business with a particular merchant whom they could know and hold responsible. Besides, it was an old feudal habit to engage merchant "retainers."

required to undergo certain military training and exercises, and many had special military duties to perform. It is indisputable, however, that the duties of the ordinary samurai rested lightly on their shoulders.

[3] Kōda Shigetomo, *Nihon Keizai Shi Kenkyū* 日本經濟史研究 [Studies in Japanese Economic History] (Tokyo: 1928), 508–11.

[4] The term *goyō* denotes official or government business. When applied to persons hired to cater to the government, it often connotes a "toady," in present usage.

[5] Kanno Watarō, "Tokugawa Jidai Shōnin no Chifu 德川時代商人の致富" [The Accumulation of Wealth by Merchants of the Tokugawa Period], *Hikone Kōshō Ronsō*, 8 (Dec., 1930), 36. This article is reprinted, with some elaborations, in Kanno's *Nihon Kaisha Kigyō Hassei Shi no Kenkyū* 日本會社企業發生史の研究 [Studies in the History of the Origination of Company Enterprises in Japan] (Tokyo: 1931), 420–499.

[6] *Ibid.*, 20; Miyamoto Mataji, "Waga Kuni Kinsei ni Okeru Shōgyō Rijun no Tokushitsu 我國近世に於ける商業利潤の特質" [The Special Characteristics of Commercial Profits in Our Country in the Early Modern Period], *KSK*, 17, 1 (Jan. 1937), 155. This article is contained, with some changes, in Miyamoto's *Kinsei Shōgyō Soshiki no Kenkyū* 近世商業組織の研究 [Studies in the Organization of Commerce in the Early Modern Period] (Tokyo: 1939), 96–119.

The *Bakufu* and the *daimyō* appointed special merchants as purveyors (*yōtatsu*)[7] to provide specific goods. But among *goyō shōnin*, the most important were those who gathered about the warehouses (*kuraya-shiki*) of the *Bakufu* and feudal lords. In Osaka, where there were the largest number of these warehouses, each *han* at first appointed a *han* official of samurai rank to supervise, called *kurayakunin* 藏役人 (literally, "warehouse official"). His duty was purely custodial in nature, and the business of the warehouse was transacted by merchants.[8] Merchants with well-established credit succeeded in having themselves appointed as *kuramoto* 藏元 and *kakeya* 掛屋 (in Edo, the so-called *fudasashi* 札差 corresponded in function to the *kakeya*). The *kuramoto* was, in principle, in charge of the warehoused goods and the *kakeya* in charge of financial duties such as receiving money for goods sold, keeping it in custody, keeping records, etc. In many cases the *kuramoto* performed both duties. These merchant functionaries were treated much the same way as were the *daimyō*'s chief retainers, receiving rice stipends.[9]

The crucial question is, why did the *daimyō* entrust these important functions to merchants? The answer appears to lie in the fact that the merchants could offer them services at low fees which they could not possibly provide for themselves by appointing samurai who knew nothing about the complicated and to them despicable workings of commerce and finance. In the first place, only two *daimyō* had permission from the *Bakufu* to own property and to build warehouses in Osaka. All the others found themselves in the anomalous position of having to buy and build in the name of some local merchant, from whom they could later claim to "rent."[10] Then, as we have seen, the actual building of warehouses was usually under the supervision of a merchant. Thus, the *daimyō* were actually dependent upon merchants for the very existence of their Osaka warehouses. However, the reason why merchants were retained by the *daimyō* and given an important role was that they could offer essential commercial and financial

[7] *NKSJ*, 11, 1648. Also called *goyōtatsu*.
[8] *Ibid.*, 422.
[9] Honjo, *Social and Economic History of Japan*, 125.
[10] *NKSJ*, 422.

services. Most of the *daimyō* marketed their excess tax rice and other products in Osaka, the central market. In exchange they received specie, most of which they had to spend in Edo and on their constant trips back and forth between Edo and their domains. For these expenses they needed money throughout the year. However, tax rice and other agricultural products were marketed at fixed times, after the crops were gathered and sent to Osaka. This was not convenient, for example, for paying expenses in Edo. Also, it was costly and inconvenient to transport large amounts of silver to Edo, where (for large transactions) gold was used primarily.[11] It was quite natural that the Osaka merchants whose credit was well established issued bills of exchange (*tegata* 手形) whenever the *daimyō* needed money in Edo. Accounts between Osaka and Edo could be settled almost entirely by bills of exchange because Edo merchants bought much of their goods from Osaka. Therefore they owed Osaka merchants, while Osaka merchants owed the *daimyō* in Edo.[12] Not only was silver heavy to transport, but the use of bills of exchange obviated the necessity of weighing and determining the quality of coins. Besides, there was an increasing scarcity of specie from the last years of the seventeenth century. Professor Nomura refers to these inconveniences when he writes, "The development of a credit system where bills of exchange were used among different localities to an extent beyond imagination, when compared to the developing money economy, was by no means the result of a pure credit system, but was because the monetary system itself fell far short of the demands placed upon it."[13] The necessity of using bills of exchange served to enhance the importance of the merchants, particularly the various rice brokers and the operators of the money exchanges.

[11] *NKSJ*, 229. Silver was most used in the Osaka area, gold in Edo. *NKSJ*, 1102–3.

[12] John Henry Wigmore, ed., "Materials for the Study of Private Law in Old Japan," *TASJ*, XX (1892), Supplement I, Introduction, 179–81. Bills of exchange were issued by the first Osaka exchange house operated by Tennojiya Gohei in the Keichō period (1596–1614). Matsuyoshi Sadao 松好 貞夫, *Nihon Ryōgae Kin'yū Shi Ron* 日本兩替金融史論 [History of Japanese Money Exchange and Money Market] (Tokyo: 1932), 11.

[13] *Tokugawa Hōken Shakai no Kenkyū* 德川封建社會の研究 [Studies in Tokugawa Feudal Society] (Tokyo: 1941), 488.

Using this means of transmitting funds to the *daimyō* in Edo, the *kakeya* in Osaka could make himself indispensable by sending money at regular times, and when needed. He could also provide an immediate advance if the market price was low. The next step, an inevitable one because the *daimyō's* incomes were fixed but their expenses were continually increasing, was for the rice brokers to provide loans at high interest secured by tax rice and other products. The fees for handling the sale of rice and remitting the proceeds in cash were low. The *kakeya* drew up statements of account at the end of the year, usually charging 2%, sometimes 3% or 4% of the total proceeds.[14]

In Edo, the pattern was similar. More than three fourths of the rice received from the domains directly controlled by the *Bakufu* was converted into money.[15] The ordinary samurai were in the same position as their lords, and had to convert their rice into money. All came to depend on merchant agents for this service and, more and more, for advances in the form of loans at high interest. *Kuramoto* and *kakeya* were found in the castle towns of the provinces as well as in the cities.[16]

Once having achieved the privileged position of a rice broker or purveyor, a merchant not only enjoyed it during his lifetime, but was in most cases able to hand it down to his heir, and the majority of these positions remained in the family throughout the Tokugawa period.[17] It should be pointed out that the protected merchants of Osaka and Edo both attained considerable influence, but those of Edo, the political center and largest single market for consumers' goods, were far more dependent upon protection than were those in Osaka,

---

[14] *NKSJ*, 229.

[15] Horie, . .*Keizai Seisaku*, 56.

[16] Endō, *Nihon Kinsei Shōgyō Shihon Hattatsu Shi Ron*, op. cit., 11.

[17] Charts in *NKSJ*, 420–441, give the names of privileged merchants retained by 125 *han* with warehouses in Osaka. For the period 1744–1868, of 103 *kuramoto* whose names are now known, 56 succeeded in maintaining the position in the family throughout this period; of 87 *kakeya*, 61, and of 77 purveyors, 60 were similarly successful. Some of the changes, moreover, were merely shifts from one position to another, as *kakeya* to *kuramoto*, or vice versa, so the general situation was one of a great deal of stability and security.

the commercial center. In Osaka, the influence of the merchants was based on their legitimate and important commercial functions which were of a nation-wide nature and upon their organizations of wholesale dealers (*toiya* 問屋, *ton'ya* in Edo dialect), trade associations (*nakama* 仲 間) and their various financial organs.[18]

About 1720, the Confucian scholar Ogyū Sorai (1666–1728) wrote: "The power and prosperity of the merchants is such that, organized together throughout the entire country, prices are maintained high, no matter whether in remote districts or in the castle towns, and it is impossible to oppose so many millions of merchants so closely organized together. Prices will continue to rise, no matter how many inspectors are placed in the castle towns to watch them."[19] This is of significance before 1720 to show the change in the economic position of the merchants since the early years of the Tokugawa period, and it is of considerable interest for the period after 1720, when various attempts to control prices and the merchants ultimately failed and proved Sorai's prediction. For the present, however, we are interested in how the merchants achieved this new position. The clue is to be found in Sorai's references to organization. For the sake of convenience, we will discuss first the organization of the commercial distribution system and then take up the subject of protective and monopolistic guilds and trade associations.

During the late Ashikaga period, "sedentary" selling in established markets began to flourish. Markets became towns, market distribution areas extended, and specialization followed. The distribution pattern of (1) producer to (2) periodic market or fair to (3) consumer tended to change to (1) producer to (2) wholesaler to (3) retailer to (4) consumer.[20] Specialization and complexity in the organization of

---

[18] Sakata, *Chōnin*, 17. As most English works use *ton'ya*, this form is adopted here.

[19] *Seidan* 政 談 [Talks on Political Economy], in *Ogyū Sorai Shū* 荻生徂徠集 [A Collection of the Works of Ogyū Sorai], in *Kinsei Shakai Keizai Gakusetsu Taikei*, op. cit., VI, 83. He refers here only to the merchants' influence through commerce. Merchants mostly began in commerce, then used excess capital in usury and investment, topics which we will treat in the next chapter.

[20] Miyamoto, *Nihon Shōgyō Shi*, 176.

commerce reached a high point during the Tokugawa period. This was in part because of the development of established retailers who required the services of middlemen and wholesalers to supply them. It was also due to the great increase in the importance of central markets such as Osaka, where goods were brought from all over the country to be sold in the population centers, and the great increases in the physical distances between the sources of supply and the consumers.

With the development of the nation-wide economy and the involvement in it of even the semi-autonomous feudal lords, there was a development of geographical specialization in products which mirrored the increased standard of living so often labeled luxury by Confucian moralists of the time. For example, the famous Nishijin fabrics of Kyoto came into demand with the various *daimyō* and *Bakufu* officials; the superior *sake* of Ikeda, Itami and Nada was transported to Shimonoseki, which became a very important collection and distribution point, and sent from there north to various points in Hokuriku and Tōhoku along the Japan Sea coast and south to Kyūshū. This *sake* also made its way around to Edo, where it was much prized. Similarly, rape seed produced in large quantities in the Kinai district was made into oil and sent to various parts of the country, including Edo; bleached linen of Nara, cotton of Kawachi, candles of Aizu, salted salmon of Tango, and other well-known specialty products of the provinces were all collected in the "three cities" and distributed throughout the country.[21]

In the first years of the Edo period, there were already wholesale dealers (*ton'ya*) in Osaka for salted sardines, lumber, cotton and oil, who carried on transactions embracing Kinai and western Japan, as well as Edo.[22] These wholesale houses were at the hub of commercial activities during the Tokugawa period. They specialized both in function and in goods handled. In production areas there were purchasing *ton'ya*, loading *ton'ya* and ship-owning *ton'ya*, and in the distribution points there were unloading *ton'ya*. In regard to commo-

---

[21] Honjō Eijirō, *Nihon Shakai Keizai Shi* 日本社會經濟史 [A Socioeconomic History of Japan] (Tokyo: 1928), 365. The Kinai 畿内 are the five provinces around Kyoto.

[22] Horie, ..*Keizai Seisaku*, 63.

dities handled, there were general *ton'ya* which tended to develop into specialized *ton'ya*, and specialized *ton'ya* which usually changed from handling goods on commission to buying goods outright and storing in anticipation of better prices. There were also various brokers or intermediary traders (*nakagai* 仲買) and middlemen (*nakadachinin* 仲立人). A typical pattern of the flow of commercial goods from individual producers to consumers was: (1) fisherman or farmer to (2) middleman to (3) loading *ton'ya*; when the goods reached the market such as Osaka, goods would ordinarily be taken over by (4) unloading *ton'ya*. If they were sold without delay, they went through a (5) middleman again, then to the (6) retailer and to the (7) consumer. (if not sold immediately, goods went first to a storage *ton'ya*, involving an additional step.) If the goods were reshipped to another market such as Edo, they could go from (1) producer to (2) middleman to (3) loading *ton'ya* to (4) unloading *ton'ya* to (5) middleman to (6) storage *ton'ya* to (7) *ton'ya* for the other market to (8) middleman to (9) retailer to (10) consumer. The pattern for rice and other goods which were collected as taxes differed in the collection phase but differed but little in the distribution phase.[23] This gives some idea of the complexity of the distribution system and the number of hands through which commodities often had to go before reaching the consumer.

There are a number of reasons why there were so many steps in collecting and distributing goods. Distances were great, considering means of transport, between production, collection and consumption points, and these distances became greater with the development of the nation-wide economy. In a period when means of communication were insufficient, middlemen were required to bind together these organs of distribution. The trading boats and boat captain-owners who connected the *ton'ya* of the production points with the *ton'ya* of the collection points are examples of this. Intermediaries among the organizations which collected goods from producers, those which relayed the goods to major collection points, and those who dispersed them to consumption centers were required "to

---

[23] Miyamoto, *Nihon Shōgyō Shi*, 168, 175. *Nakagai* often were brokers and in these cases the term can be translated "middleman."

smooth and make possible the proper relationships of producer and
ton'ya, *ton'ya* and *nakagai*, and between *nakagai* and retailer."[24] It
was safer to have a regular go-between in a period when the methods
of manufacture and quality of commercial goods were not standardized, when special skills were required in trading, and when specia
knowledge of the market was advantageous. Also, in a period when
there was no really effective advertising medium, it was impossible
to stimulate demand in an aggressive manner, and there was no better
way than merely to have a go-between handle marketing or purchasing in a negative manner. Middlemen were employed as agents for a
fee, and it was often impossible to carry on business without them.[25]

The "sedentary" organization of business made necessary a pleth-
ora of special services, to move, store, weigh and value goods. In
addition, with such a complex distribution system and with so many
middlemen, there is no wonder that prices in the cities were high, one
of the perennial complaints of the samurai class. Prices were particularly high in Edo, as the observant German physician Kaempfer
noticed in 1691: "The city of Jedo is a nursery of artists, handicraftsmen, merchants and tradesmen, and yet everything is sold dearer
than anywhere else in the Empire, by reason of the great concourse
of people, and the number of idle monks and courtiers, as also the
difficult importing of provisions and other commodities."[26] Kaempfer
was particularly impressed by the large number of stores in the cities
selling all conceivable kinds of goods. Of Kyoto he wrote, "There are
but few houses in all the chief streets, where there is not something
to be sold, and for my part, I could not help admiring, whence they
can have customers enough for such an immense quantity of goods."[27]

---

[24] Miyamoto, *Nihon Shōgyō Shi*, 202.

[25] *Ibid.*, 153, 194–204; *NKSJ*, 1146. Ingenious merchants did hit on some
very effective advertising techniques. Mitsui retail stores, for example, gave
out free umbrellas marked in large characters with the Mitsui name to
customers who were caught in their stores during a shower. Kinokuniya
Bunzaemon used a "singing commercial" to advertise a boatload of the first
mandarin oranges of the season, a song ("Mikan Bune") still sung in
Japan. Oland D. Russell, *The House of Mitsui* (Boston: 1939), 76.

[26] Engelbert Kaempfer, *History of Japan, 1690–1692* (New York: 1906 — first
published in English 1727–8), III, 76.

[27] *Ibid.*, III, 23.

The greater distances between producer and consumer, as well as the larger scale of commercial transactions in the main collection and distribution centers gave rise to markets in which merchants met with other merchants for the purpose of buying and selling. Large speculative markets existed in goods which were bought and sold in large quantities and which could easily be stored. For example, gold, silver, rice, oil and cotton exchanges were set up in Oaska, where sales on a large scale were conducted very much as they are in a modern exchange. There were speculative markets in Osaka, Nagoya, Ōtsu, Fushimi, Shimonoseki, Edo and elsewhere, but the most famous was the rice exchange at Dōjima in Osaka, where speculation in futures made and broke fortunes in a single day. Prices of rice for the entire Kinai district around Osaka were determined at this exchange, and prices as far away as Edo were strongly influenced. Smaller non-speculative markets in perishable goods such as fresh fish and vegetables were very common, and there were also important non-speculative markets for timber and various textiles.[28]

With this sketch of the organization of the commercial distribution system to give some idea of its complexity and specialization, we turn to another major factor responsible for the changed economic position of the merchant class *circa* 1720, the organization of monopolistic guilds and trade associations. The tradition of protected merchant organizations had a long history before Tokugawa times. To a large extent, Nobunaga and Hideyoshi eliminated the old type guilds (*za*) with their policy of free markets and guilds (*rakuichi-rakuza*). However, they themselves created certain new guilds under their protection, and some of the old guilds persisted in the provinces under the protection of the *daimyō*.

In the early Tokugawa period, it appears that the protected guilds (*za*) in *Bakufu* territories were mostly semi-official in nature, such as the guilds for the minting of coins[29] and the manufacture and distri-

---

[28] Miyamoto, *Nihon Shōgyō Shi*, 159–161; Endō, *Nihon Kinsei Shōgyō Shihon Hattatsu Shi Ron*, 9; also see Smith, "Materials..", *op. cit.*, 123–137, for many details about the Dōjima exchange.

[29] The *Kinza* 金座, for gold, established in 1595, the *Ginza* 銀座, for silver, in 1598, both by Ieyasu, and the *Zeniza* 錢座, for copper coins, in 1636. *NKSJ*,

bution of scales and measures. In 1609 a cinnabar guild was authorized and given the monopoly of manufacture and sale as a reward to its
operator who had secretly learned the process in China and introduced
it in Japan, but this appears to have been rather unusual. Later,
during the administration of Yoshimune, official *za* to handle imported medicinal products were set up, both to check dishonest
practices of substitution and adulteration and to give the *Bakufu* an
additional source of revenue.[30]

With the exception of these guilds which were mainly semi-official
in nature, the policy of the *Bakufu* continued throughout the early
Tokugawa period to oppose monopolistic guilds. The *Bakufu* was
particularly vigilant against any attempts to corner a market, and
any collusion among merchants and officials to make big profits. In
1642, a group of wealthy Edo merchants conspired with the highest
Bakufu financial official, the Kura Bugyō, and more than ten other
important *Bakufu* officials, cornered the Edo rice market, raised prices
and made a huge profit. This struck directly at feudal interests, and
the *Bakufu* executed all their children, exiled the merchants and confiscated their wealth.[31] As early as 1622, the *Bakufu* had prohibited
all types of merchant combinations in a proclamation for Kyoto,
explaining it as a necessary means to secure freedom for the merchants
of all parts of Japan.[32] In a general proclamation in 1657, only certain
types of combinations in specified trades are prohibited, and no mention is made of freedom for merchants, but it appears to have been
no change in basic policy.[33] Similar regulations appeared in 1629,
1666 and 1684.[34] The prohibitions of 1657 and 1684 complain of the
abuses of excluding merchants from the organizations, exacting
entrance fees, cornering markets and carrying on other monopolistic activities. The motivation for these prohibitions was not so

376, 377, 915. Guilds for the monopoly of other metals appeared later: for
copper, in 1738; iron and brass, in 1780. *Ibid.*, 1154, 1111, 1780.
[30] *Ibid.*, 606; 779; 1206–8; 1264; 1307.
[31] Sakata, *Chōnin*, 14.
[32] *Tokugawa Kinrei Kō*, op. cit., VI, 1.
[33] *Ibid.*, V, 351.
[34] Miyamoto, *Nihon Shōgyō Shi*, 205; Nomura, "Tokugawa Jidai Hōken Sei to
Shōgyō," 119–21.

much a desire to free trade as it was the *Bakufu's* hatred for such monopolistic combinations, shared wholeheartedly by samurai and peasants.[35]

The trade associations or guilds (*nakama* 仲間) which grew up in this atmosphere of official hostility were the basic monopolistic organizations of the Tokugawa period. Another important organization was the group (*kumi* 組). These groups existed either as divisions within a *nakama* or as a supra-organization made up either of *nakama* or, more commonly, *ton'ya*. The *ton'ya* themselves, although their function was wholesaling, were organized in a manner quite similar to the *nakama*.[36]

The units of these organizations were single family enterprises, usually of small scale, individually owned and managed. Companies organized along modern lines did not exist, and partnerships were apparently unknown, but two types of plural enterprises were created during the middle and late periods of the Tokugawa era. One was the large family enterprise with a main house and a number of branch families limited by the family constitution. Property was owned in common and profits and losses equally distributed, an effective means of achieving stability and security in the operation of a large enterprise. The Mitsui, Ono, and Shimada family groups are examples of this type.[37] It was common for these larger enterprisers to place one person in a *nakama* in each of the more important markets, skillfully linking them up and organizing a considerable nationwide influence.[38] Another type of plural enterprise developed in the late Tokugawa period to capitalize and manage multifarious and fairly large scale commercial enterprises. These were anonymous combinations of Ōmi

---

[35] Nomura, "Tokugawa Hōken Sei to Shogyō," 120–3.

[36] *NKSJ*, 413; Miyamoto, *Nihon Kinsei Ton'ya Sei no Kenkyū* 日本近世 問屋制の研究 [Studies in the Ton'ya System in Japan in the Early Modern Period] (Tokyo: 1951), 4.

[37] Kanno, *Nihon Kaisha..*, op. cit., 19. See also Honjo, *Social and Economic History of Japan*, 304–5. These family group enterprises were also known as "*kumi*." The Mitsui, for example, let themselves be known as Mitsuigumi only after 1721, when *Bakufu* policy was no longer hostile to such groups. *NKSJ*, 1559.

[38] Nomura, "Tokugawa Hōken Sei to Shōgyō," *op. cit.*, 133.

merchants who owned enterprises known only by the name of one of the members.[39]

Each *nakama* member owned one *kabu* 株, or membership privilege. *Kabu* has often been translated as "share," but this is not quite accurate, as ownership was hereditary and the *nakama* could restrict transfer. The only entrance to an established *nakama* was through inheritance, the purchase of *kabu* which had been "vacated" by bankruptcy or lack of an heir, and through the apprentice system, all subject to the approval of the *nakama* itself.

The apprentice system is one of much interest. It came into fullest use during the Tokugawa period, and began to disappear only gradually, after some 25 or 30 years of the Meiji period. Both merchant and artisan families took in apprentices of about ten years of age who were either related to them or recommended by relatives, customers or sometimes by employment agents. The *nakama* limited the number of apprentices to two per house, in most cases. It was the policy of large marchant houses to give precedence to children of branch employees. At first they were used to watch the master's children and do cleaning and other household chores, as well as to help the master in various minor ways. As the apprentice grew older, he was entrusted with errands. He was not called by his original name but merely called "child," "boy," or "shop-boy" (*kodomo, bōzu, kozō*). At the age of 15 or 16, he was given a name and permitted to help in more important duties. The master took responsibility for the apprentice's food, lodging, clothing, education, supervision, and treatment when ill. In return, the apprentice served without pay, except that he was provided with small gifts and new clothes twice a year, at New Year's and at the Buddhist festival for the dead (*bon*). The lower apprentices were forbidden tobacco, *sake*, and anything except simple cotton clothing.

---

[39] Cf. Kanno, "Tokugawa Jidai no Tokumei Kumiai 德川時代の匿名組合" [Anonymous Combinations of the Tokugawa Period], *KSK* 9 (July, 1930), 38–46. Essentially the same material may be found in Kanno's *Nihon Kaisha Kigyō Hassei Shi no Kenkyū*, op. cit., 22–32. Kanno considers both these types of plural enterprises as forerunners of modern companies. Western type organization of companies was known in the late Tokugawa period by scholars of Dutch, who recommended it, but the first completely Western type company was established in 1867 by Kōnoike. *NKSJ*, 524.

But these restrictions were lifted when the apprentice was given the rank of *tedai* 手 代 at the time of his coming of age ceremony, when he was 16 or 17. It then required from 8 to 14 years for him to become a *bantō*. A *bantō* was the highest ranking apprentice and could be entrusted with the shop and also put in charge of the other apprentices. Then, after a number of years of satisfactory service, he could sometimes establish a separate house (*bekke* 別 家). These separate houses were semi-independent, but still performed services for the main house, and the master-servant connection continued from generation to generation. With some capital from his master, the *bantō* could begin his own business and eventually become entirely independent, after paying off the loan. With the loan paid off, his duty to his master came to be more symbolic than real, and it was common for him to pay formal visits to his master on the first and fifteenth of each month to inquire about his health. He was still expected to help his former master in case of emergency. With the development of larger businesses, the *bantō* were often retained in the master's house and given better treatment and remuneration, but the hope of establishing their own businesses gave meaning and motivation to the apprentice system.

In peacetime, feudal loyalties among the merchants had a stronger real basis than the more idealized loyalty of the samurai to his lord. An example of the loyalty of a Mitsui "chief clerk" (*bantō*) could be cited here. The *bantō* was sent on the difficult mission to explain an "unfortunate incident" to a *daimyō* who, if displeased with the explanation, could have forced the house of Mitsui "out of existence." He took a dagger with him. "If his testimony should fail to satisfy the lord he was to disembowel himself on the spot and offer his life as a price for exoneration of his master and his house." Fortunately, the explanation was accepted, and a modern member of the Mitsui family writes, "The papers that this clerk took with him on this occasion are preserved to this day and bear testimony to the spirit with which he was serving his master."[40] Apparently it did

[40] Mitsui Takaharu, "Chonin's Life under Feudalism," *Cultural Nippon* 8, 2 (June 1940), 82–3. For the apprentice system, see *NKSJ* 1112, 1109, 1356–7, 1485, and Smith, "Materials..," 165–7.

not occur to them to send on this mission a member of the Mitsui family itself.

The *nakama* were different from the medieval *za* both in purpose and in organization. They grew out of the *rakuichi-rakuza*. Guild organization was a habit of long centuries and was a type of organization, according to Miyamoto, "inherent in the feudal system and strengthened by the closing of the country."[41] The *nakama* came to embrace all phases of economic activity. Not only artisans and traders, but those engaged in financial activities, transportation and communications, hotels and restaurants formed themselves into guilds and trade associations of persons engaged in the same activity. The most important were those of the merchants.[42]

There were two underlying emotions which appear to have motivated these organizations: the feeling of need for mutual protection and the feeling of group solidarity, augmented by religious solidarity. As Professor Miyamoto puts it:[43]

The underlying tone was a religious, protective and collective spirit which contained some elements of the uneconomic and irrational. The feeling of understanding and singleness of class status was deep. This understanding and unity was not merely an agreement or pact concluded among them, but a harmony of spirit which is most difficult to express in words.

The *nakama* maintained a meeting place with regular paid clerks, elected officers, provided for mutual aid and protection, and in some cases owned property in common. There was a feeling of fraternity among people engaged in the same economic activity, especially as they often lived in their own separate quarter of a city, where oppor-

[41] *Nihon Shōgyō Shi*, 206.

[42] Miyamoto, *ibid.* According to Professor Allen, the guilds of artisans "bore a fairly close resemblance to the European craft guilds." George C. Allen, *A Short Economic History of Modern Japan, 1867–1937* (London: 3rd impression, 1951), 13. As a matter of convenience, *nakama* may be translated as guilds in the case of artisans and as trade associations in the case of merchant *nakama*, if such a distinction is desired.

[43] "Tempō Kaikaku to Kabu Nakama 天保改革と株仲間" [The Tempō Reform and *Kabu Nakama*], *KSK*, XV, 1 (Jan. 1936), 88. Nomura, "Tokugawa Hōken Sei to Shōgyō," 131, doubts the strength of religious spirit as a motivating factor. It seems to us that the religious spirit no doubt did reinforce the feeling of solidarity.

tunities for common social activities such as pilgrimages, outings, and banquets were plentiful. They often made group pilgrimages to Shinto shrines, made donations as groups, built shrines, donated stone lanterns, etc., and frequently named clubs within the *nakama* for the god of commerce or the god of wealth.[44]

Professor Miyamoto points out that if *nakama* were interpreted merely as economic organizations, many of their activities become illogical.[45] However, immediate economic needs were no doubt of primary importance in stimulating the extraordinary proliferation of these organizations. As might be expected in a generally pre-capitalistic economy where an industrial revolution had not been experienced and where agriculture was predominant, there was apparently little idea of an expanding economy. Each merchant wanted to make secure for himself and his family and heirs his own share of the market. The merchant who was perhaps himself a fugitive from the rice paddies or whose ancestors probably were, did not like to see country bumpkins coming to the cities to engage in commerce, competing and taking business from the established merchants. The *nakama* did their best to limit the number of merchants engaged in a particular trade, using methods of withholding from non-members both credit and sources of supply controlled by *nakama* or *kumi*. However, until *nakama* achieved official recognition and backing, they no doubt had more success in controlling their own members and preventing competition among them than in preventing competition from outside. The *nakama* made themselves and their members as inconspicuous as possible by settling their differences among themselves without reference to public authority.[46]

The *nakama* fixed prices monopolistically, and met possible competition by enforcing standardization of quality and procedures, and prohibiting dishonest practices on the part of members, as well as it

---

[44] Miyamoto, *Nihon Shōgyō Shi*, 207–8.

[45] *Ibid.*, 208. Miyamoto has written in great detail on *nakama* and *kabu nakama* (their name when officially recognized and chartered). See his *Kabu Nakama no Kenkyū* 株仲間の研究 [Studies in Chartered Guilds and Trade Associations] (Tokyo: 1938), a large collection of essays first published in various periodicals.

[46] Miyamoto, *Nihon Shōgyō Shi*, 208; Sakata, *Chōnin*, 31.

could. Profits likewise were roughly standardized by means of the concept of "fair price."[47] As an organization embodying the sum of the economic power of its members, and with close connections with other *nakama*, it was able to perform important services for its members. It was vigilant against infringements of agreements with members by persons outside the *nakama*, and protected members against non-payment of bills and loans owed to members. The primary weapon appears to have been black-listing.[48]

But the most important service which the *nakama* could render was to establish and protect the credit of members. Since most single family enterprises were small, there was a problem in establishing credit. However, for members of a *nakama* this problem was solved. The *nakama* enforced responsibility upon its members with the threat of expulsion for dishonest practices and non-payment of just obligations. Once established, credit was usually carefully guarded, as merchants generally recognized that the success of the family business was not made up of separate deals but consisted of establishing continuous business relations based on credit and good will.[49] The corporate morality enforced by the *nakama* made possible the development of a highly complex system of commercial credit. Several different types of bills of exchange circulated widely among merchants very much as if they had been cash. The system of monthly billing among merchants was usual when business was continuous. Sales by sample, transactions in futures, and buying on margin, all of which were common in the speculative markets,[50] also resulted from the mutual confidence and trust among merchants whose credit had been established and was guaranteed by the *nakama, ton'ya* and *kumi* organizations.

To a very large degree, the individual liberties of merchants who joined *nakama* were absorbed into the collective will of the organization, and duties were inherent in membership. This collective will

---

[47] Miyamoto, *Nihon Shōgyō Shi*, 159, 209; Miyamoto, "Waga Kuni Kinsei ni Okeru Shōgyō Rijun no Tokushitsu," *op. cit.*, 155.

[48] Miyamoto, *Nihon Shōgyō Shi*, 209–10; Wigmore, "Materials..," *op. cit.*, 193.

[49] Miyamoto, *Nihon Shōgyō Shi*, 209–10; Sakata, *Chōnin*, 31.

[50] Miyamoto, *Nihon Shōgyō Shi*, 160–1, 202; Smith, "Materials..," 123–137; Endō, ..*Shōgyō Shihon*.., 9.

was formed at meetings and drawn up into agreements of various kinds.[51] This surrender of individual to group interest was done voluntarily, in order to gain a security not otherwise obtainable. Merchants joined organizations which were virtually underground during the first part of the Tokugawa period due to official hostility. Most members were necessarily conservative and careful, and quite willing to subordinate themselves. However, there were more restless spirits who were experts in getting around regulations in order to make extra profits. Dishonest practices, carefully covered up, meant immediate profits. Also, the use of ingenuity and farsightedness in such complicated maneuverings as transactions in futures and buying on margin, as well as the collection of fees for financial services, etc., brought additional profits.[52]

There is no doubt that the *nakama* played an important role in the settling down of business and its attainment of a degree of respectability, at least among merchants. This settling down, however, was evidently a natural product of the times, and the formation of *nakama* often a result of the merchants' fear that their field of activity was becoming overcrowded. An example of this can be seen in the development of money exchanges in Edo. In the early days of Edo, money exchangers gathered every day in one section of the city with a few *kammon* of copper coins, to exchange for gold and silver. It was common practice to mix in bad coins with the good, but one of the more enterprising exchangers opened a permanent office and gained a reputation for honesty, putting the business of money exchanging on a more responsible basis. At first, there were no more than fourteen or fifteen dealers, but when the number increased to seventy, they met, in 1679, to form a closed *nakama* to monopolize the business and to formulate the rules.[53]

Nakama were not always able to exclude non-member merchants effectively from participating in their trade. Therefore, official recognition and backing were desired. However, official policy was

---

[51] Miyamoto, "Tempō Kaikaku to Kabu Nakama," *op. cit.*, 88.

[52] Miyamoto, "Waga Kuni Kinsei ni Okeru Shōgyō Rijun no Tokushitsu," *op. cit.*, 155.

[53] Takekoshi, *Economic Aspects..*, III, 20. A *kammon* was 1,000 copper coins.

generally hostile. The *Bakufu* did permit certain monopolies by *naka-ma* for the purposes of policing and control. For example, except for a period from 1655 to 1672, the foreign trade at Nagasaki was carried on from Ieyasu's time by privileged groups of merchants. To assist the police in tracing stolen goods, chartered trade associations (*kabu nakama*) limiting the number of houses were permitted for pawn shops (in Osaka, 1642; in Edo, 1692), and for secondhand dealers (Osaka, 1645; Edo, 1702). Also for policing purposes, *kabu nakama* were permitted for public bath houses in Edo about 1650, and for peddlers and hairdressers in Edo in 1659. Each *kabu nakama* was required to pay a small annual fee (*myōga-kin* 冥加金), and each new member was required to pay this fee to the *Bakufu* upon entrance. Other *nakama* must have looked with some envy on these few privileged organizations, but they were not to achieve this status until 1721.[54]

Under this system of guilds, trade associations and groups, techniques were standardized, practiced and improved; credit operations and the transmittal of funds were made possible; production was fostered and protected, dishonest practices and the manufacture and handling of goods of poor quality were minimized, and business relations generally stabilized.[55] Since we have had to do a great deal of generalizing in this sketch of commercial organization in the Tokugawa period, it seems advisable at this point to take a closer look at commercial organization and operation through the example of the shipping business in the Osaka-Edo trade, one of the keys to the commercial history of the Tokugawa period.[56]

At the beginning of the period, with small boats hugging the dangerous coastline, without charts and without marine insurance, shipping was a hazardous business, but profits were extremely good for

---

[54] *NKSJ*, 261–2; Smith, "Materials..," 95–6; Tsuchiya, *An Economic History of Japan*, 177. This event and the circumstances surrounding it will be discussed in Chapter VI.

[55] Miyamoto, *Nihon Shōgyō Shi*, 214.

[56] The material presented here on the Osaka-Edo trade has been published in different form in my article in the *Kyoto University Economic Review*, "Some Economic Reasons for the Marked Contrast in Japanese and Chinese Modernization..," *op. cit.*, 31–4, and is used here with the kind permission of the Faculty of Economics, Kyoto University, as is the material on pages 152–160 of this monograph.

boat captains who were both skillful and lucky, as reflected in a common saying of the time, "A boat captain three years, and a secure future."[57]

The trade between Edo and Osaka was predominant throughout the Tokugawa period, especially before about 1750. The size of the boats participating in this trade during the early years of the period ranged from 200 to 400 *koku* capacity. A company called the Higaki Kaisen 菱垣廻船 was organized among successful boat captains and began offering shipping services in regularly scheduled runs in 1624. Business increased, but losses for the owners of shipped goods (the shippers) were high, due to market price fluctuations, damage and shipwreck settlements, and dishonesty of boat captains. Therefore, in 1694, a monopolistic shippers' *ton'ya* was organized in Osaka with ten groups (*kumi*) embracing all the major shippers of goods to Edo, and at the same time a purchasing *ton'ya* was organized in Edo with ten groups, called the *tokumi don'ya* 十組問屋. The two *ton'ya* federated together to supervise all settlements of losses, distributing them equally among the members. The number of groups was increased in 1716 to 22 in Edo, 24 in Osaka. Federation was facilitated by the fact that many of the Edo *kumi* were begun as branches by Osaka merchants, and the result was a type of cooperative marine insurance. With this protection, the shipping business flourished.[58] In addition, this made possible a close liaison which precluded the possibility of dishonesty on the part of boat captains. If the responsibility for loss to goods had been assumed by the owners of the goods, it might well be asked what reason there was for the shipping company and their captains to provide safe, efficient and speedy service. The answer was the development of the *bansen* 番船 system which will be described later. The problem of fluctuating market prices was dealt with by a monopolistic regulation of supply through the *bansen* system.

[57] Akabori Matajirō, *Tokugawa Jidai no Shōnin* op. cit., 204.
[58] *NKSJ*, 1360. A more detailed treatment may be found in Honjō Eijirō, ed., *Nihon Kōtsū Shi no Kenkyū* 日 本 交 通 史 の 研 究 [Studies in the History of Japanese Transportation] (Tokyo: 1929), 14–20. Legally, it would appear that the Osaka shippers and the Edo purchasers who had contracted for the goods were considered joint owners.

The exclusion edicts of 1638 limiting the size of vessels left room for exceptions in the case of merchant boats, so that vessels of 1,000 *koku* and larger could be used on some routes.[59] The Higaki Kaisen and other shipping enterprisers built vessels with capacities up to 1,000 *koku*.[60] The company owned 160 vessels in the 1770's, and specialized in the shipment of cotton, cotton textiles, oil, paper, sugar, medicines, iron, wax, and dried bonito, holding contracts with the monopolistic Osaka and Edo *kumi* which handled these commodities as part of the *ton'ya* organization.[61] One authority describes the organization of the Higaki Kaisen as "similar to the present-day Nippon Yūsen Kaisha (N.Y.K. Lines)," and adds, "There was no trouble about trans-shipment due to the long-term loading contracts with the owners of the goods."[62]

Sake was a commodity of great importance to all classes in Edo, whether fun-loving merchant, artisan or samurai. It was shipped in casks (*taru* 樽) from Osaka in the boats of the Higaki Kaisen until 1730, when the *sake* dealers broke away and formed their own shipping company, called the Taru Kaisen 樽廻船, which competed with the Higaki Kaisen, at first carrying only *sake*, but then adding other commodities. In 1772, however, the two companies amalgamated, agreeing to fix the number of membership privileges (*kabu*) and to continue operating under their own names. At this time the Taru Kaisen owned 106 boats, making a total of 266 boats between them.[63] Rates for shipment of *sake* from Osaka to Edo were quoted year by year, and were thus not on the haggling basis so common at the time.[64]

[59] Horie, "Tokugawa Jidai no Suijō Kōtsū," *op. cit.*, 85.

[60] Akabori, *Tokugawa Jidai no Shōnin*, 202; *NKSJ*, 1360.

[61] *NKSJ*, 142. For the shipping of tax rice, bids covering whole provinces were received by the authorities from contractors who hired private boats. Freight charges were paid on delivery of the rice, and elaborate regulations provided for every possible contingent. Cf. Wigmore, "Materials..," *op. cit.*, 182–6.

[62] Akabori, *op. cit.*, 202.   [63] *NKSJ*, 142, 1360.

[64] Wada Atsunori 和田篤憲, *Bansen to Seishu Torihiki no Kanrei* 番船と清酒取引の慣例 [The Customs of Bansen and Transactions in Refined Sake], in Honjō, ed., *Nihon Kōtsū Shi no Kenkyū*, op. cit., 433–4. Available records show a gradual rise in rates from 1726, almost doubling by 1835. 1726 and 1835 are the first and last dates available. The rise was from 45 to 82 *momme* silver per horse load (about 300 lbs.), but this rise may have been largely a function of inflated currency.

In the early days of the Higaki Kaisen, there was a great demand for *sake*, cotton and cotton textiles in Edo, largely unfulfilled until the new crop was harvested each year. It was difficult for producers in the Osaka area to meet the demand, and the result was that some produced inferior products in their haste to beat their competitors to the Edo market with the first cotton textiles or *sake* of the season. This was unsatisfactory to all, because hastily made goods of poor quality had the initial advantage, and the bulk of the production was dumped on the Edo market within a short period of time, with a resultant lowering of prices. There was also an overburdening of boat facilities during the rush periods. Therefore, the major producers decided to cooperate for mutual advantage. When the crops were in, an agreement was made which fixed an adequate amount of time for production, alloted to each producer a certain number of boats of similar size and type, and set a day and hour for the first fleet of the season to set sail for Edo from Nishinomiya harbor, near Osaka. There was great interest in the race. It took about three days and nights for the fastest boats, with favorable winds, to go the distance of some 400 miles. The first boat to reach Uraga was given a plaque inscribed with the date and numbered "first boat" (*ichi ban sen* 一番船). All boats were numbered as they came in, and for this reason were called *bansen*. The owners of the first boat's cargo benefited, as Edo purchasers paid a premium for "first goods." The winning boat captain was presented with a *haori* (a silk cloak) and a bonus, but most important, he gained such prestige that he never had to worry about customers to load his boat with goods. As a matter of fact, there was such competition among owners of goods to secure the services of the boats and captains with the best records that the shipping company had to limit the size of their cargoes. The number of boats in each race varied from five to fifteen, and the races were carefully spaced to avoid the disadvantages of any oversupply in Edo. This was the *bansen* system, which proved so satisfactory for cotton and *sake* to both shippers and the shipping companies that it came into quite general use, and in 1847, both the major companies put all their boats on the *bansen* system, no matter what the goods to be shipped.[65]

[65] This account is condensed from Wada, "Bansen..," 420–29. He has found

The Higaki Kaisen and the Taru Kaisen are examples of the development of pure shipping enterprises. However, they sometimes supplemented this business by acting as agents for shippers. In the case of *sake*, the producers did not maintain an agent in Edo, and relied upon the Taru Kaisen to sell the *sake* for a commission in addition to the regular shipping fees. Wada says, "The Edo *sake* trade from the first did not escape certain defects,[66] but it cannot be overlooked that it achieved a major and effective role during this period. It is perhaps enough to know how far trade had progressed, by realizing that already at this time such a large commercial enterprise was carried out on the basis of trust."[67]

The *bansen* system served to develop highly skilled boat captains and crews with considerable pride in their efficiency. The safety of their boats was in their own and their company's interest, and the safety of the goods shipped part of their pride in their efficiency. Speed, of course, was a basic ingredient of the system. The system persisted well into the Meiji period, when the old companies were pradually replaced by the steamers of such modern companies as Mitsubishi and Mitsui. It "provided for co-existence and mutual benefit, and was a good solution to problems of the time."[68]

The merchant class in the seventeenth century was very energetic. Kaempfer noticed this during his two years in Japan between 1690 and 1692. He observed that it was "scarce credible, how much trade and commerce is carried on between the several provinces and parts of the Empire! how busy and industrious the merchants are everywhere! how full their ports of ships! how many rich and flourishing towns up and down the Country! There are such multitudes of people along the coasts, and near the sea-ports, such a noise of oars and sails ... that one would be apt to imagine the whole nation had

documentary evidence of the existence of the *bansen* system in 1738, but it actually existed quite a number of years before that date. *Ibid.*, 420. In 1809, and probably earlier, *bansen* shipment could be obtained for an extra fee.

[66] Some of the vicissitudes of both shipping companies are related in Smith, "Materials..," 113–16.

[67] Wada, *op. cit.*, 447–8.

[68] *Ibid.*, 447.

settled there, and all the inland parts of the Country were left quite desart [*sic*] and empty."[69] Not only were the merchants extremely active, but they were certainly ingenious in creating new commercial and financial procedures and organizations and elaborating old ones to an unprecedented degree. In the process, merchants found a considerable degree of security, first, by making the samurai dependent upon them in a score of ways, and second, by forming themselves into protective and monopolistic organizations. These organizations made the merchants inconspicuous and more acceptable to the ruling classes by enforcing a kind of corporate morality which stabilized their commerce, their position in society and their economic power. In addition, the extreme complexity of the organization of the distribution system worked for the advantage of the merchants who controlled it, because it was quite beyond the samurai class to fathom, and all their later attempts to control it were doomed to failure.

[69] *History of Japan, 1690–1692*, op. cit., 316–17.

CHAPTER IV

THE ACCUMULATION OF COMMERCIAL AND USURY CAPITAL BY CITY MERCHANTS

ONE IS OFTEN reminded in the English literature on Japanese history[1] that the city merchants in the Tokugawa period accumulated great fortunes and attained great financial power, mostly establishing themselves before the Genroku period (1688–1703). The question left largely unanswered is, exactly how did they achieve this ? And, having achieved it, how did they use their accumulated capital ? It is the purpose of this chapter to trace this development.

Fortunes were founded in many different ways. A few examples can be cited here. The greatest of the zaibatsu houses, Mitsui, got its start about 1620 in Matsuzaka, Ise province, brewing *sake*, operating a pawn shop and lending money. With capital thus accumulated, Mitsui Hachirobei opened a dry goods store in Kyoto. This being highly successful, he began a famous dry goods store in Edo a few years later, in 1673, hanging out the sign "Cash payments and a single price." Both these policies were astonishing innovations for the day, and proved most successful.[2]

As Mitsui purchased most of his materials in Kyoto, the next logical step was for him to establish a money exchange in Edo (1683) to handle bills of exchange. With the expansion of business, he established money exchanges in Kyoto (1686), where by that time he was operating a silk wholesale house (*ton'ya*), and in Osaka (1691). It was

---

[1] Especially in Honjo's *Social and Economic History of Japan*, Takizawa's *The Penetration of Money Economy in Japan*, and Takekoshi's *Economic Aspects . .*, op. cit.

[2] *NKSJ*, 1559; Russell, *The House of Mitsui*, op. cit., 73–4. The government saw an advantage in this system of a single price. Later, injunctions were issued exhorting merchants to maintain the same prices for strangers as for regular customers, in an effort to combat the traditional personalistic and particularistic prices which were disadvantageous to the samurai class. Robert N. Bellah, *Tokugawa Religion, The Values of Pre-Industrial Japan* (The Free Press, Glencoe, Ill.: 1957), 27–8.

in 1691 that he came under official *Bakufu* protection to handle transfers of official funds by means of bills of exchange.[3] In connection with this official task, the Mitsui created a fast post system for official mail.

Retail merchants as a rule were particularly cautious and conservative, but dry goods, rice, cake and candy stores often expanded into very large enterprises.[4] Mitsui's Edo stores employed more than 1,000 men and women in the eighteenth century, under a paternalistic policy regulating their lives in minute detail.[5]

Most money exchanges made loans to *daimyō* on a large scale, but with the exception of two or three *daimyō* with whom the family had long-established and special relations, the Mitsui house was prohibited by the family constitution from making such loans. An additional source of income was the ownership of land through reclamation, with official approval.[6]

Another zaibatsu family with roots deep in the Tokugawa period, the Sumitomo, attained prominence in quite a different way. According to the family history, the founder of the merchant house,

[3] *NKSJ*, 1559; Mitsui Takakore 三井高維, "Edo Jidai ni okeru Tokushu Shōgyō to shite no Gofukuya to Ryōgaeya 江戸時代に於ける特殊商業としての呉服屋と両替屋" [The Dry Goods Business as a Special Type of Commerce in the Edo Period, and Money Exchanges], *Shakai Keizai Shi Gaku* [Studies in Social and Economic History], II, 9 (Sept. 1932), 57–62, shows the very close connections between the Mitsui dry goods business and their money exchanges.

[4] Miyamoto, *Nihon Shōgyō Shi*, 181.

[5] Russell, *The House of Mitsui*, 75, describes this paternalistic system in these words: "[It] permitted a certain amount of profit-sharing among the higher classes of employees, and strict rules governing rest periods, health, sanitation and hygiene for all others. Dormitories were set up, and the private lives of the employees were carefully looked after. They were coached in proper speech and required to be neat and clean in attire." This sounds rather like the "honoraole kindness" professed by the owner of the Omi Mills whose 1954 strike made international news. His paternalism included dormitories, free schooling, libraries, and $10 a month for thousands of girls to work in his silk mills. But it also meant that "officials penned them up in their dormitories, opened their mail, blocked romance, forced them to attend Buddhist services and recite such catechisms as: 'All this day I shall be happy to pour all my body and soul into an all-out effort.'" *Time* Magazine, September 27, 1954, 35.

[6] *NKSJ*, 1559.

Masatomo (c. 1585–1652), gave up his samurai status and opened a shop selling books and ironware, and also selling medicines on the side. His son-in-law was the son of a Kyoto copper merchant who had learned how to extract gold and silver (mostly silver) from raw copper in the refining process. This secret, which he had learned from some Europeans at Hirado, became a monopoly of the Sumitomo family, which made a fortune in copper mining and refining.[7] It was the most prominent of the merchant families which the *Bakufu* permitted after 1691 to operate mines, in the hope of increasing output.[8] The Sumitomo house was particularly active and successful in discovering new mines and operating them effectively.[9]

The founders of the present-day Daimaru Department Stores, the Shimomura family, began as modest dealers in secondhand clothing in Fushimi (near Kyoto) in the early seventeenth century. Hearing that a new theater section and gay quarters were being built in Nagoya, the head of the house decided to move there in the 1720's. He set up a clothing and tailoring shop near the gay quarters and flourished, establishing stores in Kyoto, Edo and Osaka in addition to the one in Nagoya. Generally, the policy of the Daimaru-ya was very traditional.[10] However, the Shimomura were untraditional to the extent of adopting the Mitsui policy of fixed prices "as marked," and this proved very successful.[11]

One of the most important of the Osaka merchant houses was that of Kōnoike. The founder, Kōnoike Shinroku, gave up his samurai

---

[7] *NKSJ*, 893.

[8] Horie, ..*Keizai Seisaku*, 101–2.

[9] *NKSJ*, 893. They sent agents throughout the country looking for copper, silver and gold deposits. *Ibid.*

[10] For example, the duty of the boy apprentices was to greet customers and see that they were comfortable. In summer they fanned them with a large fan, and in winter they tended the *hibachi* (charcoal brazier) to see that customers were warm while a *bantō* (head apprentice) showed goods. *Bantō* were trained to ask the age of the customer in order to know what type of clothing was appropriate. They were also instructed to accept the most unreasonable demands and, if required, to bring veritable mountains of goods from the warehouse to suit the most difficult customer's taste. This tradition was continued without change until 1904. *NKSJ*, 973.

[11] *Ibid.*

status before the Tokugawa period and went into *sake* brewing. He shipped his *sake* to Edo and sold it for good prices, as *sake* was often in short supply in the boom town of Edo, in its early years. Family tradition claims that he introduced innovations in the industry and was the first to brew "refined *sake* 清酒." When the *sankin kōtai* system, which required the *daimyō* to ship goods to Osaka and Edo, was in its infancy, he saw his opportunity, and launched into the shipping business for *daimyō* in the western part of the country. This close association with the *daimyō* gave the Kōnoike house the opportunity to lend them money, and in 1656 it established an exchange house in Osaka. It became a member of the famous Ten Exchange Houses (*Jūnin Ryōgae*) 十人両替), selected in 1663 from the Osaka exchange houses to supervise them and act as the official financial agent of the *Bakufu* in Osaka. Kōnoike was appointed *kuramoto* and *kakeya* for a number of *daimyō*, thirty-two in the Genroku period (1688–1703). About this time the Kōnoike began to participate in land reclamation projects, and by the end of the Tokugawa period, there were 121 families (750 persons) living on Kōnoike land.[12]

An equally famous Osaka merchant family was that of Yodoya. The first Yodoya moved to Osaka when Hideyoshi established it as his capital. He was for a time a purveyor for Hideyoshi, and dealt in real estate in Osaka. After Hideyoshi's time, he became a prominent timber purveyor.[13] He was the first Osaka merchant to receive permission from Ieyasu to participate in the Nagasaki trade. But he became most important as the most prominent of the rice brokers, a *kuramoto* and *kakeya* for no less than thirty-three *daimyō*. Rice

---

[12] *NKSJ*, 523. Membership in the *Jūnin Ryōgae* occasionally changed, and dropped as low as five in 1843. *Ibid.*, 771.

[13] Takekoshi, *Economic Aspects..*, II, 242, 246–7. The building of cities offered an opportunity for protected merchants to make money as purveyors of timber and by supervising large construction projects. Kōda, *Nihon Keizai Shi Kenkyū*, op. cit., 508–9, points out that Kumazawa Banzan deplored the system by which only merchants were enriched by these building projects. On the other hand, Arai Hakuseki (1666–1725), writing later, maintained that not only merchants, but officials also made money by accepting huge presents from merchants which he called bribes.

merchants' gathering at Yodoya's spacious headquarters to buy and sell was the beginning of the famous Dōjima Rice Exchange.[14]

Ingenuity and foresight were conspicuous among wealthy merchants. An example of these qualities can be seen in the life of Kawamura Zuiken (1618–1700). He began life as a coolie pushing a wagon in Edo. One day he saw a quantity of melons and eggplants bobbing about in the water near the shore at Shinagawa.[15] He gave a few coins to some beggars to gather them for him. He took the load home, pickled and sold them to day laborers congregated at the official public works and construction office in Edo. An official there talked with him, was impressed, and hired him. Zuiken showed much ability and enterprise, and before long the official put him in charge of the day laborers. He was a very clever trader, and made himself wealthy by arranging many ingenious commercial deals. He became quite famous and was often consulted by merchants on how to get rich. The day in 1657 when the great Edo fire began, he did not wait to see it demolish almost the entire city. He traveled post haste to Kiso, the major source of timber, and bought up all he could. This he sold in Edo at very high prices. Finally, the *Bakufu* put his talents to work, giving him the task of working out the best routes by which goods could be brought to Edo. He carefully surveyed all the possible alternatives himself and accomplished the mission very successfully, formulating the detailed regulations for the efficient organization of rice shipments. He was then put in charge of canal building. Taking advantage of his positions, he built up a considerable fortune.[16]

The examples given are of unusual success, and cannot be said to be entirely representative. However, they do show that there was much opportunity in the seventeenth century for men, whether of samurai or of far more humble origin, to prosper through the use of ingenuity, farsightedness and a certain enterprising spirit, coupled sometimes with a rather antisocial selfishness. Protected merchants in the seventeenth century founded the most spectacular fortunes.

[14] *NKSJ*, 1661.

[15] It was a custom to float them down the river during the festival for the dead (*bon*). *NKSJ*, 295.

[16] *NKSJ*, 295.

Of the six examples given, five fall into this category. The variety of economic activities which these enterprising merchants took up is a striking characteristic of the period. It should be remembered that the seventeenth century was an era of economic expansion through domestic trade, and it was mainly in commerce that fortunes were founded. In the years that followed, the main effort was to hold what was gained, and the adventuresome spirit of commercial enterprise declined.

It would appear that whenever samurai or peasants had economic relations with merchants, the merchants took the lion's share, taking advantage of their clients' general lack of knowledge and understanding of commerce. This was quite easy, as prices (especially retail prices) generally varied with the customer.[17] Samurai were often charged higher prices than commoners. Merchants who had direct dealings with samurai took every possible advantage of their "blindness to the way of the abacus (soroban)."[18] The author of the Seji Kemmon Roku,[19] a famous contemporary work, complains, "Because everyone from the greatest feudal lords on down to the lowest samurai uses money, the merchants make huge profits. In prosperity they far outstrip the samurai class, and enjoy far more conveniences and amenities of life. Without moving an inch, they supply the necessities to all the provinces, they act as official agents of the ruling classes down to the lowest samurai, changing money, handling rice and all other products, even military equipment, as well as providing facilities for travel, horses and trappings, etc., and merchants are indispensable for any kind of ceremony."[20] It has been suggested that those who were most successful in exploiting the

---

[17] Kōda, *Nihon Keizai Shi Kenkyū*, 516; Shōfū Katei 松風嘉定 *Zeniya Gohei Shinden* 錢屋五兵衛眞傳 [A True Biography of Zeniya Gohei] (Kyoto: 1930), 84. Merchants used a great variety of secret codes to prevent customers from knowing market prices.

[18] Kanno, "Tokugawa Jidai Shōnin no Chifu," 37.

[19] 世事見聞錄 [Record of Worldly Affairs].

[20] This work has an introduction by Buyō Inshi 武陽隱士, probably a pseudonym, written in 1816. It can be found in *Kinsei Shakai Keizai Sōsho* 近世社會經濟叢書 [Social and Economic Series, Early Modern Period] (Tokyo: 1926), Vol. I. The above quotation is on page 157.

samurai were merchants of samurai origin, due to their understanding of the samurai and their confidence in dealing with them.[21]

The wealthy merchants of the "three cities" were made up mainly
of: purveyors and protected rice merchants and brokers (*kuramoto*
and *kakeya*; in Edo, the *fudasashi*); the money exchange merchants
(*ryōgae-ya*), and the wholesale (*ton'ya*) and trade association (*nakama*)
merchants. Outside the "three cities," the wealthy merchants were
mainly purveyors and *han*-protected merchants, the privileged silk
merchants of Nagasaki, and the itinerant merchants of Ōmi. The
merchants who were in the most advantageous position were those
who had the closest connections with the feudal ruling classes. All
those listed above fall into this category, with the one exception of
the Ōmi merchants, who were not always under feudal protection.
As they were a particularly influential force in the economic history
of the time, and in many cases came to be important city merchants,
they should be discussed briefly.

The development of the money and credit economy gave great
impetus to itinerant trade. Itinerant merchants were able to go
greater distances, on foot, carrying only goods for sale, since they
sold for cash which they did not carry with them in large amounts,
as they could send money home frequently by means of bills of
exchange. Peddlers penetrated inland, carrying specialty products such
as medicines, candles, textiles, dried fish, etc., and linked even the
outlying islands by sea. As early as Hideyoshi's time, Ōmi merchants were carrying on a lucrative trade in Yezo (Hokkaidō), selling
textiles and other products to the Ainu and bringing back mainly
dried fish products.[22] One of the characteristics of the Ōmi mer-

---

[21] Kanno, "Tokugawa Jidai Shōnin no Chifu," 17. Contemporary records list
48 of 250 important Edo merchant houses as of samurai or *rōnin* descent
and over half of the most important merchants of Kyoto. *Edo Machi Kata
Kakiage* 江戸町方書上, in *Tokugawa Jidai Shōgyō Sōsho* 德川時代
商業叢書 (Tokyo: 1913–14), I 195–357. No doubt some of these warrior
ancestors were acquired for prestige purposes.

[22] Kanno, "Tokugawa Jidai..," 18. Kanno has written an important monograph on the Ōmi merchants, *Ōmi Shōnin no Kenkyū* 近江商人の研究
[A Study of Ōmi Merchants] (Tokyo: 1941), a collection of articles published
in various journals.

chants was a rare combination of caution, daring, and farsightedness. They generally built up their businesses slowly and patiently, taking care not to injure their credit. However, this is not true of all of them. The common saying, "Ōmi robber, Ise beggar" had some basis in fact. Ōmi merchants were notorious, for example, for selling mosquito nets made in Ōmi which had no tops, a discovery made only after the peddler was a safe distance away.[23]

Beginning with itinerant trade, Ōmi merchants tended to become sedentary, establishing branches all over the country, and with commerce as a base, entered and attained great importance in industry, fisheries and finance. Nihonbashi in Edo, Hommachi in Osaka and Sanjō in Kyoto were lined with Ōmi stores, all managed by men sent from Ōmi who left their families at home. The general policy was for all employees to live in back of the stores as was (and still is) customary.[24] According to the *Seji Kemmon Roku*, "Most of the merchants here in Edo are from Ōmi, Ise or Mikawa. Those from Mikawa have not been so successful, but those from Ōmi and Ise have all made their fortunes. There are now many varieties of businesses called either 'Ōmiya' or 'Iseya', ranging from pawnbrokers and money exchangers to *sake* dealers. One after another, branches are set up and prosper. Often the owner remains in his home province, sets up branches in Edo, and gathers in the profits without getting his hands wet (i.e., without much effort)."[25] The epithets "Ōmi robbers" and "Ise beggars" appear to have originated in Edo, where other merchants were envious of their success.[26]

Monopoly pricing was one of the objects of the *nakama, ton'ya*, and *kumi* organizations, and became an increasingly important source of profits. The chartered trade associations (*kabu nakama*) which multiplied after 1721 were able to exclude competition fairly effectively, with *Bakufu* support. To a certain extent, *nakama* and *ton'ya* func-

---

[23] Miyamoto, *Nihon Shōgyō Shi Gairon* 日本商業史概論 [An Outline of Japanese Commercial History] (Kyoto: 1954), 202–3.

[24] Miyamoto, *Nihon Shōgyō Shi Gairon*, 200.

[25] In *Kinsei Shakai Keizai Sōsho*, op. cit., I, 175–6.

[26] Miyamoto, *Nihon Shōgyō Shi Gairon*, 203. The Mitsui were originally from Ōmi, then moved to Matsuzaka in Ise, so they would qualify both as "robbers" and "beggars."

tioned as price-determining organs, but the existence of retail markets for such commodities as fresh fish, vegetables, timber and textiles, meant that they did not have monopolistic control of such markets. The countryside was poor, and traditionally self-sufficient, except for salt water fish, metals, salt, medicine, and miscellaneous commodities, so that the major markets in the provinces were the castle towns, where *nakama* or *kabu nakama*, according to Professor Miyamoto, controlled prices monopolistically.[27]

The *nakama* in the cities and towns had little jurisdictional trouble in dividing markets among themselves as long as they sold their goods in a single market or market area. It is true that demarcation disputes sometimes arose when the types of goods handled by different *nakama* overlapped. An example of this is where the Osaka fresh fish *nakama* quarreled for years with the dried and salted fish *nakama* over which was to handle half-dried fish.[28] However, this appears unusual, and boundaries were generally carefully defined. But difficulties did arise when *nakama* sold in markets outside their own city or town, and came into competition with *nakama* of other areas. This gave rise to a type of cartel arrangement. For example, the clothing merchants of Kyoto and Ōmi found themselves in competition for trade in the province of Kii, especially in Wakayama. They therefore formed a cartel called the Sumiyoshi Kō 住吉講 in the 1770's.[29] This cartel arrangement was only a combination of merchants with a mutual agreement which was neither public nor legal. For this reason, there were violations of the agreement, and competition again reared its ugly head. Therefore, in 1832 the cartel was revived under a new name, and solemn pledges given to abide by it. The agreement was binding only for sales in Wakayama and had no other purpose. It later increased in numbers of participants and areas affected.[30] Other *nakama* which are known to have formed cartels were the sugar

---

[27] Miyamoto, *Nihon Shōgyō Shi*, 159–160.

[28] Smith, "Materials..," 91.

[29] Kanno, "Tokugawa Jidai Shōnin no Chifu," 29. The term *kō* was used mainly for religious groups of both temples and shrines, sometimes temporary groups for pilgrimages, but was adopted by merchants to screen their monopolistic arrangements. *NKSJ*, 494.

[30] Kanno, "Tokugawa Jidai Shōnin no Chifu," 29–30.

nakama of Osaka, the innkeepers' *nakama*, and the twenty-four group shippers' *ton'ya* in Osaka. The *Bakufu* tried to control them, and the Shogun Yoshimune banned them in 1716. After this, several prohibitions were issued, but they continued to function secretly.[31]

Frequent shortages were conducive to profiteering and monopoly pricing. Any alert merchant could take advantage of them, and they were a great boon to the itinerant traders. Shortages were often quite pressing, as was the need for timber in Edo after the great fire, which was an opportunity for profiteering for people like Kawamura Zuiken. The goods involved were often essential consumers' goods, even food. Edo was particularly subject to shortages of various kinds, and there is no doubt that this gave merchants opportunities for unusual gain. Utilizing their monopolistic position, merchants could increase existing shortages, and perhaps even create them. The practice of *ne-machi*, waiting for a price, was common,[32] and the *ton'ya* were in a particularly good position to withhold goods from the market, as they were able to affect the price. The monopolistic regulation of supply from Osaka to Edo through the *bansen* system already described is a good example of this, and Kaempfer's observation that Edo prices were higher than anywhere else in Japan is evidence of it.[33]

The inconvenience of communication was an aid to monopolistic pricing. Consumers had no opportunity to learn what prices were in other parts of the country. The merchant enjoyed almost a monopoly of this knowledge, and was able to make a good thing of it.[34]

The inconveniences of transportation also helped in monopolistic pricing. The experience of an Ōmi peddler, Kawashima Matahei, is a good example of this.[35] "Once he was travelling on the Kiso road, approaching the famous Usui 碓井 peak. He and his companion were both carrying heavy loads of more than 80 pounds each. It was

---

[31] *NKSJ*, 495.

[32] Smith, "Materials..," op. cit., 87; Takizawa, *The Penetration of Money Economy in Japan*, 106.

[33] See above, p. 47.

[34] Kanno, "Tokugawa Jidai Shōnin no Chifu," 22.

[35] This anecdote is taken from Hachiman Shōgyō Gakkō 八幡商業學校, comp., *Ōmi Shōnin* 近江商人 [Ōmi Merchants], 312–4, quoted in Kanno, "Tokugawa Jidai Shōnin no Chifu," 22.

midsummer, and although a time of intense heat, that day a cool breeze came up in the morning. It was a cloudless sky, and everywhere the scenery was of surpassing beauty. They kept climbing, forgetting the fatigue of their legs, gazing about and giving voice to their admiration of the scene. By the time they were half way up the mountain, the sun was high, and it was unbearably hot. Matahei turned to his companion and asked why they should not take a rest on the grass, since the sun was very hot and they had gone far. Before he could finish saying it, his friend, already very tired, had put down his pack and was complaining, with labored breath, that since the fleeting world was wide and offered great variety, it would be better even to labor in the fields with a light heart like a peasant than to carry such a load up mountain paths in such heat, a task not even fit for an ox or a horse. Matahei listened sadly and replied that he himself had been stifling painful sighs, but that he disagreed entirely with him, because if there were five or six tall mountains like this one, the profit would be all the more, and he thought it most regrettable that there was only one. 'If it is so bad that you want to give up being a merchant and become a peasant all because of a single mountain, if happily there were five or six, then I would be the only one to cross them and trade on the other side. Thus I could carry on a flourishing trade by myself, I could prosper greatly, hand down to my sons and grandsons a thriving trade, and my house would long prosper. I am sorry there are not many such steep mountains,' he said, emphatically." The Ōmi peddlers enjoyed a special position as long-range distributors, while overland transportation conditions remained poor. Under the much improved transportation system of the Meiji period, they lost this position and were unable to continue making money as in the past. The very name of "Ōmi merchant" passed out of current usage.[36]

Capital accumulated through commerce and money transactions was often put back into the enterprise. The establishment of branches is a very common example of this type of capital utilization. Sometimes capital was used to branch out into other fields. Mitsui's setting up of money exchanges is an example of this. Besides this, excess commercial and money transaction capital could be turned into (1)

[36] Kanno, "Tokugawa Jidai Shōnin no Chifu," 23.

usury capital, or (2) it could take an important additional step, and penetrate into production through investment or speculation in such economic activities as reclaimed land, *sake* making, textile enterprises, mining, fishing and lumber industries.[37] These two roles of commercial capital were of the greatest meaning for the Tokugawa feudal society.

Of these two alternatives, there is no doubt that loans at high interest attracted by far the greater amount of capital. When excess capital which remained in the cities was used, it almost all went into usurious loans.[38] Before the Tokugawa period, the bulk of money lending was done by temples and shrines, but this function was taken over increasingly by secular merchants in the Tokugawa period and was greatly multiplied by the development of the money economy. The two types of money lending were pawning, where ownership in goods was transferred at the time the loan was made, and loans made on security, where ownership was transferred only in case of default. The most common security offered by the samurai and feudal lords was future delivery of tax rice. As permanent alienation of land was prohibited, it was illegal to use officially recorded land and temple or shrine land as security. However, this left large amounts of land which could be mortgaged under certain conditions,[39] and there were a number of ways of getting around the non-alienation laws.[40]

Usury was the quickest method of piling up capital. The great money exchange houses of Osaka such as Kōnoike, for example, made a specialty of loans to *daimyō* and never participated in usual commercial financing. This is true also, for example, of the *fudasashi* of Edo, who specialized in loans to *hatamoto* and *go-kenin* (direct vassals of the Tokugawa house).[41] Although most rice merchants and brokers as well as money exchanges lent money to *daimyō*, it was considered a dangerous business. Towards the end of the seventeenth century, Mitsui Takafusa warned that it was possible to make money for a time, but bankruptcy was never far away, as *daimyō* often defaulted

---

[37] Endō, ..*Shōgyō Shihon*.., 12; Miyamoto, "Waga Kuni Kinsei ni Okeru Shōgyō Rijun no Tokushitsu," *op. cit.*, 149.

[38] Endō, ..*Shōgyō Shihon*.., 12.   [39] *NKSJ*, 391.

[40] Takizawa, *The Penetration of Money Economy in Japan*, 73, enumerates several.   [41] Endō, ..*Shōgyō Shihon*.., 23.

on loans.[42] It is true that a number of merchant families failed through loans to *daimyō*, but the fact remains that far more capital went into loans at usurious interest rates than into industry. The close inter-relationship between commercial capital and usury is a special char-acteristic of Japanese economic development.[43]

The *daimyō* were continually in need of loans. The penetration of the money economy gradually undermined their economic position, as well as that of the Tokugawa themselves. The impoverishment of the *daimyō* was hastened by the demands of the *sankin kōtai* system, the *Bakufu* policy of shifting the positions and lands of *daimyō* as rewards or punishments, as well as the policy of ordering the *daimyō* to undertake the construction of castles, dams and emergency public works. The process of becoming indebted to merchant usurers began early. Kumazawa Banzan (1619–1691) wrote, "It is rare for a samurai these days, whether ordinary samurai or feudal lord, not to have borrowed large sums of money." He estimated that the total amount of the *daimyō*'s debts was a hundred times the amount of cash in the country.[44] There is no doubt considerable exaggeration here, but it gives some idea of the immensity of the debt.

The first and perhaps the most important of the merchants lending money to the *daimyō* were the various protected rice merchants and brokers (*kuramoto* and *kakeya*), both in the cities and in provincial towns. The large money exchanges also were important, especially in Osaka and Edo. Their loans to *daimyō*, at usurious interest rates, were only part of their many functions, including exchange of gold, silver and copper coins; receipt of deposits, issuance and collection of bills of exchange, transfers of official funds, creation of credit, etc., func-tions very like those of modern banks.[45] There was hardly one of the

[42] *Chōnin Kōken Roku* 町人考見録 [A Record of Observations of Towns-men (or, more freely) A Townsman Looks at Townsmen], in *Nihon Keizai Sōsho* 日本經濟叢書 [Japanese Economic Series], Vol. 15, 55.

[43] Endō, ..*Shōgyō Shihon*.., 24. The legal position and the historical devel-opment of the feudal-merchant struggle over loans will be discussed in Chapter VI.

[44] *Shūgi Gesho* 集義外書, in *Nihon Keizai Sōsho*, Vol. 33, 234, quoted in Takizawa, *The Penetration of Money Economy in Japan*, 94.

[45] Endō, ..*Shōgyō Shihon*.., 26. The lack of a single monetary standard with auxiliary coins gave rise in the first place to the money exchanges, but it

important money exchanges which did not make loans to *daimyō*. Besides their exchange activities, they sold rice and other commodities of their *daimyō* clients, thereby accumulating capital from three sources, all very closely inter-related: commerce, money transactions, and usury.[46] For the *fudasashi* of Edo, usury was a far more important source of capital than for the money exchanges, as the fees which the *fudasashi* collected for handling rice, their only other activity, were small.[47]

Although in the cities the bulk of money lending was to the samurai class, loans to small merchants and other commoners also comprised a big business. The most important types were: (1) "Blind money". The *Bakufu* gave special privileges to the blind money-lenders' *nakama* due to their physical handicap, permitting them to call their money "official money" and to collect high interest on it. They were most important in Edo, but similar *nakama* existed in Osaka and Kyoto as well. Interest rates in Edo were 10% to 12%, with maximum time for repayment usually three months. Using the protection of the *Bakufu*, they also extracted "thank money" by discounting it from the principal at the time the loan was made, thus adding greatly to the interest rate. They were most arbitrary in collecting loans, often on a day's notice. When a loan was overdue, they were known to gather in a group, go to the debtor's house, push their way in, and stay day and night shouting insults in order to force payment.[48] The blind money lenders could usually depend on the *machi bugyō* to give them an advantageous decision if cases were brought to litigation. There were about 3,000 members in the *nakama* in Edo, and it was common for unscrupulous capitalists to use the blind men as a front while actually operating their businesses from behind the scenes.[49]

was the great growth in commercial transactions and credit which increased their importance and caused their expansion. Horie . .*Keizai Seisaku*, 55.

[46] Endō, . .*Shōgyō Shihon*. ., 27.

[47] *Ibid.* Outside of Edo, the copper coin exchanges (*zeni ryōgae*) were the main lenders to ordinary samurai. Horie, . .*Keizai Seisaku*, 57.

[48] A practice not entirely unknown today. It is used, for example, to get unwanted tenants out of a house.

[49] *NKSJ*, 255; Honjō, "Tokugawa Jidai no Kin'yū Seido Gaisetsu," 徳川時代の金融制度概説 [An Outline of the Credit System in the Tokugawa Period], *KSK*, 10 (Sept., 1930), 62.

(2) "Crow money." These were loans made one day, to be paid back the next morning. They were called "crow money" because the loan had to be paid back when the crows began to caw at dawn. Interest was discounted when the money was lent, and amounted to well over 5% per month. Restaurants, theaters and tea houses often used this temporary means of keeping their businesses operating.

(3) "Morning to night money." A person would borrow 100 *mon* (copper coins) in the morning, and had to return 101 *mon* in the evening. Loans at this very high interest were always very small, and made mainly to peddlers who used the money to buy their wares this way every morning. Like "crow money," these loans did not require any written instrument, but did require a third party to guarantee the loan orally.

(4) "Dissipation money." Money lenders were only too happy to lend money at very high interest to the sons of families of wealth who spent their time in gay quarters and needed to be tided over from time to time. The usurers knew the family would pay and that the son would do his best to pay to keep his family from knowing of his follies.[50]

(5) "Double on death." Some money lending arrangements combined a speculative feature. Ibara Saikaku (1642–1693), the famous Osaka novelist, has described an ingenious scheme where the money-lender made secret loans to the sons of merchants to be paid back double when they came into their inheritance.[51]

If the borrower were a merchant, he was able to use his borrowed money to buy a considerable amount of goods, if he wished. For example, he could buy goods for 300 *mon*, then borrow 250 *mon* with these goods as security, buy 250 *mon* worth of goods and

---

[50] *NKSJ*, 255.

[51] Howard S. Hibbett, "Saikaku as a Realist," *Harvard Journal of Asiatic Studies*, 15, 3–4 (Dec. 1952), 411. This description is to be found in Saikaku's *Honchō Nijū Fukō* 本朝二十不孝. The term "double on death" (*shini-ichibai*) is certainly a case of calling a spade a spade. Except with Osaka townspeople, who were (and are) exceedingly forthright, words for death were generally shunned, if not tabooed. Even now, a common rejoinder, when business is bad, to the traditional Osaka greeting, "*Mōkarimakka?* (Making money?)," is "*Shini-shini!* (Dying, dying!)"

repeat the process. He could buy a total of 920 *mon* of goods by this method.[52]

Pawnbrokers also carried on flourishing businesses. The Edo pawn-brokers' *nakama*, organized first in 1642, became a chartered trade association (*kabu nakama*) in 1692. In 1723 there were 253 groups (*kumi*) with 2,731 member houses. In Osaka, the pawnbrokers, forming a *kabu nakama* as early as 1642, had 2,420 member houses in the 1850's. In Kyoto the *kabu nakama* was organized in 1699 with 628 members. Pawnbrokers were particularly numerous in the countryside due to the fact that the usual method of borrowing money was to place land in pawn.[53]

There were a number of laws governing usury, including various limitations on the interest rates. In 1736, for example, a maximum of 15% *per annum* was fixed, but in 1842, it was lowered to 10%. How-ever, these restrictions were unrealistic and not followed.[54] Actual interest was no doubt considerably higher than 15%, not only be-cause laws were paid little attention, but because it was common practice to assess additional fees, usually in the form of "thank money."[55]

Why did money-lending take the form of usury? One reason was that borrowing was mainly for the purpose of essential comsumption. The feudal classes—the *daimyō*, samurai and peasants—were forced

[52] Sakata, *Chōnin*, 17. A similar expansion of credit was effected by means of *tegata* (bills of exchange), where 60,000 or 70,000 *ryo* in *tegata* could be issued with a capital of only 10,000 *ryo*, a "dangerous expansion of commercial credit." Matsuyoshi, *Nihon Ryōgae Kin'yū Shi Ron*, op. cit., 289–90.

[53] Honjō, "Tokugawa Jidai no Kin'yū Seido Gaisetsu," 61; *NKSJ*, 708.

[54] Honjō, "Tokugawa Jidai no Kin'yū Seido Gaisetsu," 63. Fifteen percent would have been considered rather low during most of Chinese history, and very low in India. Japanese writers tend to draw European rather than Asian analogies, perhaps because they feel Japanese economic development has more in common with European than Asian experience, and also because they have been trained almost exclusively in European economics.

[55] Organizations for cooperative credit did exist. They were called *mujin kō* 無 盡 講 or simply *mujin*. Members paid a membership fee, making up a lottery fund used for (1) gambling, (2) charity, (3) loans to members. Gambling was legally prohibited, but went on secretly, often posing as charity. Use for loans seems to have been much less frequent than for gambling. *NKSJ*, 495–6; Wigmore, "Materials..," op. cit., Supplements 3–4, 322–3.

to borrow, even at high interest, because of their impoverished conditions. Also, risk of non-collection was an important factor. There was much risk of non-payment, whether loans were made to the samurai class or to the lower classes.

The two principal alternative uses for capital were commerce and usury. Profits from both were high. The fact that small merchants were willing to borrow at usurious rates in order to carry on their businesses gives proof of this. Economic conditions were comparable to those in Europe which had given rise to usury. The close and persistent inter-relationship between commercial capital and usury capital in Japan is the key, according to Endō, to the question of why commercial capital did not have an independent development as capital either for commercial or financial transactions, and why it was unable to develop into the type of industrial capital seen after the Meiji Restoration.[56]

There was only one factor which operated in favor of the debtor, and that was inflation. The rise in prices during the seventeenth century was steady, although relatively moderate. Between 1616 and 1695, the date of the first currency devaluations, rice prices increased about three and a half times.[57] Other prices tended always to follow rice prices up but seldom down, creating a problem for the feudal ruling classes, especially when fluctuations in rice prices became violent, after about 1710.[58] The general trend continued upward, however, hastened by the currency devaluations, and by the middle of the nineteenth century, the ryō had fallen to an estimated one

[56] Endō, . .Shōgyō Shihon. ., 24.

[57] Honjō, Tokugawa Bakufu no Beika Chōsetsu 德川幕府の米價調節 [The Regulation of Rice Prices by the Tokugawa Bakufu] (Kyoto: 1924), 408–10. An analysis of how this inflation was possible during a period of increasing specie scarcity will be found in my unpublished M.A. thesis, Monetary Problems of Seventeenth Century Japan (University of California, 1951), especially 63–95. The major factors were the draining of feudal treasuries, putting specie into circulation, and, more important, monetary expansion through the issuance in the han of paper currency (generally convertible), and Bakufu currency devaluations, and, perhaps most important of all, the expansion of credit by the merchants. Increasing monopolistic pressures comprised another factor.

[58] Horie, . .Keizai Seisaku, 128. See the chart in Sansom, Japan, a Short Cultural History, 470, which shows these violent fluctuations.

eighth of its purchasing power in 1661.[59] This means a price increase of something like eleven times since 1616.

"Placed in the stream of the price increase, money became capital."[60] Not only did it stimulate commerce in the form of commercial capital; it took an important step in the direction of industrial capital.[61] Ordinarily, medieval commercial capital did not touch the organization of production, and it was characteristic for it to be increased through profits in the distribution process alone.[62] The penetration of capital followed the penetration of the money economy into the traditionally self-sufficient farm communities. It began first in areas near the cities, and spread gradually to the more remote areas,[63] first reaching those places adapted to a particular type of production, for example, fishing villages and mining villages, or to those places unusually rich in farm products, especially areas where cotton was produced and those where fruit trees were cultivated.[64]

Examples of the system of loans on future production advanced

[59] A. Andreades, *Les Finances de l'Empire Japonais et leur Evolution*, 26, cited in G. C. Allen, *A Short Economic History of Japan, 1867–1937*, op. cit., 20.

[60] Miyamoto, *Nihon Shōgyō Shi*, 144.

[61] During a period of steady price rise, capital is ordinarily more attracted by investment in productive enterprises because of the hope of higher prices by the time the resulting production is ready to market. Simple loans, on the other hand, are relatively unattractive because the money repaid may not be as valuable as the money lent. During the long inflationary period of the so-called "price revolution" in Europe between about 1550 and 1650 stimulated by the inflow of precious metals from the New World, there was an important shift from usury to investment in productive enterprises. Cf. G. N. Clark, *The Wealth of England* (London: 1946), especially 57 ff.

[62] Horie, ..*Keizai Seisaku*, 127. This was true in Europe as well as in Japan. Horie argues that industrial capital does not necessarily arise from commercial capital as the next and inevitable "stage." He points out that historically, it has followed effective national unification, and cites the examples of the U. S. after the Civil War, and the late arrival of industrial capital in Italy and Germany. ..*Shihon Shugi*.., 3–4. The incomplete nature of the Tokugawa unification could be cited here as an obstacle to industrial capital development.

[63] Saikaku, in one of his *Honchō Nijūfukō* stories, is surprised at the influence of money even in the remotest mountain village "where they think dried sea-bream grow on trees, and where no one knows how to use an umbrella." Quoted in Hibbett, "Saikaku as a Realist," *op. cit.*, footnote, p. 412.

[64] Horie, ..*Keizai Seisaku*, 70–1.

by the city *ton'ya* can be seen already in the first hundred years of
the Tokugawa period. For example, the Osaka salted sardine *ton'ya*
lent silver to the fisheries in various parts of the country for them to
purchase materials for fish nets, and established an interest through
kabu (membership privileges) in new fisheries and new fish net producers. The sardines which were caught were salted and sent to the
ton'ya. The cotton *ton'ya* of Osaka, as another example, desiring to
monopolize the purchase of cotton, secretly advanced enough silver
so that when shipments arrived, they could claim them. The loading
ton'ya, having direct contact with producers, were the first
to introduce the system of advances so that they could handle
the commodities produced. Either *ton'ya* or money lenders operating
essentially wholesale enterprises sometimes lent money to small
producers in the cities and towns and to samurai whose families did
handicraft work at home, but the bulk of these loans went to producers in agricultural communities. This was because there was little
room for commercial capital to enter the handicraft industries in the
cities. In contrast to usury, this type of lending was creative of new
production, but, like usury, these advances carried quite high interest
rates, and came to absorb most of the producers' profits.[65]

Many merchants, rather than advancing loans to producers, managed their own productive enterprises. The most common example is
the manufacture of *sake*.[66] Another important example is the management of agriculture on reclaimed fields (*shinden* 新田), which made
great strides from the eighteenth century onwards.[67] By 1853, it has
been estimated that 30% of cultivated land was controlled by these
owners of new land.[68] In the examples of successful merchants given

---

[65] Horie, ..*Keizai Seisaku*, 58, 70; ..*Shihon Shugi*.., 31; "Edo Jidai no
Ōsaka no Kōgyō 江戸時代の大阪の工業" [Osaka Industry in the
Edo Period], *Keizai Ronsō*, 51, 5 (Nov. 1940), 128–147.

[66] Almost all the *sake* breweries in the Kantō (Edo area) were originated by
Ōmi merchants. Miyamoto, *Nihon Shōgyō Shi Gairon*, 202.

[67] Horie, ..*Shihon Shugi*.., 30. An important study of *shinden* has been made
by Matsuyoshi, *Shinden no Kenkyū* 新田の研究 [A Study of Reclaimed
Fields] (Tokyo: 1936).

[68] Toyoda Shirō 豊田四郎, *Nihon Shihon Shugi Hattatsu Shi* 日本資本
主義發達史 [A History of the Development of Capitalism in Japan]
(Tokyo: 1950), 17.

above, it has been noted that both the Mitsui and Kōnoike began in *sake* brewing and used excess capital extensively in establishing land ownership through land reclamation.[69]

Another significant development was the "putting-out" system, when city merchants made advances of raw materials and equipment rather than money to the producers. The tendency was to employ more and more workers rather than to rely on middlemen, thus making their own links with the producers. Provincial merchants, who were often of peasant origin, or who remained peasant landholders, also adopted the "putting-out" system. The larger merchants or peasant landholders and usurers expanded in some areas to the extent of industrializing the farm communities with subcontractors supervising the subsidiary handicraft work done there. In trades where operations were both complex and numerous, the merchants assumed responsibility for dividing the work in its various stages among the producers. This system produced large amounts of raw silk, cotton and silk textiles, paper, mats, lanterns, etc., by the end of the Tokugawa period.[70] As with capital advances to industry, the *ton'ya* was likewise most important in the "putting-out" system. The *ton'ya* became an instrument through which production was controlled by commercial capital, both by providing capital for production and by putting out the raw materials. It was through this controlling position that the *ton'ya* organizations were able to limit production and set monopolistic prices on the goods they handled.[71]

[69] For city merchants, purchase of houses offered another source of income. At first, houses were allotted to townspeople, but the authorities were unable to keep people from acquiring and renting houses. Some well-to-do merchants owned large numbers of houses and hired managers to take care of them. By the early 18th century, it was said that 60% of the houses in the large cities were rented. Kobata Jun 小葉田淳, "*Kinsei Keizai no Hattatsu* 近世經濟の發達 [The Economic Development of the Early Modern Period], in *Kinsei Shakai* 近世社會 [The Society of the Early Modern Period], (Vol. IV of *Shin Nihon Shi Taikei*) (Tokyo: 1954), 295.

[70] Miyamoto, *Nihon Shōgyō Shi*, 201; Allen, *A Short Economic History of Japan*, op. cit., 13. Thomas C. Smith, in *Political Change and Industrial Development in Japan: Government Enterprise, 1868–1880* (Stanford Univ. Press: 1955) stresses the importance of well-to-do peasants in the creation of a class of rural industrialists.

[71] *NKSJ*, 1147.

This penetration of commercial capital into the process of production meant its conversion into industrial capital, the extent and meaning of which has been for years a bone of contention among Japanese economic historians.[72] It also resulted in the development, on a small scale, of a factory system. Professor Horie writes on this question, "A development from the *ton'ya* system of cottage industry to a system of manufacture in factories without power-driven machinery can be seen in the last years of the Tokugawa period ... Putting aside as a question of definition the problem of whether or not this development meant that Japan had entered the stage of industrial capital, it must be concluded that commercial capital simply did not have the strength of its own to make a rapid transition because of fixed limits which prevented its further development."[73]

As has been suggested in the last chapter, most merchants first achieved wealth through commerce carried on either under direct feudal protection or within the protective walls of a monopolistic organization like the *nakama*. The money thus accumulated was to some extent hoarded[74] or spent for legally forbidden luxuries and high life, especially in the gay quarters. However, such employment of capital has more relevance for social than for economic history. Merchants used their capital in two very important economic ways: lending money at usurious interest rates, a traditional role for excess capital, and a means to gain long-range security which was difficult through commerce alone; and investing in productive enterprises, including land. Such investment was a new role for commercial capital which meant an important shift in the direction of industrial capital. All these uses of capital were destructive of the feudal society.

---

[72] See the short article by Nobutaka Ike, "The Development of Capitalism in Japan," *Pacific Affairs* 22, 2 (June, 1949), 185–90, devoted to the "manufacture controversy."

[73] ..*Shihon Shugi*.., 45–6. The limits referred to here will be discussed in Chapter IX.

[74] Sansom, *Japan, a Short Cultural History*, 472, describes the great wealth hoarded by Yodoya.

CHAPTER V

THE "HAPPY SOCIETY" OF THE GENROKU PERIOD
(1688–1703)

The period called Genroku may be looked upon as the zenith of Tokugawa prosperity, and perhaps even the justification of feudal rule, for here was peace and plenty and a great flourishing of the arts — a happy society as human societies go.[1]

After many years of active effort to achieve a degree of security in a hostile feudal atmosphere, the merchant class finally emerged into an era of prosperity and confidence. The merchants were favored by the samurai's contempt for commerce, the softening, with years of peace, of the harshness of military rule and feudal discipline, and the increased standard of living and luxury enjoyed by a large percentage of the population, particularly in the cities.

The fact that the standard of living was increasing throughout the century which culminated in the Genroku period seems to be subject to little doubt. It was a period of free spending and thriving business, and the merchants whose services were indispensable to their "betters" profited in increasing numbers from the lavish spending of the Shogun and his retainers, of the *daimyō*, and, to a lesser extent, of the ordinary samurai. By the Genroku period, everyone was involved in the flourishing money economy,[2] and even the downtrodden peasants who did not follow their brothers to the cities in search of a better life, seem to have come in for a small share in the prosperity.[3] Muro Kyūso (1658–1734), an influential Confucianist, in an essay written in 1711, said that no one tied his hair up in paper cords as had always been the custom, but bought aloes-wood oil for the hair and many fancy ornaments. Husbands even gave these things to their wives and children, to make them happy, showing that commercial enterprises had been

[1] Sansom, *The Western World and Japan*, 197.

[2] Takizawa, *The Penetration of Money Economy in Japan*, 49.

[3] Cf. Tsuchiya, *An Economic History of Japan*, op. cit., 158, who states, "Food was better and the farmers' incomes increased."

formed to sell manufactured goods to peasants.[4] There were well-to-do peasants in the agricultural villages, often concerned with local administration, who lived a life whose amenities were hardly less than those of the upper samurai and the well-to-do merchants. It was natural that the common peasants were affected by the example of this prosperity at such close hand, as well as news about the gay life of the cities. The authorities looked upon this as rampant luxury, but, according to Horie, "it should really be thought of as a rise in the standard of living."[5]

The inflation seems to have been gradual enough not to have created grave maladjustments. Honjō has shown how the factor of higher or lower prices of rice did not affect the *Bakufu* and samurai finances really adversely until the fluctuations became sharp, after the Genroku period, and that the poverty of the samurai became extreme only after the middle of the Tokugawa period.[6] Moreover, it should be remembered that the poverty of the samurai class was only comparative, and was on a different level from that of the peasants. The samurai never had to worry about obtaining sufficient food.[7]

By the beginning of the Genroku period, evidence of the increasing standard of living can be seen in the flood of specialty products reaching the city markets and in the appearance in the cities of many shops selling things formerly made by women in their homes. Examples are split-toe socks (*tabi*), paper cords for tying the hair (*motoyui*), and other articles of personal and household use.[8] During the general economic expansion of the early Tokugawa period, there is no doubt that the increasing standard of living began among all the city dwellers, whether *chōnin* or samurai, and then extended even to the agricultural communities.[9]

[4] ..*Keizai Seisaku*, 70, citing *Nihon Zaisei Keizai Shiryō* 日本財政經濟史料 [Materials of Japanese Financial and Economic History] (Compiled by the Finance Ministry, Tokyo: 1922-3), VII, 861. Aloes-wood produces an aromatic oil. The reference to paper cords (*motoyui*) is an exaggeration, as they remained in common use.

[5] Horie, ..*Shihon Shugi*.., 31-2. "Luxury" meant living beyond the standard assigned to the classes by the feudal rulers. Horie, ..*Keizai Seisaku*, 80.

[6] *The Social and Economic History of Japan*, 217, 281-3.

[7] Sakata, *Chōnin*, 96.

[8] Miyamoto, *Nihon Shōgyō Shi Gairon*, 188.   [9] Horie, ..*Keizai Seisaku*, 80.

The samurai class participated in this increased standard of living only by going into debt to the merchant class. The *Bakufu* policy of keeping the *daimyō* in an impoverished state was paralleled by a policy of actually encouraging luxury and extravagance on the part of the outer *han* and their retainers, as part of the policy of weakening potential enemies, while taking strong measures to discourage it in their own direct retainers and in the inner *han*. Ironically, the first policy was as successful as the second was unsuccessful. The inner *han* and the retainers of the Tokugawa house were quite unable, and certainly unwilling, to remain outside the tendencies of the time. Furthermore, as if to heighten the irony, natural disasters, a financial system created under the assumption of unchanging conditions, and spendthrift Shoguns combined to exhaust even the *Bakufu* treasury.

Ieyasu understood the power of money and piled up a considerable treasure. Hidetada, Shogun from 1605 to 1622, was conservative and economical, but the third Shogun, Iemitsu (1622–1651), the fourth Shogun Ietsuna (1651–1680) and the fifth Shogun Tsunayoshi (1680 to 1709), for a variety of reasons, all spent a great deal more than the income of the *Bakufu*. During the reign of Iemitsu, the construction of the Nikkō mausoleum, the reconstruction of the Imperial Palace at Kyoto and of the Edo castle after its destruction by fire, as well as the cost of the Shimabara Rebellion of 1637–8, took much of the accumulated reserves. In addition, Iemitsu gave lavish gifts in money to relatives and feudal lords.[10]

During the time of Ietsuna, Edo was almost wiped out in the famous Meireki fire of 1657, and much money was expended in rebuilding and in lending to the sufferers.[11]

But it was not until the reign of Tsunayoshi that the impoverishment of the Edo government became more and more pronounced. Tsunayoshi was a lover of luxury and extravagance and spent tremendous amounts of money in charity, music and public works, and, a devout Buddhist, he spent large amounts of money for the

---

[10] Sawada, "Financial Difficulties of the Edo Bakufu," *op. cit.*, 314. For example, in 1632, he gave away 288,050 *ryō* in gold and 17,200 *kan* in silver, as a memento of his father, Hidetada. Takekoshi, *Economic Aspects..*, II, 217.   [11] Sawada, 314.

construction of temples and monasteries.[12] To aggravate the financial
embarrassment of the government, there were frequent earthquakes
and conflagrations, requiring the expenditure of a vast amount of
money for relief and reconstruction, and corrupt officials increased
the government's difficulties.[13]

In principle, the Tokugawa government was very much the same
as the governments of the various *han*, and financing was of the
"family" type, the expenditure fixed according to income, in contrast
to modern governments. For this reason, when the *Bakufu* treasury
was found unable to meet a demand for 100,000 *ryō* for Tsunayoshi's
proposed pilgrimage to Nikkō, in 1695, the *Bakufu* turned in desperation to a policy of devaluation of the currency through recoinage.[14]
This impoverishment of the *Bakufu* as well as the *han* meant that the
money formerly in their treasuries found its way permanently into
the control of the merchants. The Genroku period saw the completion
of this process. This reckless spending had important effects other
than to encourage general extravagance. It strengthened the foundations of the commercial money economy, permitted the sound
establishment of the credit system, and the resultant increase in the
material standard of living had a lasting effect in stimulating productive power.[15]

The Genroku era was the critical period in the development of the
merchant class, because it was during this time that it consolidated
its economic strength, and emerged as a force which the feudal ruling
classes could no longer overlook. In the process of this consolidation,
the merchant for the first time seemed to feel a security for which he
had long strived. The security of the merchants of Osaka was established earlier, was of longer duration and was more solidly based on
their essential nation-wide commercial and financial functions and
ingenious organizations. That of the merchants of Edo was of a dif-

---

[12] Honjo, *The Social and Economic History of Japan*, 271; Sawada, 314.
[13] Honjo, *The Social and Economic History of Japan*, 271.
[14] Recoinage was resorted to many times to stave off bankruptcy. The *han*
    policy analogous to this in both cause and effect, was the issuance of paper
    money (*hansatsu*). See Horie's article on *hansatsu* in *NKSJ*, 634–44, or my
    Master's Thesis, *op. cit.*, 69–76, and 84–5 on similarities to the recoinages.
[15] Sakata, *Chōnin*, 40.

ferent kind. Living in a samurai-dominated city, they were devoted to the task of furnishing the samurai with money or whatever could be had for money. For this reason, they were far more dependent upon their samurai clients, and their security was to prove of a more ephemeral sort.

Although the Genroku period was one of certain important and permanent gains for the merchants, to the extent that these gains stemmed from the *Bakufu's* extravagance and financial chaos, they were unnatural and unhealthy. The protected merchants of Edo were in the best position to benefit from the overspending of the Shoguns. Those who benefited most directly were the timber merchants and the merchants of the gold and silver mints (*Kinza* and *Ginza*). Kinokuniya Bunzaemon and Naraya Mōzaemon are notable examples of protected merchants who made their fortunes in timber during the Genroku period, in part from Tsunayoshi's fondness for building magnificent temples and other buildings, for example, the one to house his large harem. The protected merchants of the gold and silver mints who proposed and carried through the devaluation made huge illegal profits from it.[16]

The so-called "Genroku style" was set by the protected merchants of Edo. They made money easily and spent it with prodigality. They were able to ingratiate themselves with the samurai bureaucrats mainly by a liberal use of money, and to win concessions from them. They spent large amounts of money in the gay quarters without the slightest compunction. The *daimyō*, bound by moral conventions (and, perhaps more, by lack of funds) usually stayed away from the gay quarters, but the merchants were under no such restrictions. A contemporary observer described the Genroku gay quarters as "a splendor which was by day like paradise and by night like the palace of the dragon king. Luxuries from every part of the country are brought first to these bad places. Unusual perfumes fill one house after another,

---

[16] This comparison of Osaka and Edo merchants derives mainly from Sakata, *Chōnin*, 17, 22–23, 25–26, 40. Fires, always frequent and destructive in the crowded tinderbox of Edo, were especially so during the Genroku era, and timber merchants profited accordingly. Tsuchiya Takao, *Nihon no Seishō* 日本の政商 [Political Merchants of Japan] (Tokyo: 1956), 51.

there are entertainments of all types, and guests rival each other in spending. When one spends a hundred, another spends a thousand."[17]

The operation of courtesan establishments came to be an important business in itself, and was a significant factor in the building up of large fortunes.[18] The existence of prostitutes in Japan in pre-Nara times is established historically, but the development of the gay quarters did not reach completion until the Edo period.[19] Professor Sakata gives credit to the cleverness of the operators of the famous Edo gay quarters, the Yoshiwara, for preserving a strict hierarchy among the courtesans, to cover the market. Those of the highest rank were popularly called the playthings of *daimyō*.[20] Much of the popular literature of the Genroku period, especially the metrical romances called *Jōruri* 淨瑠璃, depicted life in the gay quarters, and most of the woodblock prints of the *ukiyo-e* school pictured the colorful worlds of the theater and the gay quarters, where the townsmen were supreme.[21]

There was a clear connection between the merchants' new-found confidence based on their economic position and their development of new artistic forms. Norman writes, "The nascent merchant class growing confident in its economic position was creating rich and sensual art forms, liberating the theatre from the stiff conventions of the past, breathing life onto the stage so that drama enacted not only the rancorous feuds of warriors, but the lives and loves of common citizens."[22] The new art forms made their appearance and matured in Osaka, where the townspeople were the first to attain security and the leisure to devote themselves to culture. As one cul-

---

[17] *Waga Koromo* 我衣 by Ei Bian 曳尾庵, in *Enseki Jisshu* 燕石十種 Vol. I, 141–2, quoted in Sakata, *Chōnin*, 25. This is a treatise devoted mainly to the evolution of clothing and hair styles, with comments about what was considered proper.

[18] Tsuchiya, *An Economic History of Japan*, op. cit., 267–8, note 72.

[19] Takigawa, *Nihon Shakai Shi*, op. cit., 327.

[20] Sakata, *Chōnin*, 19–20. Prof. Tsuchiya compares the Yoshiwara with the *machiai* (assignation houses) of later years as a useful place for the "political merchants" of Edo to arrange deals and, by lavish spending, to compete in gaining contracts. *Nihon no Seishō, op. cit.*, 56.

[21] Takigawa, *Nihon Shakai Shi*, 327.

[22] "Andō Shōeki and the Anatomy of Japanese Feudalism," *op. cit.*, 68.

tural historian has noted, "It can be said of all the townspeople that they had desire for money, ambition for power, and love for culture. They differed in the different cities, with Osaka people emphasizing money, Edo people, power, and Kyoto people, culture."[23] The Osaka merchant is well described by the famous Osaka novelist Ibara Saikaku (1642–1693), the most representative of Genroku writers. According to Saikaku, the Osaka merchant's sole aim and special privilege in society was to make money. Once this was achieved, he was expected to turn to the cultivation of the arts, poetry, music, tea ceremony, archery, to participate in incense meetings, and to lose his vulgar speech.[24] A kind of merchant nobility appeared early in Osaka. When the family business was firmly established, sometimes after two or three generations, it was common for the head of the family to retire at a comparatively early age, putting an able man, usually his heir, in charge.[25] In the merchant society, heads of important merchant houses were at the top of their social hierarchy, and were the objects of the personal loyalty and service of apprentices, shop supervisors and branch house heads, all brought up in the paternalistic tradition of the apprentice system. The retirement or semi-retirement of the heads of houses did not damage their position, but rather gave them more prestige and increased their influence. The devotion of important Osaka merchants to culture was an important stimulus to the development of the brilliant Genroku culture.[26]

The expansive air of the Edo merchant who spent his money with abandon and was always ready to risk his money in some new and promising venture was much admired among the Edo townspeople. However, this "expansive air" was too often his only distinctive attribute, and compared to the merchants of Kyoto and Osaka, un-

[23] Ishida Ichirō 石田一郎, *Kinsei Bunka no Tenkai* 近世文化の展開 [The Unfolding of the Early Modern Culture], in *Kinsei Shakai*, op. cit., 409.
[24] Quoted from Saikaku's *Nihon Eitaigura* 日本永代藏 [A Warehouse of Wealth], in Sakata, *Chōnin*, 30. Incense meetings (Kō-awase 香會) were genteel contests in identifying various incenses.
[25] *Ibid.*, 70.
[26] *Ibid.* This culture has been skillfully described by Sir George Sansom in *Japan, a Short Cultural History*, 471–93, and in *The Western World and Japan*, 192–4.

leavened by the influence of culture and education. This was the major difference between Edo merchants and those of the Kansai region. The expansive Edo merchant was a chance product of the unusual atmosphere of Genroku society. Osaka merchants, on the other hand, had a long and natural growth based on the social and economic development of Osaka. They made their money more by commercial ingenuity and ability than by chance killings in speculative schemes.[27]

The culture of the Osaka merchant stemmed from the townspeople's culture created in Sakai, and was on a far higher plane than that of the Edo merchants. The Sakai merchants, after assimilating the culture of the court nobles of nearby Kyoto, had gone on to create their own special culture. But with the appearance in Osaka in the Genroku period of the two great literary figures, Saikaku and Chikamatsu, there was born a culture which came directly from the townspeople of Osaka and can properly be called Osaka culture.[28]

A striking feature of Genroku culture was the awakening of a new and deep interest and concern for people. It is natural that a commoner's art for commoners would depict their lives. For the first time, common people appear in literature and in art portrayed with sympathy. For example, in Saikaku's *Kōshoku Nidai Otoko* 好色二代男 [Two Generations of Men who Loved Love], the hero, on the point of death due to his dissolute life, is visited by a prostitute rather than by a Bodhisattva from heaven. According to Professor Ishida, this scene evokes not only sympathy but a contempt for any feeling of superiority, and reveals Saikaku's feeling that man's life is entirely in this world.[29]

Among Confucian schools, the recognition of the human personality was emphasized most by the School of Ancient Learning (*kogaku-ha* 古學派), the only important Confucian school of the period which represented a Japanese re-interpretation of the classics. The main members of this school, Yamaga Sokō (1622–1685), Itō Jinsai (1627–1705) and Ogyū Sorai (1666–1728) all rejected the Chu

[27] Sakata, *Chōnin*, 17, 28.
[28] *Ibid.*, 98–9.
[29] *Kinsei Bunka no Tenkai*, op. cit., 377–81.

Hsi concentration on knowing heaven, and shifted the emphasis to knowing man. Sorai expressed this idea when he wrote, "The way is not in heaven nor in earth, but in man," and went on to point out that it does not come to man from a superior person, but through self-cultivation.[30] The nativist school (kokugaku-ha), although anti-Confucian, continued the humanistic emphasis of the Confucianists. Their main motivation from their first beginnings in the Genroku period was to discover the "pure feelings" of the Japanese personality, while still untainted by the influx of foreign ideas, particularly Buddhist and Confucian. Their works abound in such phrases as "the sincerity of human feelings" and "peoples' cherished desires," and they sought to liberate human nature from unnatural restraints, and to enhance the interest in human personality. Ishida emphasizes the close relationship which existed between the kogaku-ha and the kokugaku-ha as seen in the fact that Kamo Mabuchi (1697-1769) and other kokugakusha began as members of the kogaku-ha.[31] Kokugaku has been described as "a naturalistic ideological system ... opposed to the feudal society, having as its point of origin the consciousness of a new way of life on the part of townspeople."[32]

Related to the new humanism stimulated by city life was a feeling of individualism seen throughout Genroku life and culture. Money consistently demands realism and rationality, and, according to Miyamoto, although the merchants were strictly limited status-wise in their relations with superiors, they gradually began to acquire a certain individualistic sense of the equality of all men, through repeated contracts and transactions which were essentially of a levelling nature among the parties.[33] In art, an expression of the rise of individual consciousness can be seen in the portrayal of individual per-

---

[30] Ishida, Kinsei Bunka no Tenkai, 382-3. Chu Hsi 朱熹 (1130-1200) was the chief founder of the Neo-Confucian school which became the orthodox Bakufu school.

[31] Ibid., 383-4. Kamo Mabuchi and Motoori Norinaga, the most famous Kokugakusha, were both of merchant stock.

[32] Yamamoto Masahide 山本正秀 and Watanabe Shū 渡邊秀, Kokugaku Ron 國學論 [An Essay on Kokugaku], Vol. 19 of Nihon Rekishi Zensho (Tokyo: 1939), 9. A short summary of kokugaku ideas can be found in Bellah, Tokugawa Religion, op. cit., 99-102.

[33] Nihon Shōgyō Shi, 141.

sonality in the *ukiyo-e*. For the first time an art depicted the personalities of mere commoners, especially those prostitutes and actors who were the most famous and admired of the time. Pictures of famous courtesan beauties and portraits of actors in famous scenes attained great popularity, in part because they often depicted actual persons. In sculpture, there was a shift from religious and "monumental" art to the carving of small and remarkably intricate and expressive objects for individual use and appreciation.[34]

The fads which swept through the cities are interpreted by Ishida as illustrative of the feeling of individualism of the period. Many of these fads came from the gay quarters, such as kimono styles and hair styles like the "Shimada," or from the theater.[35] The samurai author of the *Seji Kemmon Roku* lamented the fact that the *kabuki* set the style and influenced the behavior of people: "All the women in the cities, married or unmarried, take no greater pleasure than in the *kabuki*. No one is more idolized than the *kabuki* actors, and women never cease in their constant infatuation with them. The plays no longer imitate society, but society imitates the plays as models for life."[36]

But there is a sense of frustration and restriction in the avenues open to the merchant class for self-expression. There is in Saikaku's novels, according to Norman, "a yearning for greater social or cultural opportunities, for a wider arena in which to spend energy and develop talent."[37] There is a certain air of futility in the almost frenzied competition in conspicuous consumption typical of the behavior of the merchants in the gay quarters. Professor Honjō has described[38] the protected Edo timber merchants, Kinokuniya Bun-

---

[34] Ishida, *Kinsei Bunka no Tenkai*, 395–6. Prof. Ishida stresses the depiction of actual persons by such artists as Suzuki Harunobu (1718–1770) as a unique and meaningful aspect of Genroku and later art. It should be kept in mind, however, that perhaps the majority of the people depicted in *ukiyo-e* art were idealizations or stylizations of types (or in the case of actors, the Kabuki style) rather than a conscious and realistic representation of individuals.

[35] Ishida, *Kinsei Bunka no Tenkai*, 395.

[36] In *Kinsei Shakai Keizai Sōsho*, op. cit., I, 242.

[37] Norman, "Andō Shōeki and the Anatomy of Japanese Feudalism," 74.

[38] *The Social and Economic History of Japan*, 262–4.

zaemon and Naraya Mōzaemon and others gaining the admiration of all in the gay quarters by throwing away money with an air of utmost nonchalance, the wives of Edo and Kyoto merchants parading their expensive clothes in the streets, and the sumptuous mansion of Yodoya in Osaka where care seems to have been taken to violate every regulation prohibiting the use of lacquer furnishings, gold, silk, etc.[39] These merchants expended their energies in "endless sexual adventures, in continual experiment with luxury and extravagance; this is the only field in which the new *chōnin* class could express its increased power with impunity."[40]

But even in the amorous adventures and in the luxuries in which the merchants could indulge and which were the rewards of money-making, there were certain dangers against which the elder merchants often warned. Many merchant families were ruined by spendthrift sons who frequented the gay quarters, referred to in merchant family constitutions as "bad places" (*akusho* 惡所). Sons were warned against spending time there, not so much from moral considerations, but as a violation of the frugality insisted upon by the merchant code. However, the principle of subduing the desires was at odds with the principle of making money. The merchants seldom denied themselves pleasure. "Up to thirteen, a boy does not know it; up to twenty-four or twenty-five, he is under his parents' direction, but from then on, to age forty-five, he establishes his own family and is free to pursue pleasure to his utmost."[41]

[39] It is interesting to compare his description of Yodoya's mansion with the regulations found on page 255 of Honjo's *Social and Economic History of Japan*. Many anecdotes about throwing away money are probably mythical. Tsuchiya, however, is ready to believe some of them, such as the story about Kinokuniya's disturbing Naraya's enjoyment of a snow scene by throwing coins into the snow and watching gleefully while a mob trampled and scattered the snow in frantic searching. *Nihon no Seishō*, op. cit., 56.

[40] Norman, "Andō Shōeki and the Anatomy of Japanese Feudalism," 74–5. During the Genroku period, the *Bakufu* had not yet declared war on merchant extravagance. It only "checked the more brazen displays of eroticism and luxury not so much on moral grounds as to protect from contagious exposure the Spartan spirit of the samurai class, unaware all the time that the power and prestige of this class were being undermined by causes far beyond the reach of legislation or exhortation." *Ibid.*, 76.

[41] Sakata, *Chōnin*, 36, quoting Saikaku's *Nihon Eitaigura*.

The merchant code evolved as the result of years of experience by Sakai and Osaka merchants, expressing the commonly accepted merchant morality. Modern Japanese writers call this code the "way of the merchant" (chōnin dō 町人道). The most important rules were to revere the family enterprise and to practice economy in all things. This was a personal code emphasizing the virtues of hard work and sincerity as well as frugality, handed down in family instructions and constitutions. There was a social side to this code as well. Particularly in Osaka, merchants generally recognized that success was not made up of separate deals but of continuous business. Therefore, good will and credit were strongly emphasized, and this emphasis was made effective largely through merchant organizations, especially the nakama.[42]

Within the family enterprise, relations between employers and employees were strictly as superior to inferior. Loyalty of a feudal type was expected of all inferiors towards their superiors, and ultimately to the master of the enterprise. This loyalty was an integral part of the merchant code. It was an emotion cultivated throughout the apprentice system, and together with the paternalistic benevolence expected of the superior to the inferior, it was among the merchants "exactly the same phenomenon as the reciprocal feeling between lord and vassal which was seen, very much alive, in the Kamakura and sengoku periods, in the samurai class."[43] All the participants in a merchant family enterprise, from the lowliest apprentice up, formed an organic unit, and the economic success of the enterprise meant success for all its members. This gave the merchant code a real motivation not seen in peacetime in the code of the warriors (bushidō).[44]

A discussion of the Osaka merchant code, however, is insufficient without looking at their actual mode of life. Although there was a larger degree of security and stability in their lives, and a primary emphasis of their code was frugality, they sought pleasures in much

[42] Sakata, Chōnin, 31.
[43] Ibid., 61, 68–9.
[44] Ibid., 70–1. Like chōnin dō, the term is the creation of modern Japanese writers.

the same way as their Edo counterparts. They had as much enthusiasm for the theater and the gay quarters as the Edo merchants. The Yoshiwara of Osaka was Shimmachi, opened up in the 1620's, where prostitutes were graded in a strict hierarchy and those of the highest rank were as admired as in Edo.[45]

According to Professor Sakata, the Edo merchants violated the merchant code completely. But it was considered a foreign thing, as it had been formulated in Sakai and elaborated in Osaka. The Edo merchants, strongly influenced by the samurai, had a code of their own, in which the most important element was manly spirit (*kyōki* 俠氣). They separated the moral from the economic life, whereas the Osaka merchant code integrated them. This attitude was never consciously formulated by the Edo merchants as was the Osaka merchant code. It was emotional rather than theoretical. In actual practice, this idea of separation became vulgarized into the expedient view that a person should concern himself about ethics only after he was well fed and well clothed. This did not mean that the Edo merchants had no ideals, but that if they did, they were apt to be at war with reality.[46]

The merchant code which emerged from the long experience of the Osaka merchants contributed to their success and to their feeling of security, importance and integration in the feudal system. Calling themselves "merchants of the empire" (*tenka no shōnin* 天下の商人), they actually had a certain pride in being merchants because they considered themselves as unique in the country. The Edo merchants, on the other hand, had no such important position and no such stabilizing code, and were seldom able to achieve any lasting success. They were always hard pressed by the activities of the *kamigata* merchants[47] who established branches in Edo and whose influence, always strong, continually increased. Besides, Edo, the consumption center, was always under a huge debt to Osaka, the supply center. The Edo merchants had no chance of beating the Osaka merchants in this economic battle, and in Edo, they had to content themselves with hurling insults at them and at other *kamigata* merchants. The

---

[45] *Ibid.*, 34.   [46] Sakata, *Chōnin*, 125–6.
[47] 上方. From the Kyoto-Osaka area, including Ōmi and Ise.

epithets "Ōmi robbers" and "Ise beggars" were most current among Edo merchants.[48]

Generalizing about the merchant mentality of the Tokugawa period, Professor Miyamoto sees both positive and negative aspects. As positive aspects, Miyamoto lists frugality, careful calculation of profits, and resourcefulness. These qualities were seen in varying degrees in all merchants, and most strikingly exemplified by such merchant families as Mitsui, Kōnoike and Sumitomo. The frank profit-seeking of merchants has been despised by many Japanese writers, both contemporary and recent, but Miyamoto believes it was not so much for themselves or merely for the sake of profit itself, but for their families.[49] As negative aspects, he points out that all merchants lived in a feudal society and naturally reflected the prevalent concepts of the duty of service to superiors, honor (or "face," *taimen* 體面), and the recognition of the limitations of social position. These concepts permeated the merchant mentality. The respect and obligation (*on* 恩) felt by the samurai who received land in fief from feudal lords was paralleled among merchants who generally thought of participation in commerce as a privilege granted from above. This was an idea especially strong among members of chartered trade associations (*kabu nakama*), where this privilege was expressed concretely in the membership privileges (*kabu*) which they held. The first sentence in *nakama* regulations almost always expressed this feeling, and pledged absolute adherence to law. As for "face," this feeling was as strong as among samurai.[50] The limitations of social position were strongly felt. One of the basic official instructions of the Tokugawa period was, "Know your place!"[51] This emphasis on knowing the limitations of status reinforced precedent and family tradition and opposed innovations, discoveries, inventions, aggressive competition, new markets, and new types of transactions.[52]

---

[48] Sakata, *Chōnin*, 128–9.   [49] *Nihon Shōgyō Shi*, 186–8.   [50] *Ibid.*, 184–5.

[51] *Mi no hodo wo shire*, written in *kana* so that everyone could read it, it was known as the seven-character instruction. Akabori, *Tokugawa Jidai no Shōnin*, 191.

[52] Miyamoto, *Nihon Shōgyō Shi*, 186. These points are elaborated in Miyamoto's *Kinsei Shōnin Ishiki no Kenkyū* 近世商人意識の研究 [Studies in the Merchant Mentality of the Early Modern Period] (Tokyo: 1941), 27–42.

The general prosperity and increased standard of living experienced in the Genroku period meant a great increase in the manufacturing and sale of commercial goods. Not only did the merchants benefit from this, but the Genroku period saw the draining of feudal treasuries into merchant coffers. The *daimyō* and ordinary samurai alike became more deeply indebted to the merchant money lenders. This gave the merchants a high degree of economic security and permitted the development of a type of merchant nobility with the leisure and inclination not only for amusements but for experimenting in or patronizing new artistic and literary forms. These new cultural forms which sprang from the new city society and which colored and glorified for the first time the lives of townspeople were doubtless factors in the stimulation of certain humanistic and individualistic trends in thought seen, for example, in the *kogaku-ha* and the *kokugaku-ha*. But Genroku culture was more the expression of an emotional than an intellectual emancipation. Theaters and gay quarters could flourish, and fads could sweep the cities. Merchants could win the admiration and envy of lesser townspeople with their amorous adventures and by their indulgence in extravagance for the sake of extravagance, largely within the narrow confines of the gay quarters.[53] However, this did not menace the prerogatives of the feudal rulers, but instead provided harmless outlets for ambition and energy, and the *Bakufu* did not attempt to suppress it.

The elder and wiser merchants cautioned against extravagance, and insisted on conformance with the "way of the merchant." This merchant code was most effective in Osaka. However, it combined with the essentially conservative mentality of the great majority of the city merchants of the period, a feeling fostered by their privileged economic position, their close and advantageous connections with the samurai class, and an understandable fear of arbitrary reprisals from an easily aroused tyranny. The self-expression of the merchants bloomed spectacularly, much like a hothouse flower, in the special conditions of the Genroku period, but this combination of conservative forces was sufficient to prevent it from taking a dangerous antifeudal turn.

[53] Takigawa, *Nihon Shakai Shi*, 327, calls the theaters and the gay quarters the "heavens of the townspeople."

CHAPTER VI

THE TOKUGAWA DEADLOCK—
ALTERNATIONS IN CITY AND FEUDAL PREDOMINANCE
(1703–1843)

THE "HAPPY SOCIETY" of the Genroku period was bound to be temporary. The limits of the economic expansion of the first century of Tokugawa rule were reached and could not be extended far without basic changes. The increase of the population of the cities which had been so rapid began to slow down after the Genroku period and by about 1735 came to a virtual standstill.[1] Opportunities for employment in the cities for peasants escaping from the countryside disappeared after the construction boom which Tsunayoshi had extended with his fondness for lavish building.[2] The area of land under cultivation continued to increase somewhat due to land reclamation, but total agricultural production made but small gains after about 1730.[3] The peasants, subjected to increasing exploitation, and virtually denied the recourse of flight to the cities, resorted to two desperate methods of alleviating their extreme poverty: limitation of population by birth control, abortion and infanticide—a negative means, and peasant uprisings—a positive means.[4] The result was a general stagnation of both population and production levels.

Markets were almost entirely limited by the exclusion policy to domestic markets, which expanded greatly during the first hundred years largely due to the great increases in city and castle town population. When these increases slowed to a virtual halt, there was little room for further expansion of markets due to the very low purchasing power of the agricultural villages. Through the application of capital, provincial production could gradually be increased, but the actual

---

[1] Horie, ..Shihon Shugi.., 47.

[2] Ibid.

[3] Matsuyoshi Sadao, "Tokugawa Bakufu no Kaikon Seisaku Kanken," op. cit., 14.

[4] Horie, ..Shihon Shugi.., 47; Takahashi Kamekichi 高橋龜吉, Nihon Shihon Shugi Hattatsu Shi 日本資本主義發達史 [A History of the Development of Capitalism in Japan] (Tokyo: 6th ed., 1939), 10 ff.

expansion was small.[5] The issuance by the *han* of paper money (*han-satsu*) and the *Bakufu* currency devaluations served to expand the limits of the markets somewhat, but only temporarily. From the first, the development of monopolistic *nakama* and especially *kabu nakama* by the merchants gave rise to an artificial limitation of the markets. The inefficiencies of transport hampered the expansion of markets and aided monopolistic merchant organizations in securing and holding their own markets against competition.[6] Most merchants, having achieved monopolistic control of a particular market, were content with it, and did not strive to expand it. Also, their policies of controlling production by advancing capital or through the "putting-out" system led to an absorption of the producers' profits which discouraged an increase in purchasing power in the countryside.[7]

The factors which contributed to the economic contraction did not arise full blown after the Genroku period. They are evident in the Genroku period, but became gradually more and more prominent as the eighteenth century progressed. With this development came a change in the attitude of the samurai toward the merchant class. During the Genroku period, the samurai displayed irritation at the luxury of a class supposed to be the lowest in the social hierarchy. Townsmen, especially merchants, spent money which the samurai felt should rightfully belong to them, and which they felt was taken from them by dishonest merchants. The samurai were especially incensed at high interest rates on loans and monopolistic control of prices by the merchants. As these conditions undermined the samurais' economic security, irritation at the merchants deepened into enmity,[8] and a struggle ensued.

It is possible to trace, in very general terms, a constant alternation

---

[5] Nomura, "Tokugawa Hōken Sei to Shōgyō," op. *cit.*, 124; 128–9.

[6] *Ibid.*, 124, 129.

[7] Horie, ..*Shihon Shugi*.., 31.

[8] Takahashi, *Nihon Shihon Shugi Hattatsu Shi*, op. cit., 10, lists four sources of social dislocation: (1) *Kuge* (court nobles) and the court against the *Bakufu*, (2) *Bakufu* and allies against the outer *han*, (3) Upper class samurai against lower class samurai, and (4) Samurai against peasants and townsmen. All of these inherent hostilities increased with the decline of the feudal institutions and the rise of the money economy.

throughout the Tokugawa period between feudal and city influences in the position of cultural and economic predominance:

1. 1600–1687 First years of the period   Feudal
2. 1688–1703 Genroku period   City
3. 1716–1735 "Kyōhō reform" (Shogun Yoshimune)   Feudal
4. 1751–1786 "Tanumà period"   City
5. 1787–1793 "Kansei reform" (Councillor Matsudaira)   Feudal
6. 1804–1829 Bunka-Bunsei periods   City
7. 1841–1843 "Tempō reform" (Councillor Mizuno)   Feudal

Neither won a definite victory. In the final analysis, the feudal rulers, always politically predominant, were able to require the cities and the merchants to conform to their rules, while the cities and the merchants were able to exist and flourish only by relying upon the existing feudal relationships.[9] It was an uneasy kind of coexistence of closely interdependent but at the same time incompatible forces.

The first period was definitely one of feudal predominance, when the feudal authorities often asserted their prerogatives and the merchant class, aware of the dangers inherent in their position, were nonetheless able eventually to achieve a considerable degree of security, working almost underground. The Genroku period was the first and most striking period of city and merchant predominance in the cultural and economic spheres.

In the struggle which followed the Genroku period, the first blow was struck in 1705 by the *Bakufu* when it accused the house of Yodoya, the most prominent in Osaka, of ostentatious luxury not befitting a member of the merchant class, and confiscated its entire wealth. The successive heads of the house of Yodoya enjoyed rice stipends, wore swords as the agents of some thirty-three *daimyō*, and lived in a mansion which was more luxurious than those of most of the *daimyō* themselves.[10] This was enough to give a pretext for the confiscation. However, the Yodoya family could not be accused of the type of conspicuous consumption practiced in Edo by such protected merchants as Kinokuniya and Naraya. Moreover, Yodoya's mode of life was duplicated by such protected Osaka merchants as Kōnoike,

---

[9] Ishida, *Kinsei Bunka no Tenkai*, op. cit., 414.
[10] *NKSJ*, 1661, 469; Honjo, *The Social and Economic History of Japan*, 264.

Tennōjiya and Hiranoya.[11] Also, the head of the house of Yodoya was a mere boy of eighteen and was not personally culpable. The real reason for the confiscation was the fact that Yodoya had come to control the finances of many of the *daimyō* of Kyūshū and western Honshū who found themselves in an intolerable situation, so deeply in debt to Yodoya as to have lost their freedom of action in financial affairs. According to Matsuyoshi, "There is no doubt that it was a resolute action taken to break this financial and economic stalemate."[12]

The confiscation not only served to cancel the huge debts owed Yodoya by the *daimyō*, but it gave the *Bakufu* a nice profit, estimated by a contemporary source at no less than 121,867,610 *ryō*,[13] probably an exaggeration, but even a fraction of this amount would have been a fabulous sum for the time. Saburōemon, the unfortunate boy who had come into this fortune not long before, was imprisoned. He was later permitted to spend the rest of his life under house arrest in a Shinto shrine which had made a plea for him, but it was the end of the house of Yodoya.[14]

It was the Yodoya incident which reminded the merchants forcibly that they were only merchants, just at the time when they were gaining a new degree of independence and influence. The blow had fallen where it was perhaps least expected, on the well established, honored and comparatively conservative house of Yodoya, not only the greatest of Osaka merchant families but known for its cultural activities and great interest in the arts, especially in linking verses (*renga*) and in the tea ceremony.[15] The confiscation made a deep im-

---

[11] Kanno, "Tokugawa Jidai Shōnin no Chifu," 44.

[12] *NKSJ*, 1661–2.

[13] Takigawa, *Nihon Shakai Shi*, 244. It included "fifty pairs of gold screens, three hundred and sixty carpets, innumerable precious stones, mansions, granaries and storehouses, and gold pieces by the hundred thousand." Sansom, *Japan, a Short Cultural History*, 472. A complete inventory can be found in Takekoshi, *Economic Aspects..*, II, 251–5.

[14] *NKSJ*, 1662. Confiscation (*kessho* 闕所) was connected with punishments for all types of crimes, and varied in extent with the gravity of the crime. *NKSJ*, 469. It always accompanied banishment, a punishment often meted out during the *sengoku* period. The *Bakufu* made use of this tradition. Takigawa, *Nihon Shakai Shi*, 325.   [15] *NKSJ*, 1661.

pression on the merchants of the entire country. It had a sobering effect even on the *nouveaux riches* of Edo, and underlined the warnings of the elder merchants. It threw a shadow over the more important merchant families in the cities and forced them to be more careful.[16]

The complete subjection of the merchants to the political power of the *Bakufu* and their impotence in the face of confiscation emphasizes the separation between political and economic power. The separation becomes more striking with the increase in merchant wealth and the attendant impoverishment of the ruling classes, because needless to say, such isolated events as the Yodoya confiscation did not change the trend of the times.[17]

The first of the "three great reforms" of the Tokugawa period was that of Yoshimune in the Kyōhō period (1716–1735). They were undertaken not to improve the national economy but primarily to lift the *Bakufu* out of its financial impoverishment and, as a secondary purpose, to restrain the merchant class. Considering these limited aims, they all achieved a degree of success, but none of them remedied the basic conditions which gave rise to these pressing problems.[18] Looking back at Ieyasu's time when the feudal power based on the land was as yet unchallenged and the financial position of the *Bakufu* a truly enviable one, Yoshimune set in motion a "back-to-Ieyasu" movement, emulating his great ancestor by first economizing on *Bakufu* expenses. As part of this effort, he suspended all construction projects and prohibited new contracts for a time. The first to feel the brunt of Yoshimune's economic retrenchment were the protected merchants of Edo. The Edo merchants lived primarily by supplying the economic needs of the samurai class for consumers' goods. Their livelihood was almost entirely dependent upon these needs of the samurai. The wealth of the Edo merchants was due largely to pro-

[16] Sakata, *Chōnin*, 37.

[17] *Ibid.*, 38. Sakata calls this separation of economic and political power one of the basic "contradictions" (*mujun* 矛盾) of the Tokugawa society, a term in common use among Japanese writers on Tokugawa Japan, even though not of Marxist orientation.

[18] These three reforms are treated in a series of articles in the *KSK*, XV, 1 (Jan. 1936), 1–111.

tection and the corruption of the political power. When this protection was withdrawn and the political power reverted to its original
form, their special privileges were destroyed.[19]

Under Yoshimune, the samurai went even further into debt. Yoshimune attempted to discourage samurai from borrowing money by
exhorting them to frugality while enforcing strict economy in the
Bakufu itself. He also legislated against the samurais' practice of ex-
tricating themselves from financial distress by selling their samurai
status to rich merchants or peasants. This was obviously destructive
of the feudal system. It was effected usually by adopting a commoner
as heir (often marrying a daughter to him), for a large sum of money.
Although no doubt rare in Yoshimune's time, it became more frequent toward the end of the Tokugawa period, with the accelerating
decay of the samurai's finances, integrity, and pride.[20]

Some scholars advocated that the merchants be thoroughly suppressed. Ogyū Sorai, for example, blamed the merchants for the lack
of order in society, and he had the ear of Yoshimune. His attitude is
seen in his *Seidan*,[21] written about 1720: "The samurai and peasants
have no means of subsistence besides their land. They are constant
factors in government and it is the duty and basic principle of government to see always to their well-being. Merchants, on the other
hand, carry on an insignificant occupation ... it should be no concern
of government if they ruin themselves." No doubt influenced by this
kind of advice, Yoshimune decided that the *Bakufu* officials should
stop accepting litigation concerning loans to members of the samurai
class by merchants in *Bakufu* cities.[22]

This policy of refusing resort to litigation by merchants was not
without precedent. The *Bakufu* had refused in 1685 and in 1702 to
hear cases brought by *fudasashi* against *hatamoto* and *go-kenin* as a
means of assisting their direct vassals.[23] Even without this official

---

[19] Sakata, *Chōnin*, 45.
[20] Sansom, *Japan, a Short Cultural History*, 521; Honjo, *The Social and Economic History of Japan*, 204–6. Prices of samurai status eventually fluctu-
ated with changes in economic conditions, like any commodity bought
and sold.
[21] In *Nihon Keizai Sōsho*, op. cit., III, 427.
[22] Sakata, *Chōnin*, 54.   [23] *NKSJ*, 322.

106 THE MERCHANT CLASS IN TOKUGAWA JAPAN

policy, officials sometimes found means to dismiss cases against samurai. For example, a samurai who owed a heavy debt to a merchant money-lender absconded. His lord decided his family name should be ended, but the authorities decided the heir should begin a "new" samurai family with the same name which would not be subject to the debt. They argued that the heir knew nothing about the loans and should not be burdened with them.[24] When *daimyō* refused to pay debts and the merchant money-lender appealed to the *Bakufu*, the *Bakufu* often arranged for payment by installments over a long period, if they did not wish or could not find justification for dismissing the case. In the final analysis, the *Bakufu* "could not force the bankruptcy of a *daimyō* due to debts."[25] In Edo, excuses were often found for refusing to hear complaints. In one case, the house of Mori refused to repay a Kyoto money exchange a loan of 10,000 *ryō*. The exchange was forced to close, and the head of the house went to Edo to appeal to the *Bakufu*, only to be told that since he had once received a rice stipend from the Mori house, it would be "unprincipled and unpardonable" for him to bring a suit against his master. The *daimyō* who most frequently refused to repay loans in the early Tokugawa period were Shimazu of Satsuma and Hosokawa of Higo.[26]

The finances of the various *daimyō* were temporarily aided by Yoshimune's policies, but as there was no longer any guarantee against defaulting on loans, they found it more difficult to get loans.[27] The decision to stop accepting litigation was a blow principally felt by the financiers who specialized in loans to *daimyō*, but it disturbed the financial world generally. Those who suffered most were the money exchanges (*ryōgae-ya*) who had used deposits collected from merchants to lend to *daimyō*.[28]

In 1722, as part of his effort to improve *Bakufu* finances, Yoshimune levied a tax on all feudal lords of one hundredth of their annual

[24] Wigmore, "Materials..," *op. cit.*, Supplements 3–4, 333–337. Also see *ibid.*, 9–10; 210; 301–303; 370–378 for other cases, in which the officials seem to have been quite conscientious, and did not decide in favor of samurai without some justification.
[25] Takigawa, *Nihon Shakai Shi*, op. cit., 322.
[26] Ibid., 324, citing the *Chōnin Kōken Roku* of Mitsui Takafusa.
[27] Sakata, *Chōnin*, 73.   [28] Sakata, *Chōnin*, 48.

rice incomes. At the same time, so that they could pay this, he reduced by half the required period of residence of *daimyō* in Edo. This reform lasted for nine years, but was abolished under the criticisms of Muro Kyusō (1658–1734) and other scholars who believed in maintaining the *sankin kōtai* system intact for strategic reasons.[29] While it lasted, it decreased the expenditures of the *daimyō* and likewise the profits of the merchants.

In an attempt to bring down usurious interest rates and help out his direct vassals (the *hatamoto* and *go-kenin*), Yoshimune limited the number of *fudasashi* to 109 in 1724, giving them a monopoly of the business, and at the same time set a ceiling on interest rates of 15% per annum. Not wishing to be limited to a mere 15%, the *fudasashi* appealed on the grounds that there was a tendency for financial backers to repay loans negotiated by the *fudasashi* in order to minimize the interest charges, thus decreasing the income of the *fudasashi*. This was only a pretext, however, and the appeal contained a reference to the willingness of the *fudasashi* to provide the *Bakufu* with loans (*goyō-kin*).[30] The *Bakufu* reply to the appeal was so ambiguous as to mean silent assent to higher interest rates and a victory for the *fudasashi*.[31]

For merchants who made loans to members of the samurai class, the honor which the samurai cherished was important security. However, in cases where samurai defaulted, merchants had had the right to a hearing from *Bakufu* officials, if they resided in a *Bakufu*-controlled area. This had been their last and very important recourse, although to take a case to court required of the merchant a good deal of courage and the firm conviction of being in the right.[32] As the *daimyō* became

[29] *NKSJ*, 13. This tax on *daimyō* was called *agemai* 上げ米.

[30] 御用金. These were loans to feudal rulers with no necessary obligation for repayment. This term is usually translated "forced loans." They were often "requested" by the feudal authorities.

[31] Sakata, *Chōnin*, 113.

[32] In the first place, settlement out of court was always attempted, and exhaustive efforts at conciliation were made before resort was had to the authorities. Even then, judgments were largely personal ones, as written laws were (no doubt purposely) vague. It was the rule of man rather than the rule of law. Another deterrent, perhaps, for a merchant petitioner, was the requirement that he crawl on hands and knees from the door of the court

more and more impoverished, the number of merchants forced into bankruptcy due to defaulting *daimyō* increased, even with this *Bakufu* protection. The *daimyō* saw this as merely a hard necessity, and when the *Bakufu* under Yoshimune abolished this recourse to litigation, the *daimyō* were freed from ultimate legal responsibility. Loans to *daimyō* became far more dangerous, and the weak position of the merchant in the face of political power was once more revealed. However, at the same time the basically unsound financial policy of the *Bakufu* was not to be changed by Yoshimune's policies. This was the weakness of the samurai class and the strength of the merchant class.[33]

The Edo merchants were dealt a serious blow by Yoshimune's economic retrenchment, but the failure of some of the protected merchants in Edo was no real loss to the economy, as these merchants were the temporary creations of a period of reckless spending. With them disappeared the "expansive atmosphere" of the Genroku period, and merchants reverted to their pre-Genroku type.[34] A contemporary observer describes it this way: "Instead of a merchant spending 100 and his companion 1000, now, the first spends 10 and his companion 5, and they go home."[35] The Osaka merchants, on the other hand, protected by their essential soundness, scarcely were touched by the economic retrenchment.

Although many of Yoshimune's policies were disadvantageous to the merchant class, he gave the *nakama* organizations just what they had wanted for many years—official recognition. Yoshimune not only recognized existing *nakama* and made provisions for chartering them as *kabu nakama*, but he actually took steps to have merchants and

to the judgment room to present his case. See Dan F. Henderson, "Some Aspects of Tokugawa Law," *Washington Law Review* 27, 1 (Feb. 1952), especially 96, 98–102.
[33] Sakata, *Chōnin*, 50–1.
[34] *Ibid.*, 45–6.
[35] *Waga Koromo*, in *Enseki Jisshu*, I, 142, quoted in Sakata, *Chōnin*, 45. This source goes on to say, "For the men of the Genroku period, bad places (*akusho*) were places to throw away money. Those who had not the heart to throw away money did not enter there ... for the men of today, they risk being laughed at if they set their foot inside such a place."

artisans who were not members join them.[36] Speculative exchanges were given official approval for the first time, *ton'ya* were recognized as well, and all types of *kabu* could be legally bought and sold and used as security on loans.[37]

The organization of *ton'ya* and *nakama* into *kabu nakama* gave the members exclusive rights and the means to protect them. If infringements of these rights were discovered, the *kabu nakama* would appeal to the authorities. These requests, often complaining, "We are being hindered by the actions of non-members," would usually be supported by the officials.[38] This gave to the *ton'ya* in particular immense prestige to inspire confidence and almost unlimited credit. Its exclusive position enabled members to stabilize their family enterprises. Profits from monopoly pricing enriched *kabu nakama* members, and there was no fear of bankruptcy. Management of the family enterprise could usually be passed on from generation to generation without trouble, although there were cases where families split, brought in other families, sometimes selling *kabu* or increasing their number. However, these changes were made only after a strict investigation and discussion by the *kabu nakama* assembly, and permitted only when the credit or ability of the family management was at a very low ebb. Also, these cases arose seldom because weak enterprises were not accepted into membership, and business stability of members plus the supervision of the experienced merchants of the *kabu nakama*

---

[36] Nomura, "Tokugawa Hōken Sei to Shōgyō," *op. cit.*, 126. Non-members were required to report to the authorities if they wished to enter an organization. This did not mean they were prohibited from participating in an enterprise outside a *nakama*, but "it would appear that if those who neither entered a *nakama* nor reported to the authorities did not make some arrangements themselves, they were made for them. Since the prohibition is not specific on this point, it is impossible to know what arrangements were made, but it probably meant ultimately that they were forced to enter. However, in actual fact, merchants and artisans probably found it possible to carry on enterprises without entering." In principle, it was possible for outside merchants to form new competing *kabu nakama*, but it was probably almost impossible in practice. *Ibid.*

[37] Yoshimura, "Edo Jidai ni okeru Shōgyō no Seishitsu," *op. cit.*, 199; Nomura, "Tokugawa Hōken Sei to Shōgyō," 127.

[38] Smith, "Materials..," 90.

made it almost difficult to lose money.[39] In short, it was a most comforting kind of security.

The recognition of these essentially monopolistic organizations was a reversal of the policy of non-interference and it created the conditions under which commerce was to develop until 1843. For this reason, it requires some discussion. Early in the Tokugawa period, when commerce was considered a servant of the feudal order rather than a danger to it, the Confucian theory of free circulation of goods was generally accepted. Later, however, adapting to the conditions, the policy changed to simply an emphasis on the abolition of monopolistic combinations. However, repeated prohibitions had little effect on the organization of monopolistic *nakama*, and a change of policy was inevitable. Since the *Bakufu* was unable to abolish the *nakama*, it decided to utilize them. By granting official recognition, the *Bakufu* meant to regulate prices through the chartered trade associations (*kabu nakama*) thus created, and was able to utilize them for the transmission and enforcement of orders to the merchants.[40]

Besides the means of control which this policy provided to the *Bakufu*, the policy of recognition provided a new source of revenue. Charter fees called *unjō-kin* were required when the *kabu nakama* were first organized,[41] and regular contributions were also required, called *myōga-kin*.[42] The amount of these fees was usually determined by discussion between the town magistrate (*machi bugyō*) and representatives of the *nakama*, on a price-haggling basis. The merchants

---

[39] Miyamoto, *Nihon Kinsei Ton'ya Sei no Kenkyū*, op. cit., 367.

[40] Nomura, "Tokugawa Hōken Sei to Shōgyō," 123. Miyamoto, *Kabu Nakama no Kenkyū*, op. cit., 252.

[41] *Unjō-kin* 運上金 (or simply *unjō*), "thank money," was collected on occasions other than chartering. These fees were known from the first of the Tokugawa period, but used regularly only from the Genroku era, when Ogiwara levied one on *sake*. Periodic *unjō* were connected with goods in the Nagasaki foreign trade and gold and silver foil before Yoshimune's time. Sakata, *Chōnin*, 58.

[42] 冥加金 (or *myōga*). Generally, there were two types: (1) collected from *kabu nakama*, sometimes came to be a fixed amount each year, and (2) collected from individual enterprises, based roughly on the amount of production in the case of *sake*, soy sauce, and pressed oil. From inns which furnished prostitutes on request, and from pawn shops, amounts were determined separately for each establishment. *NKSJ*, 1577–8.

usually succeeded in keeping these fees quite low.[43] Nevertheless, they were a new source of revenue, although a comparatively minor one.

This reversal of policy indicates a realistic reappraisal of the role of the *nakama*. The objective situation, namely, the *Bakufu*'s failure in its attempt to prohibit the *nakama*, was admitted, and the *nakama* used as a means to control prices and production and also as a source of revenue. Group control of both merchant and artisan enterprises sprang first from the merchants and artisans themselves, and the *Bakufu* came to recognize the *nakama* for a variety of reasons, always as a matter of immediate convenience. This was also generally true in the various *han*. From the first, *nakama* or *kabu nakama*, besides providing security to their members, prevented the production of inferior goods, and provided a certain standardization and guarantee of quality. In this way they were advantageous to the consumers. The official policy of utilizing them was a reasonable means of stabilizing economic relations generally. However, *nakama* prohibited competition both within the organization, among members, and outside, preventing free entry to trade.[44] This discouraged individual initiative and the expansion of individual enterprises. For example, members of the Osaka guild of hand-operated lathe workers limited themselves voluntarily to no more than two lathes for each house.[45] This type of limitation of commercial goods was in harmony with Yoshimune's policy of frugality, and the 1721 order recognizing and encouraging *kabu nakama* specifically forbids the manufacture

[43] Smith, "Materials..," 91. For example, as a result of such a discussion, which "became rather troublesome," it was decided that the 24-group *ton'ya* of Osaka, the largest in the country, would pay only 300 *ryō* the first year, 100 *ryō* in following years, "with the prospect of some increases in later years." *Ibid.*, 112. This is an indication of the influence of the Osaka merchants. The *Tokumi Don'ya* of Edo was not nearly so lucky, paying at one time 10,200 *ryō* in *myōga-kin* annually. Yoshimura, "Edo Jidai..," 200.

[44] The idea of economic competition was so strange to the Japanese in pre-Restoration days that scholars translating Western economic works into Japanese could find no word for "competition." Fukuzawa Yukichi, the famous Westernizer, coined the word *kyōsō* 競争, combining the words for "race" and fight," and has related "how shocked his colleagues were by such harsh terminology." Sansom, *The Western World and Japan*, 235.

[45] Horie, ..*Keizai Seisaku*, 107. These lathes were used for making a variety of goods, including pottery.

of "new things." The control of production which was one of the objects of the recognition and encouragement of *kabu nakama* in a way assisted production at first, but in time the limitation of supply and the control of prices restricted production.[46]

Besides its role as a stabilizing factor in the economic field of production and prices, the *nakama* was recognized as a means of making *Bakufu* class policy more effective. The *nakama* built up the apprentice system, and entrance came to be generally limited to heredity and completion of apprenticeship, in both industrial and commercial enterprises. Also, the number of apprentices was limited and they were almost always chosen from relatives of members. This left little opportunity for peasants who had fled their native places to get into trade except outside the *nakama*, and this was made even more difficult by the policy of recognizing the *nakama* and giving them tighter monopolies. The recognition policy undoubtedly contributed to the rigidity of class lines and helped to discourage peasants from going to the cities and castle towns.

Yoshimune's economic policies, although unpopular with samurai, whose stipends were reduced, as well as with merchants, restored the solvency of the *Bakufu* and the social balance generally which had existed before the Genroku period.[47] His period as Shogun is an important one in economic history because most of the economic policies of the middle and late Tokugawa were originated by him or took definite form under his regime.[48] Yoshimune was more nearly successful in his attempts to restore an effective feudal rule than any of his successors. However, the merchant class had been successful in gaining a real and permanent influence during the Genroku period, and once this had happened, the principles of feudal rule were no longer valid.

[46] Horie, . . *Keizai Seisaku*, 107.

[47] Sakata, *Chōnin*, 55.

[48] The most important of these new policies were: encouragement of agriculture, land reclamation, and local specialty products; the general recognition and fostering of *kabu nakama*; the regulation of the price of rice and other commodities, and, in addition to these efforts to stimulate production, Yoshimune attempted to decrease consumption by continuing Arai Hakuseki's policy of strenuous frugality which was urged upon all, and actually practiced by the Shogun himself. Horie, . . *Keizai Seisaku*, 168–9.

The time had already come when social and economic forces could not expand without breaking through the feudal structure. At the same time, Yoshimune was unable to push back the forces which had evolved for more than a hundred years, forces which were not understood by the feudal rulers because of their newness in Japanese history and because of their complexity. Even if they had been understood, any real remedy would have been the very denial of the feudal basis of the Tokugawa regime.

It is probably true, as Professor Sakata suggests, that the overspending of the *Bakufu* in the middle and late seventeenth century, especially during the Genroku period, made further development of an enlightened feudal regime almost impossible. This "inexcusable" policy meant that the role of reaction fell to Yoshimune, who was forced to stop the spending policy and revert to feudal simplicity.[49] It would appear, though, that the overspending of the *Bakufu* merely hastened the tendencies towards a deadlock between feudal and money power. Yoshimune's attempts to restore the old balance were futile, although he did achieve a temporary success in restoring *Bakufu* solvency, and in increasing production and decreasing expenditures. His policy towards *nakama* made them an additional, although rather small, source of revenue, but failed ultimately as a means for price regulating. The price regulating function of the *kabu nakama* worked in the one direction of raising prices. The practice of shifting the burden of the *Bakufu* fees to the consumer intensified this tendency. The *nakama* monopolies, moreover, were made secure and this eventually began to restrict the development of the economy.

Yoshimune's economic retrenchment eliminated many of the protected merchants of Edo, especially those connected with lumber and the building trades. His refusal of litigation for cases of money lenders against samurai was hard on the city money lenders.[50] However, the merchants found means to protect themselves. Denial of the right of litigation forced the merchant money lenders to insist upon security

---

[49] *Chōnin*, 40.
[50] The fact that this principle was repeated in edicts of 1736, 1746, 1797 and 1843 makes one wonder if there were lapses, as there often were with Tokugawa exhortatory legislation. *NKSJ*, 322.

for most loans[51] and to make a principle of not lending to members of the samurai class who had defaulted on loans in the past. Members of *nakama* undertook not to lend to anyone who had broken his connection with another *nakama* member unless the consent of the latter was obtained, and all arrears due him repaid.[52] Other pressures were applied. According to Professor Honjō, "In the Kyōhō era (1716 to 1735) already, there were cases of reprisals adopted by aggrieved *chōnin* against samurai. It often happened in Edo that *chōnin* insulted the samurai who had failed either to pay their debts or to pay for articles bought, by planting paper banners or putting up defamatory placards at the doors of the defaulters."[53] It was the fear of boycott that Gamō Kumpei (1768–1813) described in his oft-quoted lines, "The anger of the wealthy merchants of Osaka strikes terror into the hearts of the *daimyō*."[54]

After his death in 1751, Yoshimune's unpopular policies were reversed, in part as a natural reaction from the moralistic repression of the Yoshimune period.[55] The so-called Tanuma period (c. 1751–1786), named after the able politician and official, Tanuma Okitsugu (1719 to 1788), was characterized by bribery (or gift-giving for a more or less definite purpose) and other official corruption on a large scale.[56] During the period of Tanuma Okitsugu's dominant position in the *Bakufu*, an unprecedented number of monopolistic rights were granted to merchants and merchant organizations in return for the payment of *unjō* and *myōga*. As an example, houses of prostitution

---

[51] Sakata, "Meiji Ishin to Tempō Kaikaku," *op. cit.*, 6.

[52] Wigmore, "Materials..," 193.

[53] *A Social and Economic History of Japan*, 125–6.

[54] In a memorial contained in *Nihon Keizai Sōsho*, XXXIV, 528. The spectacle of a *daimyo* afraid that mere merchants would not grant him a loan was such an anomaly and so far from the feudal ideal as to excite a statement like this which no doubt uses exaggeration for effect.

[55] Yoshimune was Shogun from 1716 to 1745, almost thirty years. Like Ieyasu, he resigned in favor of his son.

[56] An interesting example of this gift-giving as evidence of official decadence is often cited by Japanese writers. Dolls made in Kyoto (Miyako *ningyō*) were justly famous, and made popular gifts. In one case, a Miyako singing girl was purchased, dressed in beautiful kimono, put in a box and presented as a gift to a high official, together with a memorial. Sakata, *Chōnin*, 56.

were legalized by paying *unjō*, and signs put up indicating their official status. In many ways the payment of *unjō* was by no means a disadvantage. It made monopolistic prices possible, and the *unjō* fees were passed on to the consumers.[57]

The Tanuma period revived the Edo merchants. Their influence, especially that of the *fudasashi*, reached its highest peak, as the samurai, high and low, were at the time particularly addicted to pleasures and extravagances.[58] For the samurai in Edo, money was something to use, and no sooner did the samurai get his hands on some than he poured it into the outstretched hands of the Edo merchants. This gave rise to the expression, "They scorn money left over from the night before."[59] Merchants always dealt indirectly with the *daimyō* in lending money, but they dealt directly with the lower samurai. Since some of the samurai in this period resorted to force against the merchants, the merchants retaliated by actually hiring *rōnin* (masterless samurai) and samurai hangers-on to protect their establishments. With the protection of these hired gangs, the *fudasashi* tended to display a particular type of arrogance known popularly as the *kuramae-fū* 藏 前 風, literally, "the warehouse front style," an imitation of the Genroku style, but rather less agreeable.[60]

With a series of natural disasters unprecedented even in the Tokugawa period, the *Bakufu* finances which Yoshimune had bolstered fell again into dire straits. Tanuma not only utilized the methods originated by Yoshimune—especially the encouragement of all types of *kabu nakama* in order to collect *unjō* and *myōga*—but he moved cautiously towards the development of semi-official monopolies.[61] Here he took the initiative in setting up new monopolies for the sale of silver and copper where the *Bakufu* before had controlled the mines and the minting only. He minted brass and iron coins for the first

---

[57] *Ibid.*, 57. Temples which kept prostitutes were also taxed. John W. Hall, *Tanuma Okitsugu, Forerunner of Modern Japan* (Harvard University Press: 1955), 80.

[58] Sakata, *Chōnin*, 60; 114.

[59] *Ibid.*, 120. *Yogoshi no kane wa tsukawanu* 宵越しの金は使はぬ, still used, often for Tokyo people.

[60] Sakata, *Chōnin*, 114; Kōda, *Nihon Keizaishi Kenkyū*, 52.

[61] *NKSJ*, 1026–7.

time, and set up similar monopolies for these metals, in this case paying a regular handling fee to a *ton'ya* for wholesaling. He encouraged domestic production of ginseng and other medicinal herbs by setting up monopolies, and gave monopoly privileges to an Edo merchant to handle all the cement for the city. In no case did he break precedent and put officials in control, and pay merchants regular wages so that the *Bakufu* would reap all the profits. This would be going into business and would have excited great opposition. He relied on fees from these various monopolies to help bolster finances, and the merchants took both the risks, which were very small, and the profits, which were usually very good.[62]

Tanuma has been called the most realistic of Tokugawa administrators, but his schemes sometimes showed little understanding of economics. For example, oil prices went very high in 1781 and there was much discontent in the cities, particularly in Edo, where large amounts were used for lighting purposes. Tanuma set up a new monopoly of Osaka merchants, exhorted producers to greater production, and then ordered them to send all their oil and oil seeds to Osaka, without selling anything in their own provinces or on the way, and without hiding any. The idea was that so much oil coming to the Osaka exchange would send prices down. But Tanuma evidently did not consider the great inconvenience and expense of sending oil first to Osaka and then back to the provincial buyers and the increase in the gap between supply and demand due to the loss of time. The arrangement was more violated than followed and it did not, of course, serve to bring prices down, so producers in the provinces were finally given specific permission to produce and sell their own oil.[63]

In 1781, Tanuma attempted to control the sale of silk by sending officials to the market to record sales and collect a high tax from

---

[62] Tsuji Zennosuke 辻善之助, *Tanuma Jidai* 田沼時代 [The Tanuma Period] (Tokyo: 1936), 190–198. This book seems to have been written mainly to disprove the facile generalization propounded by generations of Confucian moralists and uncritical historians, that the decadence of his period was caused entirely by Tanuma's corruption and his frank love of money and gifts. A recent monograph by John W. Hall, *Tanuma Okitsugu, Forerunner of Modern Japan* (op. cit.), lends further weight to Tsuji's thesis.

[63] Tsuji, *Tanuma Jidai*, 199–201.

buyers. Mitsui, Daimaru, and other large buyers simply decided to stay away from the market when it was opened. The peasants who had brought their silk to market were desperate as they were unable to sell anything. Led by some old men who "would soon die anyway," a crowd of some one thousand aroused peasants demolished the house of the unfortunate person who had suggested this new system. The leaders were taken as hostages, but were finally released, and the new system was abolished soon afterwards.[64]

Tanuma was willing to experiment to find new sources of revenue for the *Bakufu*, and was untraditional enough even to consider the general question of foreign trade. He seems to have discussed it with other officials, who were opposed to any increase. The prospect of trade relations with the Russians was considered seriously. Secret trade with the Russians was carried on in Yezo (Hokkaidō) and the Kuriles under the patronage of the *daimyō* of Matsumae probably as early as 1777, with Osaka merchants participating. Word got around that 12 *ryō* of goods were traded for goods which could be sold for 100 *ryō* in Osaka, and the opening of trade was discussed at length in *Bakufu* circles, the argument being brought forward that it would be better for the *Bakufu* to benefit from this trade than some of the *daimyō*. Conservatives continued to argue that Japan did not need foreign trade, and in any event, the matter was dropped with the fall of Tanuma and his replacement by Matsudaira Sadanobu (1758–1815) who was entirely opposed to foreign trade. During Tanuma's period in power he increased the trade in Nagasaki and encouraged the production of goods to replace precious metals as exports, by lifting the *unjō* and other fees from the production of sea foods and other commodities for which there was a demand in foreign trade.[65]

Violence, which was seen already in Yoshimune's time, became more frequent during the Tanuma period. Peasant uprisings were increasing in number in the countryside, with the abuses and maladministration which characterized the period,[66] and in the towns

---

[64] Tsuji, *Tanuma Jidai*, 204–7.

[65] *Ibid.*, 296, 300–313, 328.

[66] Hugh Borton, "Peasant Uprisings in Japan of the Tokugawa Period," *TASJ*, Second Series, XVI (May, 1938), 49.

and cities, uprisings usually known as *uchi-kowashi* 打毀 ("smashing up") became more frequent.[67] It is here that the antisocial nature of the merchants is most strikingly revealed. In times of shortage, especially when there were bad crops, merchants held their rice and other food products in the expectation of higher and higher prices. This occurred in 1733, when the *Bakufu* was forced to issue several decrees between January and May ordering all *ton'ya* to sell out all their stored rice directly to retailers so that it would not pass through the hands of middlemen, increasing its price, and that "if anybody held rice, the whole street should accuse him and his rice should be forfeited."[68] In many cases the hungry townspeople took direct action. Mobs of impoverished townspeople, including lesser tradespeople, driven to desperation by shortages and sudden increases in rice prices, attacked and often demolished the establishments of rice and *sake* dealers and pawn shops, as well as those of merchants known to be wealthy. The victims were sometimes forced to sell their rice and other products to the mob at very low prices, and usually the shops were stripped of all valuable belongings. These disturbances were directed against the monopolists who were popularly regarded as causing the price rises.[69] The first major rising in Edo was in the first month of 1733, when a plague of locusts in the western part of the country had caused a bad harvest the previous fall and greatly increased rice prices. Most of these risings were associated with bad harvests due to various natural catastrophes, increasing in frequency towards the end of the Tokugawa period. The worst occurred in the last years of Tanuma's regime, in the Temmei era (1781–8), when great famines swept the country.[70] The worst year of these riots

---

[67] They were also called *chōnin ikki* 町人一揆, uprisings of townspeople.

[68] Quoted in Takizawa, *The Penetration of Money Economy in Japan*, op. cit., 106, from *Koji Ruien*, IX, 582. "Whole street" would be better translated "whole district" (*chōchū* 町中).

[69] They were therefore quite different from the peasant uprisings which were generally directed against the feudal authorities.

[70] *NKSJ*, 90–91. The people who broke into rice markets and shops for food were largely laborers and "back-room renters," who rented rooms in the back of shops and eked out a bare living selling vegetables, old paper, etc., and hiring themselves out as day laborers. Takigawa, *Nihon Shakai Shi*, 315.

was 1787, a year of the most widespread famine when most of the large towns and cities were terrorized for days by looting mobs.[71]

Pressed by the *Bakufu*'s deteriorating finances, Tanuma broke a precedent and levied forced loans (*goyō-kin*) from wealthy merchants, a new emergency source of funds which was used sixteen times by the *Bakufu*, more and more frequently towards the end of the Tokugawa period. In 1761, he asked 305 Osaka merchants for 1,703,000 *ryō*, as rice prices were low and this sum was needed to make up the loss in income of the *Bakufu* and its retainers. The merchants then offered to supply 700,000 *ryō*. The actual amount provided is not known' but it probably was close to the figure offered by the merchants.[72] In principle, *goyō-kin* were to be repaid, but appear in most cases not to

With unemployment in the cities and people still coming from the country-side because of worsening conditions there, the *Bakufu* made use of the traditional punishment of banishment, rounding up vagrants from time to time and sending them back to the place of their birth, where they were placed on the census rolls, because in the cities they constituted a menace to public peace. Those whom they could charge with minor offences were placed in laborer's barracks and set to manual labor, manufacturing work, etc. (The similarities with the treatment of the poor in England under the Elizabethan Poor Laws are quite striking here.) Many of those committed to workhouses were petty gamblers who loitered around the gay quarters and theaters and were called "kabuki fellows" (*kabuki mono*). There were cases where unscrupulous officials used them or their women for their own purposes, according to the *Seji Kemmon Roku*, in *Kinsei Shakai Keizai Sōsho*, I, 211, cited in Takigawa, 326.

[71] Takigawa, *Nihon Shakai Shi*, 315; *NKSJ*, 91. Also see Honjo, *A Social and Economic History of Japan*, 56–8. Merchants were not the only antisocial creatures to withhold food during periods of famine. For example, a contemporary account records that in 1783, "in a year of severe famine the lord of the Nambu clan whose income was 200,000 *koku* of rice a year, and the lord of Hachinohe of 20,000, had their godowns packed with rice so that not only the higher feudal authorities but even the castle samurai who received rice stipends were able to make a handsome profit from the high price of rice." Norman, "Andō Shōeki and the Anatomy of Japanese Feudalism," 63, citing *Kisai Ryōkan* 飢歳凌鑑 [A Treatise on How to Survive the Years of Great Famine] (Hachinohe: 1926), 11 et seq.

[72] *NKSJ*, 596–7. The largest in Tokugawa times, in 1843, reached something over a million *ryō*. Takigawa, *Nihon Shakai Shi*, 325. *Goyō-kin* had previously been levied by *daimyō*, but not by the *Bakufu*.

have been. Tanuma levied two more *goyō-kin*, in 1785 and 1786,[73] and after this time both the *Bakufu* and *daimyō* used them as both an emergency and sometimes even as a regular source of revenue. There was a feeling, no doubt, as in the payment of *myōga-kin*, that the right to engage in trade was granted by the ruling classes and that the recipients of this privilege should be grateful for it, as they should also be grateful to the military class for having established the peace and order in which the merchant class could prosper. At the same time, it was generally thought that the usual burden on the well-to-do merchants was very light, and it was no more than just to make up financial deficits by ordering them to make emergency contributions.[74]

Tanuma's policies were both advantageous and disadvantageous to the merchants. As was the case with all Tokugawa administrators, his policies toward them were motivated primarily by the need to bolster *Bakufu* finances. He encouraged certain enterprises by granting monopoly rights in order to collect fees from them. This served to make the monopolists' position more secure. On the other hand, he introduced a new type of imposition—forced loans—which had quite a different effect. *Unjō* and *myōga* fees were fixed for some years at a time by discussion among officials and merchants, and the merchants could operate their enterprises making allowance for these regular fees. Forced loans, however, could be imposed at any time, and the amount was not fixed. Therefore, merchants were always afraid of them and had to be prepared. When a forced loan was ordered, the merchants paled with fear, according to Takigawa.[75] This fear cer-

---

[73] *NKSJ*, 596–7. Requests for large sums were always made, and the merchants then made an offer of a much smaller amount, always securing reductions. Osaka merchants were most often required to furnish "loans." Eight of the seventeen *Bakufu* requests were to Osaka merchants alone, and they were included in three others, along with other city merchants. *Ibid.*, 597.

[74] Horie, ..*Keizai Seisaku*, 145–6.

[75] *Nihon Shakai Shi*, 325. Takigawa, writing in 1928, cautioned those who complained about the arbitrary power of the Mitsui, Sumitomo and other capitalists not to forget that they had to go through almost three hundred years of ordeal. *Ibid.*

tainly contributed to the extreme carefulness which was characteristic of the established merchants of the time.

A powerful opposition faction headed by Matsudaira Sadanobu (1758–1829), horrified at the corruption of the Tanuma regime and at his innovations, finally accomplished the feat of overthrowing him when, in the midst of the unprecedented natural disasters of the 1780's, new scandals came to light.[76] Sadanobu presided over a reaction which attempted to put the merchant back in his place. He believed that the organization of commerce was good, and the method of exercising control through merchant organizations, collecting fees and seeing that goods were standardized and improved (Yoshimune's policy) was also good. He attributed the rises in prices entirely to one cause, the selfishness of the merchants.[77] He set about restricting the influence of the merchants, enacting strenuous frugality measures, dissolving some of the monopolies created by Tanuma, attempting to control prices, annulling some of the contracts for foreign trade in Nagasaki, and retracting the privilege of sword-wearing for certain merchants.[78] Sadanobu's regime lasted from 1786 to 1793, and was

---

[76] One of the scandals involved a friend of Tanuma. This friend had a concubine who happened to be the sister of a concubine of Tanuma's. The friend was appointed as magistrate of Fushimi, with Tanuma's help. He spent so much money in gay quarters that he had to pawn a famous family heirloom. An important official requested to see it. He agreed to show it later, but he did not have the necessary 2,000 ryō to get it back from the pawnbroker. The concubine suggested a very easy solution — merely assess a forced loan on the merchants of Fushimi. Overjoyed at this simple way to get out of his predicament, he soon got the money and was able to show the heirloom. But the story got out, and the fact that Tanuma took no steps when informed of this misuse of forced loans (goyō-kin) was naturally held against him. Tsuji, Tanuma Jidai, 222–3. Sadanobu was so incensed at Tanuma that he plotted several times to assassinate him, but finally thought better of it, not because he thought it would have been wrong, but, as he explained in a secret memorial, because he decided it would be disloyal to the Shogun who had appointed Tanuma. Ibid., 224. This from the Confucian moralist whom Sansom describes (with considerable justification) as a "benevolent statesman"! Japan, a Short Cultural History, 494.

[77] Tsuji, Tanuma Jidai, 213.

[78] Hall, "The Tokugawa Bakufu and the Merchant Class," op. cit., 31; Takigawa, Nihon Shakai Shi, 325.

called the Kansei reform. He issued one *goyō-kin* order, in 1788,[79] but the *fudasashi* bore the brunt of his attack on the merchants. In 1789 all 109 of them were called together, given a tongue-lashing for their immoral and grasping commercial conduct, and told that all old debts owed to them which had been incurred before 1784 were cancelled, and that interest on all loans contracted since that time must henceforth be less than 12% per annum.[80] The cancellation of debts (*kien*) completed the arsenal of economic weapons which the ruling classes could use against the merchants, including confiscation (*kessho*), forced loans (*goyō-kin*), refusal to pay debts (*o kotowari* お 斷 り) plus refusal to hear cases involving debts, and now cancellation of debts (*kien*).[81]

The *fudasashi* are said to have lost more than 1,187,000 *ryō* in these old debts which were cancelled. Since it was "not politic" for the *fudasashi* to bear this loss by themselves, Sadanobu granted them a loan of 10,000 *ryō* (about 92 *ryō* apiece), to be repaid in twenty years, with a ten-year delay in the beginning of payment. At the same time, he established with another 10,000 *ryō* the Saruya-chō Kaisho 猿屋町會所 as a lending organ to *fudasashi* who needed loans.[82] The reason why Yoshimune, Sadanobu and other *Bakufu* administrators took such pains to protect the financial position of

---

[79] Horie, "San Dai Kaikaku to Zaisei 三 大 改 革 と 財 政" [The Three Great Reforms and Finances], *KSK*, XV, 1 (Jan. 1936), 32.

[80] Sakata, *Chōnin*, 115. It will be remembered that Yoshimune had set a ceiling of 15%, which was not effective. See above, p. 107. The cancellation of debts (*kien* 棄捐) issued by the *Bakufu* affected only the territory under direct control, and only debts which the *hatamoto* and *go-kenin* owed to the *fudasashi*. This was not a general cancellation of samurai debts, as Hall interprets it (The Tokugawa Bakufu and the Merchant Class," 31), although it is true that some of the *han* issued similar cancellations of their samurais' debts. For example, Kaga issued four, in 1785, 1786, 1837 and 1838, and Tosa, Saga, and Tsu are also known to have issued them. *NKSJ*, 322.

[81] Takigawa, *Nihon Shakai Shakai Shi*, 322.

[82] Horie, "San Dai Kaikaku to Zaisei," *op. cit.*, 37. Interest was 12%, 1% to go to operating expenses, 5% to pay off the *Bakufu* in 20 years, 3% to add to the principal as interest, the remaining 3% to the *fudasashi* who were to operate the agency. *Ibid.* This aid to the injured *fudasashi* implies an admission that the retainers of the *Bakufu* would continue to depend on them in financial matters.

the *hatamoto* and *go-kenin* is not hard to find, as the *Bakufu* took ultimate responsibility for the debts of these direct retainers. The *kien* of Sadanobu was indirectly a lightening of the *Bakufu's* own burden of debt.[83]

As the result of the *kien*, the *fudasashi* became very careful in making loans, and often refused them. Those *hatamoto* and *go-kenin* who were badly in need of funds also suffered from this policy. Some resorted to sending persuasive merchants or energetic *rōnin* as go-betweens who would sometimes threaten violence if refused. The *fudasashi* again hired bodyguards, and the atmosphere was very tense. The *Bakufu* tried to assure them that no other *kien* would be issued, but the *fudasashi* were still wary. No doubt this promise was recalled when forty-three years later, a second *kien* was prepared by Mizuno Tadakuni and issued immediately after his resignation.[84]

Although Sadanobu's financial measures were not nearly so success-ful as Yoshimune's had been, they did succeed in giving the *Bakufu* treasury a surplus. Sadanobu himself was in power for barely seven years (1787–1793), but his influence was felt for several years, and the treasury excess reached a total of something like 338,000 *ryō*, according to a contemporary source, in 1797.[85] But people soon be-came tired of such excesses of frugality and strict Confucian morality which ran counter to the social and economic forces of the time and to the people's enjoyment of pleasure. A popular song heard in the

[83] Horie, "San Dai Kaikaku to Zaisei," 38. Having set up one loan agency, Sasanobu later, in 1791, organized another to lend money to poor people. This was called the Edo Machi Kaisho 江戶町會所, and was a semi-official organ run by nine appointed merchants. It was not successful and almost never made a loan to "poor people" evidently because of nameless abuses which sprang up. Horie, "San Dai Kaikaku to Zaisei," 29. Some of Sadanobu's other measures were to store grain for emergencies; to prohibit gambling, the new construction of houses of prostitution, intermingling of the sexes in public baths; to censor literature by destroying the blocks of licentious novels and plays; and to encourage children to be filial, wives to be chaste and servants to be loyal, by offering prizes. He established a workhouse for unemployed persons and prisoners, and closed the avenues to official positions to all who did not accept the official Chu Hsi Confucian orthodoxy. *NKSJ*, 310–11.

[84] *NKSJ*, 322.

[85] Horie, "San Dai Kaikaku to Zaisei," 32; *NKSJ*, 311.

cities during Sadanobu's time reflects the opinion of townspeople of this period:[86]

In the White River's* pure waters, the fish can live no more;

They long for the muddy waters of the paddy fields** of yore.

* Shirakawa — one of Sadanobu's names.

** Tanuma

The reforms of Sadanobu threw a shadow over the "warehouse front style," but this was only as long as he lived. The *fudasashi* soon recovered after his death.[87] After Sadanobu's time, *Bakufu* income was not equal to expenses, and treasury shortages year by year had to be made up by recoinages and by squeezing the merchants.

The period between Sadanobu's Kansei reform and the Tempō reform of Mizuno Tadakuni was one of city predominance. It was during this period (especially during the Bunka-Bunsei periods, 1804 to 1829) that the center of popular literature shifted from Osaka to Edo,[88] and Edo culture which was in its formative stage during the Tanuma period reached its full maturity.[89] Perhaps due in part to censorship and feudal displeasure with the eroticism of Genroku culture, the trend of the more highly cultivated Osaka townspeople's culture was towards a "life of taste" after passing through a "life of pleasure." The trend in all the major cities was from a concentration on eroticism (*iro* 色) to the wider and more universal field of human feelings (*jō* 情).[90]

---

[86] This song, which plays cleverly on the two names, is quoted by most everyone who writes on this period. It can be found in Tsuji, *Tanuma Jidai*, 341–2; Horie, "San Dai Kaikaku to Zaisei," 33, and in *NKSJ*, 1027: "Shirakawa no kiyoki ni sakana mo sumikanete, Moto no nigori no Tanuma koishiki."

[87] Sakata, *Chōnin*, 116. According to Sakata, Sadanobu was universally recognized as a true samurai, and "In the presence of a true samurai, the merchants were nothing but merchants." In their dealings with the *hatamoto* and *go-kenin*, however, the *fudasashi* did not consider them as real samurai. *Ibid.*

[88] *Ibid.*, 103. Sakata is careful to point out, however, that the center of *chōnin* culture still remained in Osaka.

[89] Tsuji, *Tanuma Jidai*, 289.

[90] Sakata, *Chōnin*, 100–103; Miyamoto, *Nihon Shōgyō Shi*, 191.

The Tempō reform (1841–3) of Mizuno Tadakuni (1794–1851) was the third and last attempt at reform, and followed the tradition of Yoshimune and Sadanobu. It was still possible to put some order in the Tokugawa house, but the martial virtue and feudal frugality of the samurai class had reached such a level of deterioration as to be most difficult to reform, and the social and economic structure was more complex than that which existed in the time of Yoshimune and Sadanobu, whose heroic efforts to turn back the clock were Tadakuni's ideal. When the Shogun Ienari died, a reform was long overdue and the feudal society as well as the continued existence of the *Bakufu* were at stake. Tadakuni began his reform immediately after Ienari's death with a new exhortation to frugality, in the tradition of Yoshimune and Sadanobu. Sadanobu, for example, had told people to serve dried fish rather than sea-bream (*tai*, a delicious but expensive fish) on special occasions. Tadakuni took the next logical step and ordered that no fish be bought at all on these occasions. Instead, the amount that would have gone to buy sea-bream should be offered as a gift to the Shogun.[91]

Besides enforcing frugality, the major objectives of Tadakuni's reform were to bring down prices of commodities other than rice,[92] and increase *Bakufu* income. All these policies were doomed to dismal failure. The first step in Tadakuni's campaign against high prices was a drastic one. He ordered the dissolution of the *ton'ya* and *kabu nakama*, whose monopolistic activities were blamed for the increasing commodity prices, and called for freedom in buying and selling. With this, he attempted to restore the conditions previous to 1721, and combined an attack on the interests of the merchants with an attempt

[91] Horie, "San Dai Kaikaku to Zaisei," 33. The great demand for *tai* on festive days was (and still is) an artificial one, and fish dealers could easily take advantage of it. Tadakuni confiscated the property of merchants and other townspeople who violated any of his many prohibitions against luxury. He also reenacted many of Sadanobu's puritanical measures such as the prohibition of mixed bathing in public bath houses, although the idea that it was wrong seems more Chinese than Japanese. See *NKSJ*, 1137, for a description of these reforms.

[92] Price policy was aimed at maintaining rice prices relatively stable and the prices of other commodities low relative to rice prices, a policy to benefit the samurai classes. Horie, ..*Keizai Seisaku*, 127–8.

to lower prices.[93] Actually, by 1841 the discipline of the *kabu nakama* both over their members and over outsiders had declined considerably and their monopolies were not so tight, although this was probably not apparent to the authorities.[94] The rise in prices at that particular time seems to have been more due to increasing trouble on the part of Osaka merchants to get Edo merchants to pay up their accounts with them and they were resorting to withholding shipments.[95] Tadakuni not only dissolved the *kabu nakama*, including the *ton'ya*, which were specifically named as an evil type of *nakama* due to their monopolistic control of markets,[96] but he also attempted to cut out some of the middlemen in the complicated distribution system. Wholesalers were instructed to sell at retail, and all merchants were warned not to hold goods for higher prices.[97]

The dissolution of the *kabu nakama* meant the destruction of the organization of commerce. It interfered with transport because Osaka merchants were given no assurance of being paid by Edo merchants for goods or for shipwreck settlements. It caused a dislocation in the money market because *kabu*, the most important securities, were no longer acceptable.[98] In addition, new merchants were not sufficiently familiar with the intricacies of commercial methods, and the established merchants, disturbed at the instability of prices and not knowing what to expect from official policy, tended to be especially careful,

[93] Nomura, "Tokugawa Hōken Sei to Shōgyō," *op. cit.*, 131. Nomura points out that Tadakuni did not mean free trade in any modern sense as can be seen when other provisions are examined. *Ibid.* Tadakuni also decreed the abolition of *han* monopolies, but it seems doubtful if this had much effect. Horie, "San Dai Kaikaku to Zaisei," 34.

[94] Nomura, "Tokugawa Hōken Sei to Shōgyō," 130.

[95] Smith, "Materials..," 81–2.

[96] *NKSJ*, 1147. Cartels (*kō*) were not affected because they were not organized as *kabu nakama* but were merely agreements for the purpose of allotting markets. Kanno, "Tokugawa Jidai Shōnin no Chifu," 32.

[97] Smith, "Materials..," 97. Yoshimune had also tried to cut out middlemen (see above, p. 118). In Tadakuni's reform, for example, a merchant dealing in charcoal, whether wholesaler, middleman or retailer, was to call himself merely a "dealer in charcoal" (*sumi-ya*). *Ibid.* For details of some aspects of the Tempō reform, see *ibid.*, 96–104, taken from Kōda's *Edo to Ōsaka*.

[98] *Ibid.*, 104.

often withholding goods for the storm to pass. In the free markets created when the *kabu nakama* were dissolved, open bidding drove prices up at the production points. The result was that prices did not fall as expected, and the *Bakufu* turned in desperation to forceful lowering of prices by decree, requiring the merchants of semi-official standing such as the *nanushi* to see that they were enforced.[99] Price cuts were ordered in all the cities, but merchants promptly complied by giving short weight or measure or by selling goods of poorer quality, nullifying to a large extent the effect of the order.[100] In Osaka, a cut of 20% was ordered on all goods, wages, rents, etc., resulting in a general avoidance of the Osaka market by sellers. The shortages which inevitably developed caused even higher prices. Ironically, the policy of price reduction by dissolution of the *kabu nakama* on behalf of freer trade resulted in a retreat from this freer trade to the imposition of stringent controls, a policy which was likewise bound to fail.[101] After the resignation of Tadakuni in 1843, the legal restoration of the *ton'ya* and *kabu nakama* was seriously considered. The restoration, however, did not actually become policy until 1851 when it was decided that it was the only way to restore the commercial distribution system to working order.[102]

To relieve the direct retainers of the Tokugawa house who were again deeply in debt to the *fudasashi*, another partial cancellation (*kien*) was considered, but it was decided in 1842 to revise the Saruya-chō Kaisho lending law to provide loans to *hatamoto* and *go-kenin* so that they could pay off their debts.[103] At the same time, a ceiling of 10% was set on the interest rates *fudasashi* could demand, a reduction of 2% compared to previous legislation.[104] However, before this program could get well under way, Tadakuni was forced to resign, and his successor put into effect the plan which Tadakuni had been holding in reserve. This was a new kind of *kien* which cancelled

[99] *NKSJ*, 1137.
[100] Smith, "Materials..," 99.
[101] Cf. *NKSJ*, 1137.
[102] Horie, ..*Keizai Seisaku*, 116.
[103] Interest was 7% and loans were to be paid off in 26 years. Horie, "San Dai Kaikaku to Zaisei," 38.
[104] *Ibid.*

all interest rather than principal. It ordered all *hatamoto* and *go-kenin*
to pay off their loans to the *fudasashi* without interest at the rate of
roughly 5% a year over a period of twenty years. "It is said that
approximately half of the *fudasashi* closed their doors."[105] This plan
was not without precedent. In 1806, for example, disputes over debts
had been ordered to be settled out of court with both parties making
concessions. If no settlement was made within 30 days, magistrates
were to settle the dispute by reducing the amount of the debt and
giving a number of years to repay, according to a schedule.[106]

Bakufu finances had reached the point where unless a basic change
in policy were carried through, financial ruin was only a matter of
time. But no such policy emerged. The reforms were entirely reactionary in nature, and did nothing to increase production or prosperity. Tadakuni relied on recoinages and *goyō-kin*. In 1841, a good
profit of 1,155,000 *ryō* was obtained from a recoinage, and 500,000 *ryō*
in 1842. As this was insufficient to make up the treasury deficit in
1843, the largest *goyō-kin* of the Tokugawa period was demanded,
1,902,500 *ryō* from 705 prominent merchants of the "three cities,"
as well as Sakai, Hyōgo, Nishinomiya and other *Bakufu* towns.
The amount actually collected is not known, but was probably over a
million *ryō*.[107] Despite these measures, Tadakuni's shortlived reform
must have bestowed little financial benefit to the *Bakufu*.[108]

One of the justifications for raising prices which the *kabu nakama*
used was the fact that they had to pay *unjō* and *myōga* fees. This
shifting of the burden to the consumer was recognized as one of the
causes of high prices, and Tadakuni dissolved the *kabu nakama* without much thought about the loss of this source of revenue.[109] Nevertheless, he proposed a means of making up this loss. He planned for
the Shogun to rearrange fiefs, reducing them enough so that areas
within a radius of 24.4 miles (ten *ri*) around the three cities would become *Bakufu* land, under direct control. These were areas of high

---

[105] *NKSJ*, 1137. Honjō's description of this *kien*, in *The Social and Economic
History of Japan*, 40–1, is rather difficult to understand due to the poor
translation.   [106] Cf. Wigmore, "Materials..," Supplements 3–4, 349–362.
[107] *NKSJ*, 1137; Takigawa, *Nihon Shakai Shi*, 325.
[108] Horie, "San Dai Kaikaku to Zaisai," 33.   [109] Horie, ..*Keizai Seisaku*, 115.

agricultural production and would have added to the *Bakufu's* feudal revenues. However, this was not carried through due to the vocal opposition of the *daimyō* involved, and particularly the powerful lord of Kishū, the head of one of the three Tokugawa branch families, whose lands were involved. This was the immediate cause for Tadakuni's fall.[110]

The failure of the Tempō reform was hastened by the fact that Mizuno Tadakuni did not have the authority of a Yoshimune nor the friends of a Sadanobu, and the severity of his reforms served only to multiply the number of his enemies. He also lacked able assistance and advice. But no matter how excellent the implementation of his reforms might have been, they were bound to fail because they could not undo more than two hundred years of development in commerce and production.[111] It is natural that Tadakuni became the object of the Edo merchants' hatred. Finally, after almost three years, and with his work half done, he was forced to relinquish his post by the plots of his political opponents and betrayal by his subordinates. When, in 1843, the news was spread that he had resigned, a shouting crowd of several thousand Edo townsmen gathered and pushed their way to the Mizuno residence. They threw stones at the residence and demolished one of the guardhouses outside the gate, "thus expressing their long-accumulated resentment towards Tadakuni. The failure of the Tempō reform showed that the Tokugawa *Bakufu* had lost its right to exist. The history of the Meiji Restoration had already begun."[112]

Commerce and money transactions offered new sources of income and an opportunity to shift the basis of the feudal regime with its heavy burden of a non-productive samurai population to support.

[110] Horie, "San Dai Kaikaku to Zaisei," 34–5. The Lord of Kishū, who was benefiting from a shipping *nakama*, had already been alienated by Tadakuni's dissolution of the *kabu nakama*. *Ibid.*

[111] Sakata, *Chōnin*, 131; *NKSJ*, 1138.

[112] Sakata, *Chōnin*, 131. Tadakuni's reforms were really a remarkable succession of failures. Besides those discussed here, his policy of sending people back to the countryside had a similar fate. Previously, this policy had been to prevent the depopulation of the agricultural communities, but in the Tempō reform it took on the added purpose of decreasing the population of Edo. This policy was only very temporarily effective and ended in failure. *NKSJ*, 1137.

However, utilization of these sources caused higher prices and larger official disbursements. Moreover, to shift the basis of government from its traditional feudal base was unthinkable to those who followed the almost universally accepted orthodoxy of the agricultural state where commerce was a fruitless and despised occupation. Resort to *goyō-kin* and *kien* had the double purpose of suppressing the power and influence of the merchants and saving *Bakufu* (or *han*) finances. These expedients could never be really successful, and ironically enough, reveal the fact that the feudal finances, in the final analysis, had to depend in some way upon the financial power of the merchants for the difference between bankruptcy and solvency.

The three reforms of the Tokugawa period were similar in intent but different in methods and results. Yoshimune was successful both in effecting economies and in increasing revenues. Sadanobu, however, pursued a largely negative policy, spending most of his effort on economies and frugality, perhaps finding little room for increasing revenues. The fact that he increased the merchants' burden through emergency measures such as the *goyō-kin* and *kien* reveals a lack of understanding of realities. On this point, the policies of the Tanuma period are of greater interest. However, the Kansei reforms of Sadanobu did bolster *Bakufu* finances, even if temporarily. But the Tempō reforms did not result even in financial improvement. Rather, they revealed the lack of agreement among the *Bakufu* authorities and the fact that it had become almost impossible to carry through a feudal policy. Each of the three reforms followed what were considered periods of extravagance and luxury, when the *Bakufu* treasury became exhausted. For this reason, the reforms were necessarily economic retrenchments. However, the differences in methods and effects were a function of changing conditions. In the Kyōhō period, it was still possible for the *Bakufu* finances to be based on agriculture. Later, it was no longer possible.[113] In terms of impersonal forces, the difference was the increased strength of the money and commercial economy. In human terms, it was the continued rise of the merchant class.

[113] It is noteworthy that Yoshimune had nineteen years to enact his reforms and another ten years to preside over them, a total of twenty-nine years. Sadanobu had seven years to put through his reforms; Tadakuni had less than three.

CHAPTER VII

IDEAS OF SAMURAI AND MERCHANT SCHOLARS ABOUT COMMERCE AND MERCHANTS

IN THE PRECEDING chapter, we outlined historically the alternations in feudal and city predominance largely from the standpoint of the authorities, as the role played by the merchant class throughout was necessarily a passive one. As Sakata points out, all attempts to coerce the merchants served only to make them more wary. They could not oppose the samurai actively, but were able to oppose them passively.[1] But an important question remains unconsidered. In view of the failure on the part of the feudal ruling classes to cope with the problems created by the new commercial and money economy, was there no one to suggest a different approach? Were there no scholars to analyze the economic and social phenomena of the day correctly and prescribe a remedy? Since the history of thought is a legitimate part of history, we shall attempt to outline some of the more influential thought directed towards the problems posed by the rise of commerce and the merchant class.

Samurai Confucian scholars of the early Tokugawa period, during a time of feudal predominance, generally reaffirmed the official class policy and allowed the merchant his role as distributor of the necessities of life. But when the merchants gradually became the hated wielders of economic power, there was a general shift to the position that commerce was necessary but merchants were evil.[2] It is typical of Confucian thinking to blame all ills not on the system or organization of the society, but on defects of personal morality. Writers were apt to complain that the merchant forgot his duty to society in his scramble for personal gain, and they branded him as an immoral creature. This typical attitude can be seen in the writings of Yamaga Sokō (1622-1685). There was reason for this

---

[1] *Chōnin*, 92.

[2] Honjo, *Economic Theory and History of Japan in the Tokugawa Period* Tokyo: 1943), 104, 106–8.

view, as the commerce of the time was to a large extent the art of bilking both producers and consumers, or at least buying cheap and selling dear, using the pressures of monopolistic devices.[3]

As the penetration of money economy and the rise of the merchant class came to be recognized as subversive to the feudal system, definite measures to remedy the situation were demanded and were debated thoroughly among contemporary scholars. Most scholars recognized the necessity of commerce, but their contempt for the merchants coupled with envy for their success gave rise to two common types of proposals: (1) Those who detested the scramble for profits advocated the restriction of the merchants and a return to a simple rice economy; (2) Those who, although disliking the profit motive, could find some justification for it which could be expressed in acceptable moral terms (e.g., to save the people from poverty, or to assure provision of sufficient food, etc.) advocated official control of commerce. Some scholars stood between these two schools, and advised both the restriction of the money economy and the utilization of it, even though restricted. Both schools opposed merchant prosperity and attacked monopolistic profits. These continued attacks finally resulted in Tadakuni's ill-fated reforms.[4]

Among those who advocated a return to a self-sufficient rice economy, thus restraining the influence of the merchant class, were Kumazawa Banzan (1619–1691) and Ogyū Sorai (1666–1728), who wanted the samurai sent back to the country-side and reintegrated into the land economy as peasant-soldiers (nōhei 農兵). Banzan, as part of his program for preventing rapid drops in rice prices, advocated that rice and other grains should be used in buying and selling and should be used together with currency in paying interest on loans. He wrote, "If the five grains are used as media of exchange, when they are either in oversupply or undersupply it will be difficult to profiteer. Therefore, prices will be lower, and without being extra-

---

[3] Endō, ..Shōgyō Shihon.., 14, citing Yamaga Gorui, in Yamaga Sokō Shū, op. cit., 288.

[4] Cf. Nomura Kanetarō, Tokugawa Jidai no Keizai Shisō 德川時代の經濟思想 [The Economic Thought of the Tokugawa Period] (Tokyo: 1939) 104.

vagant, both samurai and commoners will have enough, and artisans and merchants will be productive."[5] Sorai expressed his attitude toward the merchants in this way: "Merchants carry on an insignificant occupation ... it should be no concern of ours if they ruin themselves."[6]

Miura Baien (1725–1789) explained that due to the penetration of the money economy, the rich were getting richer, the poor poorer. In order to remedy this, he maintained that the use of money as an instrument of exchange must be stopped in spite of all opposition, and insisted that a policy be adopted to carry this out by causing the feudal lords to economize and avoid borrowing money from merchants, at the same time as accumulating stores of goods and giving surpluses to the peasants.[7] Motoori Norinaga (1730–1801) also pointed out various evils arising from the development of money transactions, and urged that the practice be restricted. He maintained that if it were restricted and reduced, human feelings would be alienated from gold and silver, and the people would become diligent in the pursuit of their proper occupations. These arguments that the development of a money economy be suppressed were closely connected with the prevalent idea of "revere grain, despise money" (kikoku senkin 貴穀賤金). Although the methods suggested were often not feasible, these writers asserted that the merchants had grasped economic prerogatives and insisted that this situation had to be rectified.[8]

Kumazawa Banzan, an unorthodox and original thinker, advocated a return to the use of rice and other grains as media of exchange, but realized that the money economy to some extent was bound to stay. He represents an early view that the feudal authorities should control it. He wrote, "Money is to be despised by the superior man (kunshi 君子), but the right to control wealth is not to be given over to inferiors. The masses are low-minded, and the right to control them

[5] Shūgi Gesho, in Nihon Rinri Ihen, op. cit., II, 220. See also "Dai Gaku Wakumon, a Discussion of Public Questions in the Light of the Great Learning, by Kumazawa Banzan," translated by Galen M. Fisher, TASJ, XVI, 2nd Series (May 1938), 259–356.

[6] Seidan, in Nihon Keizai Sōsho, III, 427.

[7] Horie, ..Keizai Seisaku, 177.

[8] Ibid.

rests with the rulers. The superior man reverences virtue and despises money, but the right to control the nation's money rests with the rulers."[9] Satō Shin'en (1769–1850) wrote: "From early times the occupation of trade in commodities has been only in a general way under the supervision of the ruling authorities. Due to the fact that they left the merchants even such an important power as control of the market, merchants and others have given free rein to their cleverness and greed, have caused prices to go up and down at will, all making huge profits, many making themselves extremely wealthy, and they are confronting the authorities with their wealth. ... Despite the high position of the ruling class, the wealth is all falling into the hands of merchants. It has become difficult to control them, and rulers have come to bow their heads before them. By this it should be recognized what a great loss to the country has resulted from leaving to merchants the privileges of trade ... For these reasons, the power of the merchants should be crushed, privileges of trade taken away and made the possession of the rulers, the *ton'ya* all put under their supervision and operated by their appointees. Also, merchants should be ordered to build markets, live there, and they should be strictly forbidden to be in the fields."[10]

The development of the argument for samurai participation in, or at least control over, commercial activities paralleled the rise of *han* monopolies, and gave these monopolies an aura of Confucian justification. Those who opposed samurai participation still admitted the great development of commerce and realized that profits could be made from it. They opposed it on the grounds that exploitation of profits from such an immoral and detestable source as commerce was beneath the samurai class, and would result in intensified exploitation and impoverishment of the peasants. Those who favored it insisted that since profits were clearly made in commerce, it was better for the feudal rulers than for the merchant class to benefit from

---

[9] *Shūgi Gesho*, in *Nihon Rinri Ihen*, op. cit., II, 224. The translation of this quotation in Horie Yasuzo, "An Outline of Economic Policy in the Tokugawa Period," *KUER*, 64–5 is freer, but farther from the original text.

[10] *Keizai Teiyō* 經濟提要 [A Manual of Political Economy], *Satō Shin'en-ka Gaku Zenshū*, II, 582–5.

such profits.[11] This argument can be seen, for instance, in the *Kei-zairoku* 經濟錄 of Dazai Shundai (1680–1747).[12] Kaiho Seiryō (1755–1818) justified samurai participation in commerce with an interesting rationalistic argument. He pointed out that it was not logical that a samurai could buy whatever he needed without being considered strange by anyone, but if he once sold something, it was a great disgrace. Seiryō insisted there was no great difference between buying and selling, and it was quite just for samurai to make profits by selling his stipend rice openly rather than through merchants.[13]

There are many examples where the export of goods from the *han* and the import of specie to pay for them was advocated. The scholar of Dutch, Hayashi Shihei (1754–1793), denounced the merchants in stinging terms, "Townspeople only soak up the stipends of the samurai. They are otherwise profitless things, really useless destroyers of grain!"[14] However, he went on to advocate commercial monopolies to be controlled by the *han* authorities: "When the products of your land are plentiful, they are a profit to your domain; when scarce, they become a loss. When products are exported, gold and silver can be imported. On the other hand, if many products are imported from other *han*, there is an outflow of gold and silver. At present, since more goods are imported than exported, all gold and silver has been lost to other *han*. Therefore, local products must be increased, prepared and sold to other *han* for gold and silver, to fill the treasury

---

[11] Endō, ..*Shōgyō Shihon*.., 15.

[12] In *Nihon Keizai Sōsho*, op. cit., XI, 291.

[13] *Masukodan* 升古談, in *Nihon Keizai Sōsho*, XVIII, 217–18. He satirized the samurai's unrealistic ideas about money: "The members of a samurai family think that money and rice fall from heaven, so all merely eat. It is like a house infested with mice — the rice just disappears... They do not know how to value the money with which to buy rice, as it is the samurai style to despise money, and it quickly vanishes. It is the universal fashion to scoff at people who value money, calling them mercenary creatures." *Zen-chūdan* 善中談, in *Nihon Keizai Taiten* (Tokyo: 1928), XXVII, cited in Sakata, *Chōnin*, 81. Related to Seiryū's attack on the ethic which permitted merchants to buy but not sell was the opposition of Tanaka Kyūgu (1663–1729) to the prohibition against the buying and selling of land. *Minkan Seiyō* 民間省要 in *Nihon Keizai Sōsho*, I, 673–4.

[14] *Jōsho* 上書 [Memorial] (the first of a series presented to Date, the *daimyō* of Sendai), in *Nihon Keizai Sōsho*, XII, 25.

of the lord of Sendai."[15] As late as the period 1853–67, memorialists were urging *daimyō* to pursue mercantilist policies.[16] During the Tempō reform, the idea of establishing a *Bakufu* monopoly system in *Bakufu* territories like that of Satsuma was actually considered, but given up because it appeared that more squeezing of the already rebellious farmers would have been necessary, and the result of such a monopoly promised to be higher prices.[17] These examples show that the feudal authorities could despise the merchants and still plan to use commerce to enrich themselves.

The success of many of the *han* monopolies served as a stimulus to the idea that foreign trade could be beneficial to the country, and it was easy to apply mercantilistic ideas about the *han* to the entire country. Despite the feudal bonds of commerce, there was a gradual development of the realization that foreign trade was necessary. This idea is seen first in the eighteenth century, after commerce had experienced a great expansion internally. An example is the argument of Yamagata Bantō (1789–1821), the merchant scholar, that as an inevitable result of the money and commercial economy, not only should domestic commerce be expanded, but foreign trade should be resumed.[18] A more complete and thorough-going argument for foreign trade was made by Honda Toshiaki (1744–1821), a scholar of Dutch who attained a considerable knowledge of foreign countries. He proposed to standardize prices on all commodities and do away with profits due to merchants' dishonesty and monopolistic activities. He wrote, "By opening up the seaways to other countries, and setting standard prices on all our produce, both samurai and peasants would be saved, profits for the country would multiply day by day...Beginning with the rice from all parts of the country, and applying to all products, an average uniform price should be assigned to each category, valuing equally the industry of all the people upon which

---

[15] *Jōsho*, in *Nihon Keizai Sōsho*, XII, 25.

[16] An example is the memorial of Ueno Shōjū to the *daimyō* of Fukuoka in this period, in which the writer cautions against the draining away of gold and silver by the importation of paper currency of other *han*. Endō, ..*Shōgyō Shihon*.., 18, citing a manuscript of Ueno Shōjū.

[17] Sakata, "Meiji Ishin to Tempō Kaikaku," *op. cit.*, 14–15.

[18] Endō, ..*Shōgyō Shihon*.., 18–19.

they depend for their existence. In this way all the people, without exception, can hope for long life ... There is no way to make the nation prosperous except through the importation of gold, silver and copper from other countries."[19] Another famous advocate of foreign trade was Satō Shin'en, who pointed at England as a country with limited resources which had become both wealthy and powerful through foreign trade.[20] It should be noted here that these proposals for opening up foreign trade were not made to the *Bakufu*. They were usually unpublished and circulated secretly among a few persons of advanced views.

A major dilemma of *Bakufu* commercial policy was the problem of whether to permit monopolies and tax them, giving rise to higher prices, or to abolish them and forego the taxes in the interest of lower prices. It was a dilemma because feudal sources of revenue were no longer sufficient, and squeezing of the peasants had reached a point of diminishing returns, when peasants left the land and resorted to rebellion. In the conditions of the early nineteenth century, to abolish the monopolies was virtually to disorganize the commerce upon which the feudal classes living in cities and castle towns were dependent. It was attempted only once, and with disastrous results, by Tadakuni. The only alternative to financial ruin, under the conditions which obtained, was to continue Yoshimune's policies which included the recognition of the monopolies. However, revenues from commerce were limited by the haggling of the merchants, who used their superior knowledge of the complexity of commerce effectively to decrease all types of levies. Moreover, there were limits to the squeezing of the merchants. Public opinion, in the form of city mobs, was feared, and there was no desire to remove the sources of the loans so needed by the samurai class.

Scholars generally did not like the idea of taxing merchants, and often opposed *myōga* and *unjō* fees because they caused prices to rise.[21] Another important reason was reluctance to accept money

---

[19] *Keisei Hisaku* 經世秘策 [A Secret Plan of Government], in Vol. X, *Kinsei Shakai Keizai Gakusetsu Taikei*, op. cit., 13–15.

[20] *Kaibō Saku* 海防策 [A Policy for Coastal Defense], *Satō Shin'en-ka Gaku Zenshū*, op. cit., II, 821.   [21] Nomura, *Tokugawa Jidai no Keizai Shisō*, 101.

from merchants. A representative view is that of Shingū Ryōtei (1787–1854), who wrote, "There have been cases of late where vassals of various feudal lords have caused losses to *chōnin* without any qualm of conscience or even defrauded them. This is a very deplorable state of affairs... Besides, the frequent imposition of *goyō-kin* on *chōnin* and peasants is regrettable as it is tantamount to seeking alms from those below and it reflects discredit on the feudal lords concerned."[22] The theory that the right to participate in commerce was a privilege justified merchants' "gifts" to the ruling classes in the form of *unjō* and *myōga-kin*. This put the feudal rulers in a difficult moral position to dictate the amounts and put the system on an impersonal basis. Moreover, it might be added that impersonality in economic relations had not yet been discovered. This distaste for accepting favors from inferiors no doubt played a part in the advocacy by many scholars of the kind of control of commerce which had proved successful in some of the *han*. But to carry out effectively such a policy in *Bakufu* territories where commerce was so complex and on so large a scale was entirely impossible. The minimum program of control attempted was the regulation of prices, but in this there was no success whatever.[23] The merchant scholars Kusama Naokata (1753–1831) and Yamagata Bantō, both of whom started as apprentices and worked up in the commercial world, explained (Bantō for the first time) the working of the market, supply and demand, and the effect of bad crops on the price of rice. They did their best to discourage attempts to regulate rice prices as an impossibility.[24]

A traditional Confucian attitude towards commercial profits was that the superior man kept righteousness and rejected profits, but the merchant kept profits and rejected righteousness. An interesting contrast to this view is found in some writings of teachers of the Shin sect of Buddhism (Jōdo Shinshū 淨土眞宗) which justified profits which were not gained from selfish motives. A Shin writer of the

---

[22] Honjo, *Economic Theory and History of Japan*, 201, quoting from Ryōtei's *Yabureya no Tsuzukuri Banashi*.

[23] Nomura, *Tokugawa Jidai no Keizai Shisō*. 101.

[24] *Ibid.*

period described justifiable profits in terms of a doctrine of *jiri-rita* (自 利 利 他), profiting self and others:

> In merchandising we receive remuneration for supplying the consumer with manufactured goods. The artisans receive their remuneration by producing the goods and supplying them to the consumer. What the world calls this remuneration is profit. But the basis of receiving this profit depends on profiting others. Thus both the business of merchants and of artisans is the profiting of others. By profiting others they receive the right to profit themselves. This is the virtue of the harmony of *jiri-rita*. The spirit of profiting others is the Bodhisattva spirit. Having a Bodhisattva spirit and saving all beings, this is called Bodhisattva deeds. Thus Bodhisattva deeds are just the deeds of merchants and artisans. In general the secret of merchants' and artisans' business lies in obtaining confidence through Bodhisattva deeds.[25]

One might expect merchant scholars to strive for the stabilization and enhancement of commerce, but this expectation is not fulfilled. Merchant scholars, including the *shingaku* school established by Ishida Baigan (1685–1744), made no attempt to glorify trade or to make a more realistic (i. e., higher) place in society for the merchant class. Rather, they tried to harmonize commerce and the merchants within the feudal system, and to make the merchants satisfied with the social structure as it was.[26] The *shingaku* school elaborated the common-sense morality of the Osaka merchant code, the "way of the

---

[25] As quoted in Bellah, *Tokugawa Religion*, op. cit., 120. Ōmi merchants were very often Shin believers. Shin doctrine gave strong emphasis to frugality and the value of hard work, ideas found in merchant house rules. *Ibid.*, 117–126. Bellah finds that Shin was "the closest analogue to Western Protestantism and its ethic most similar to the Protestant ethic." *Ibid.*, 122.

[26] Nomura, *Tokugawa Jidai no Keizai Shisō*, 103. This merchant *shingaku* school, which drew from Shintō, Buddhism and Confucianism, should not be confused with the Ōyōmei (Wang Yang-ming) Confucian school, also called *shingaku*, whose most important proponents were Nakae Tōju (1608–1648) and Kumazawa Banzan (1619–1691). For a recent study of Ishida Baigan and his *shingaku* movement, see Bellah, *Tokugawa Religion*, 133–176; 199–215. This interesting movement, begun in Kyoto and Osaka, became an important ethical and religious force, and was later embraced by the *Bakufu* to give greater effect to its moral injunctions.

merchant." Nishikawa Joken (1648–1724), a merchant-astronomer-mathematician, laid the foundations for this school by suggesting a basis upon which the merchants could attain a degree of self-respect within the feudal society. He wrote, "A true merchant is one who calculates things of all kinds, in large and small amounts, of high and low value, considering gain and loss, and without taking a high profit for himself, fulfills an important function for the country by taking things from where they are plentiful to where they are scarce, trans-porting them from one province to another, linking together the wealth of the nation."[27] Ishida Baigan, the founder of *shingaku*, whose early training was in Shin Buddhism, emphasized the attainment of a just, organic society with an identification of interests and goals of all segments, in which all classes had their proper places, and all lower classes, including the merchants, were aids to the ruling class.[28] This teaching is in agreement with concepts prevalent among merchants, who, for example, joined samurai moralists in deploring the social chaos caused by merchants who were adopted into samurai families. Among the established merchants, "For a merchant to acquire a higher status was looked upon as a vice of egotism. Such a person was thought to have lost his mind and was to be avoided at all costs."[29] Baigan believed that although all classes of men were the same in principle, they differed in form. He would have agreed with the common expression, "The off-spring of a toad is a toad; the offspring of a merchant is a merchant."[30]

The acceptance by merchant scholars of a subordinate role for merchants is no doubt based in part on the recognition of the close interdependence of the merchant and samurai classes. It was also strongly influenced by powerful social pressures for the sacrifice of individual, family or smaller group interests to the larger group interest, ultimately, to the interests of the society as a whole.[31] For scholars of merchant origin, there may also have been an element of

---

[27] *Chōnin Bukuro* 町人囊, Vol. I, cited in Nomura, *Tokugawa Jidai no Kei-zai Shisō*, 78.

[28] Bamba Masatomo 萬羽正朋, *Nihon Jukyō Ron* 日本儒教論 [An Essay on Japanese Confucianism] (Tokyo: 1939), 283.

[29] Miyamoto, *Nihon Shōgyō Shi*, 186.

[30] *Ibid.*, 178.

[31] For an interpretation of the continuing priority given in Tokugawa Japan to "polity" over economic or any other motivation, and its increased em-

fear in proposing drastic changes to the ruling classes whom they often advised and memorialized, as the only method for putting their ideas into practice. This may furnish some explanation for the strange ambivalence in the attitude of a Yamagata Bantō who argued for an expansion and extension of commerce and against official interference in the market, but who could embrace the prevalent theory of the agrarian state and advocate the suppression of the merchant class of which he was a member.[32]

Ishida Baigan attempted to justify commercial profits as the same thing, in principle, as the stipends of the samurai. He emphasized a cardinal point of the merchant code, loyalty to one's master, and his insistence on frugality for merchants as well for all classes struck a chord with the *Bakufu*. His writings on frugality, as well as those of another famous merchant scholar, Nakai Chikuzan (1730–1804), and those of Matsudaira Sadanobu sound like echoes of one another.[33]

Both samurai and merchant writers on economic subjects seem to have thought it immoral to stimulate demand for commercial goods. No one appears to have considered the possibility of a general expansion of production, purchasing power and commerce, through more efficient use of land and labor and through the stimulation of technological innovations.[34] This is perhaps understandable during a period

phasis in the Meiji period and since, see Bellah, *Tokugawa Religion*, especially pp. 5–6, 13–30.

[32] In his principal work, Yume no Shiro 夢之代, Bantō wrote, "Agriculture should be encouraged while commerce should be discouraged. Farmers are the essence of the country... They are more important than any other class of people. Farmers cannot be dispensed with, though we can do without merchants and artisans... Efforts should be made to increase the number of farmers and to reduce that of merchants. It is the prerequisite of statesmanship to advance the interests of the farming population at the expense of the townspeople." In *Nihon Keizai Taiten*, XXXVII, 302, as translated in Norman, "Andō Shōeki..," 279. A full-scale study of Bantō, a brilliant but apparently erratic scholar, might be most fruitful.

[33] Sakata, *Chōnin*, 106–7. An important element in the merchant culture of Osaka was the Confucian school of the Nakai family known as the Kaitokudō 懐徳堂 (Cf. *NKSJ*, 212–13). It was unique in that members of different classes — samurai, peasant, artisan and merchant — sat together at the feet of merchant Confucianists. Sakata, *Chōnin*, 106–7.

[34] This is not to say that there was no thought of the improvement of agriculture. On the contrary, there was a huge output of treatises, and some of the

when production, population and purchasing power had reached a virtual standstill and the city merchants who controlled most of the production and marketing relied upon monopoly to secure their share and upon limitation of production (sometimes even the destruction of goods) to maintain a profitable price.[35] Also, it was a period when the methods of modern science which could improve technology were virtually unknown.

Most of those who opposed the utilization of commercial monopolies by the *Bakufu* and the *han* were in favor, like Miura Baien, of reverting to a rice economy. However, Professor Horie has found two rather obscure writers who opposed these monopolies and at the same time advocated the encouragement of taxation of commerce. These two scholars, Sakurada Tada and Ōshima Kōnin, [36] writing in the last years of the Tokugawa period, after the failure of the Tempō reform, used the Confucian precept, "The prosperity of the people means the prosperity of the ruler," as a point of departure. They advocated bolstering the feudal treasuries through taxes on commerce, as the existence of well-to-do peasants and wealthy merchants was a source of national wealth. Kōnin in particular pointed out that merely following the traditional line that the basis of the country was agriculture and its prosperity lay in the exercise of frugality, and neglecting to encourage commerce and production would never bring prosperity to the nation.[37] This indicates a step towards a reappraisal

feudal lords and Shoguns (notably Yoshimune) were quick to put new ideas into effect, primarily to improve their own finances, but perhaps also, in a general way, to benefit the people.

[35] *Han* monopolies were often tighter than the merchant monopolies. Cf. Horie, "Clan Monopoly Policy in the Tokugawa Period," *KUER* XVII, 1 (Jan. 1942), 31–52.

[36] Kōnin (1826–1901) was a samurai student of Dutch who became an expert in military science, ordinance, metalurgy and mining. *Dai Nihon Jimmei Jisho* 大日本人名辭書 (Tokyo: 1937 ed.), I, 576. Sakurada is not listed in any of the standard biographical dictionaries.

[37] ..*Keizai Seisaku*, 178–9. Kanda Takahira (1830–1898), writing on the eve of the Restoration, pointed out disadvantages of relying entirely on agriculture, especially emphasizing that there were no means to expand revenues when the taxes on land were so high that peasants could exist only by cultivating the most productive land, leaving the rest to go to waste. Honjo, *Economic Theory and History of Japan*, 212–3. A plan to tax commerce proposed

of the relationship between feudal and commercial power, as the arguments for foreign trade represented a challenge to the cherished policy of the closed country. Perhaps a reason why a more realistic policy toward commerce was not more strongly advocated was that the person who had taken a few faltering steps towards the encouragement and utilization of commerce was Tanuma, and he was under a dark Confucian cloud of moralistic denunciation.

It is apparent from this short outline that economic thought was important in shaping official policies. Where it did not support official policy, it often was unacceptable because it overlooked strategic considerations, as did the proposal of sending samurai back to the land, or because it opposed sacrosanct policies such as the closed country. Proposals almost all assumed strong state control to carry them out, a state control which was no longer effective in practice. Most proposals of a revolutionary nature were reactionary,[38] although it is possible to find some hesitating steps towards a more progressive policy. However, even assuming that such proposals reached the authorities, the chances against their adoption were formidable. Only when the foreign powers, by forcing the *Bakufu* to abandon its exclusion policy, created a gaping hole in its feudal armor, was the *Bakufu* compelled to experiment with new economic policies.

by Léon Roches, the French Minister in Japan from 1864 to 1868, was considered by the *Bakufu* but not put into effect. There was a small business tax levied by prefectures after the Restoration, but it became a national tax only in 1896.

[38] The obscure scholar Andō Shōeki furnishes a remarkable example of revolutionary reactionary thought. He wanted a return to a simple, self-sufficient agrarian society, and his condemnation of the merchants was perhaps the most sweeping of all: "The merchants shun physical labor such as the peasants have to endure even in stormy weather, confidently expecting to pass their life in ease and comfort. With fair words and a plausible manner they tell deliberate lies, flatter the upper and lower classes, deceive each other and even their own parents and brothers. Yet it is this class which grows richer than the other three classes of samurai, peasants and artisans. Hence the merchants wish to live without physical effort, expending only smooth words. A very few make an honest living by direct cultivation, but most of them thirst for name and gain. Thus greed, envy and error reign supreme." Quoted in Norman, "Andō Shōeki..", 71.

CHAPTER VIII

A NEW CHALLENGE TO THE CITY MERCHANTS:
THE RISE OF PROVINCIAL MERCHANTS

THE DEVELOPMENT of the money economy and the accompanying rise of the merchants did not affect all parts of the country in the same way or at the same time. Barter economy and the use of rice as money was seen throughout the period in the outlying sections, and even in the central areas in the first years of the period, but the money economy soon took precedence in the central areas, extending first around the cities, then gradually to the remotest villages.[1] From the middle Tokugawa period onward, the larger part of commercial capital in the major cities turned into usury capital, while in the provinces it tended to evolve away from simple commercial and money transaction capital. It turned rather towards production capital.[2] Through the "putting-out" system, the city ton'ya reached out to some extent into the country-side for both raw materials and finished products. But the markets exploited by the city merchants were mainly the city markets. It was left largely to provincial merchants to extend selling operations to the countryside. The chief method was sending out itinerant traders. The next step was to establish branches in various parts of the country. This sometimes led to investment in productive enterprises. The best example of this is the Ōmi merchants. One of the areas in which they traded even as early as the time of Hideyoshi was Yezo (Hokkaidō). When the daimyō of Matsumae needed money, Ōmi merchants lent to him in return for commercial privileges, and whenever he refused to repay a loan, they received additional privileges. They established many branches in Hokkaidō and even in the Kurile Islands, and embarked upon a very successful program of encouragement to fisheries, resulting in great increases in the amounts of sea foods which they

---

[1] Miyamoto, *Nihon Shōgyō Shi*, 138.
[2] Endō, ..*Shōgyō Shihon*.., 12.

marketed in Edo and elsewhere. According to Kanno, "They can be called really the first economic developers of Hokkaidō."[3]

The Toyama medicine salesmen were very famous itinerant traders and deserve mention here. About 1682, the lord of Toyama on the Japan Sea coast was treated effectively with a new medicine made from a secret formula. It was called "spirit-restoring medicine" (*hankontan* 反 魂 丹). The feudal lord gave permission to a merchant of his castle town to manufacture and sell it throughout Japan. The business was organized as a *nakama* and paid regular fees to the *daimyō*, and its operation is most interesting. Each peddler was sent out to his territory carrying prepared kits containing a fixed assortment of medicines. He simply left a kit or two with the customer and made a record on his register. The next time he called, perhaps six months or a year later, he collected only for those medicines used, and replaced them. Sales resistance must have been very low against this psychologically persuasive technique, and the business thrived throughout the country. As the formulas were secrets and competed only in those *han* where local production was fostered, the Toyama peddlers were permitted to sell in most of the feudal domains, sometimes gaining admission by paying for licenses.[4]

The influence of the city *ton'ya* was generally limited to the areas around the *Bakufu* cities, and there were many obstacles in the way of the expansion of commercial enterprises into the various *han*. It will be remembered that early *Bakufu* policy was to prevent as much as possible the restriction of commerce by the *daimyō*. This policy, never effective in the *han*, was soon dropped. It has been suggested

---

[3] *NKSJ*, 157.

[4] *NKSJ*, 1196–8; Miyamoto, *Nihon Shōgyō Shi Gairon*, 197–8. The business continued to flourish, and increased during the Meiji period. There were 5,000 peddlers in 1875, and Toyama medicines were also exported in fairly large amounts. In 1904 Toyama manufactured about one quarter of all medicines produced in Japan. Royds, W. M., "Japanese Patent Medicines," *TASJ*, XXXV, Part I (Aug. 1907), 2, 4, 7. The business has made adjustments to the times. Some modern scientific medicines are now sold along with the old remedies, many women are employed as peddlers, and all use modern means of transportation, but the old system of collecting only for what is used is still unchanged, according to informants in Tokyo and Karuizawa, where I saw Toyama medicines being peddled in 1954.

that one of the purposes of this change of policy was to restrain the further expansion of the merchants.[5] It was not usually easy for merchants of other *han* to enter castle towns to sell their products at the markets. In some *han*, merchants from other *han* were actually forbidden from entering the markets in the castle town.[6] When merchants were permitted to trade in the markets of the *han*, they were usually required to stay in designated inns where their activities could be under observation.[7] It was common practice to levy a tax on imports into the *han*, which permitted some goods to come in, but often prohibited particular goods. For example, Toyama medicines were permitted to enter the Kumamoto *han* (in Kyūshū) as they did not compete with local products. However, the Toyama merchants were forbidden to take in any goods which were banned, and were permitted to take out only Kumamoto goods, and no money, except for travelling expenses.[8] All these restrictions were not necessarily to protect local merchants, but were intended primarily to prevent specie from going out of the *han*. However, the initiative for restrictions sometimes came from local merchants, who, fearing for their profits, successfully petitioned the *machi bugyō* of the castle town for expulsion of "foreign" merchants and branch shops based outside the *han*.[9]

Commerce of all types which provided goods to peasants was under a great variety of restrictions. Purchases by merchants of both raw materials and finished products from the peasants were subject to restrictions in some domains due to the fear on the part of the feudal lords of the penetration of the money economy into the peasant villages.[10] Frequency of fairs and trips of itinerant traders as well as types of goods were regulated for reasons of economic self-sufficiency

---

[5] Nomura, "Tokugawa Hōken Sei to Shōgyō," 124.

[6] Miyamoto, *Nihon Shōgyō Shi Gairon*, 179. In Satsuma (Kyūshū), which had one of the most thorough-going monopoly systems, "foreign" merchants were not even allowed within the boundaries of the *han*. *Ibid*.

[7] *Ibid.*, 179. Miyamoto points out the similarity with the Wirtzwang inns in medieval Germany. *Ibid.*, 180.

[8] Horie, . .*Keizai Seisaku*, 122–3.

[9] Miyamoto, *Nihon Shōgyō Shi Gairon*, 180.

[10] *Ibid.*, 181–2.

and to protect the position of privileged merchants.[11] This no doubt favored the merchants in the castle towns and prevented the city merchants from expanding into the *han*. However, there were cases where the city merchants exercised strong influence within the *han*. As many of the *daimyō* were deeply in debt to rice and money exchange merchants of Osaka, these merchants came to have considerable influence on *han* finances. They offered economic advice, as they were interested in bolstering *han* finances to assure the repayment of loans.[12] They also aided in programs of encouraging production in those *han* where industry was late in developing, mainly in the northern and eastern part of Honshū.[13] For example, there are some cases where *daimyō* arranged loans with these city merchants to be used in encouraging production, with the understanding that this excess production would be handled exclusively by the merchants who lent the money.[14]

Where *han* monopolies were established, a close collaboration is seen between *daimyō* and provincial merchants who were usually organized in protected *nakama* similar to those in the cities. Most of these *han* monopolies were in western and southern Japan where industry was comparatively early in developing.[15] Of the total of some 260 *han* in Japan, 53 were known to have had monopolies, 16 of which were begun during or before the Kyōhō period (1716–1735).

[11] *Ibid.*, 180.

[12] Honjo, *Social and Economic History of Japan*, quotes Kaiho Seiryō's description of the Osaka merchant Masuya Heiemon as "having taken unto himself the management of the household finances of the Lord of Sendai." This reference is from Seiryō's *Keizai Dan* 經濟談, written in 1816, to be found in *Nihon Keizai Sōsho*, op. cit., XVII, 376. Yamagata Bantō began as a Masuya apprentice, and his best known work, *Yume no Shiro*, was a treatise presented to Date, the *daimyō* of Sendai.

[13] Kobata, *Kinsei Keizai no Hattatsu*, op. cit., 267.

[14] *Ibid.*

[15] *Ibid.* See the article by Horie, "Clan Monopoly Policy in the Tokugawa Period," *KUER* XVII, 1 (Jan. 1942), 31–52. Horie's monograph, *Waga Kuni Kinsei no Sembai Seido* 我國近世の專賣制度 [The Monopoly System in Japan in the Early Modern Period] (Tokyo: 1933) is the standard work on this subject. "Outer" *han*, especially those most active in the Restoration movement, enjoyed the greatest degree of economic autonomy and had the strongest and most lucrative monopolies.

In the north and west where crop encouragement plans were carried out, monopolies were generally limited to rice, but in the south and west, they embraced a wide variety of goods.[16] Local *han* merchants were usually limited in their activities to the territory of the *han* itself. If they wished to expand, they had to do so with the permission of the *daimyō*. This is because the *daimyō* were the first to market excess commodities, especially rice, in the mercantile centers, the most important of which was Osaka. This business was handled by protected merchants, because the *daimyō* had to depend upon them for all business activities. Thus it was advantageous for local merchants to receive such protection.[17] The experience of the provincial merchants in commercial transactions and their role as money lenders made them indispensable to the *daimyō* in carrying out their monopoly policies. In some cases the functions were delegated to such an extent to the merchants that they proved to be "the absolute controllers of this policy."[18] On the other hand, there were isolated cases where *daimyō* attempted to exclude merchants from monopoly activities. The Aizu *han*, for example, tried to exclude the local wholesale merchants (*ton'ya*) from the monopolistic distribution of imported salt within the *han*, and the Wakayama *han* tried to exclude the Edo *ton'ya* from participation in the monopolistic distribution of mandarin oranges in Edo. Such attempts invariably failed, thereby indicating that the cooperation of the merchants was essential.[19]

Another activity in which local protected merchants were closely associated with the *daimyō* was the issuance of paper currency (*hansatsu*). Well-to-do local merchants were appointed as the originators and guarantors of the notes, and they took charge of the exchange of the notes for specie. For this special privilege, from which they were in a position to benefit financially, the *daimyō* obliged them to pay *unjō* fees, or to provide loans in the form of *goyō-kin*, sometimes a combination of both.[20] The issuance of *hansatsu* was often associated

[16] Kobata, *Kinsei Keizai no Hattatsu*, 267.
[17] Horie, "Clan Monopoly Policy in the Tokugawa Period," 36.
[18] *Ibid.*
[19] *Ibid.*, 37.
[20] *NKSJ*, 635.

with *han* monopolies, but was carried out by most of the *han* at some time during the Tokugawa period.[21]

Provincial rice merchants and money lenders in points of importance in the distribution system came into prominence in the later years of the Tokugawa period. An indication of the commercial development of the provinces is the growth of speculative markets. Not only were they to be found in such towns as Nagoya, Ōtsu and Fushimi, but by the end of the period were scattered throughout Japan. The rice market of Shimonoseki is a notable example.[22] Illustrative of the rise of protected provincial merchants are the rice brokers and financial agents (*kakeya*) in Hida, Bungo province, Kyūshū. Living in the most important of the *Bakufu* territories in Kyūshū, and with *Bakufu* protection, they exploited the twin fields of commerce and usury with unusual thoroughness and success. They sold local timber in the cities and towns of Kyūshū and in Osaka, and came to control the production of *sake*, oil, soy sauce and other products which they sold both in the agricultural villages of Kyūshū at monopoly prices and in the three cities.[23] Later, when they gained *Bakufu* protection, they made loans to *Bakufu* officials and *daimyō*. The local *Bakufu* administration placed in their hands the collection and sale of all excess rice and local specialty products. The money collected was remitted by bills of exchange (*tegata*) directly to Edo, Nagasaki, Osaka and other *Bakufu* offices within a fixed period after collection. Closely connected with their commercial operations, they made advances to

---

[21] See the list of *han* and the types and time of issue, in *NKSJ*, 634–645. Major *han*, especially *tozama*, were the first to issue *hansatsu*, after about 1670, ordering all coins converted, at a premium. Reconversion was either prohibited or discouraged by setting a disadvantageous rate. *Ibid.*

[22] Endō, ..*Shōgyō Shihon*.., 9. Ueno Shōjū, a local scholar, wrote a memorial in the Tempō period (1830–43) to Mōri, the *daimyō* of Chōshū whose domains included Shimonoseki, in which he laments the fact that peasants as well as merchants in the neighborhood of Shimonoseki were wasting much time and getting involved in rice market "gambling." He describes their watching with binoculars for the flags which were raised above the exchange at closing, denoting the closing quotations by their colors. Those successful enough to make a fortune overnight were welcomed back to the villages "like famous and victorious warriors." *Ibid.*, 10–11.

[23] Endō, ..*Shōgyō Shihon*.., 22. *NKSJ*, 1372 contains a short summary taken from Endō's study.

the local *Bakufu* deputy and eventually to almost all the *daimyō* of Kyūshū in the form of usurious loans, and their loans to peasants and other commoners throughout Kyūshū brought an annual return of from 20 % to 40 %.[24]

Most of the major merchant houses in the cities, such as Mitsui, Sumitomo, and Kōnoike established themselves in the period of economic expansion during the first hundred years of the Tokugawa period. From that time on, there was little further expansion in the cities. Commerce and usury came to be extremely monopolistic and rigid, offering little opportunity for new merchants. However, the castle towns and agricultural communities did present an opportunity, because economic activities were not so monopolized and merchants were closer to the increasingly important source of commercial commodities, the agricultural village. Outside of the so-called skilled artisans (*shokunin*)[25] such as carpenters and metal workers, the larger part of the production of both luxury and everyday goods came to be carried on in the agricultural communities.[26]

Provincial merchants existed in the early days of the Tokugawa period but came into prominence only in the later years, especially from the end of the eighteenth century onwards, when *han* monopolies grew to large proportions and when the countryside became predominant in the production of commercial commodities. As has been pointed out before, the agricultural villages presented a limited market due to low purchasing power. However, they did furnish a market which was capable of some expansion.[27] Although feudal taxes and impositions on agriculture were very heavy, they did not absorb all surpluses.[28] Moreover, a class of well-to-do landowners who were at once peasants and local merchant-usurers was increasing in importance in the countryside. They enjoyed many of the amenities of life and provided a market for commercial goods.[29]

---

[24] Endō, ..*Shōgyō Shihon*.., 28. For a detailed study of the Hida merchants, see *ibid.*, 137–339.

[25] 職人. Professor Allen translates this term "journeyman." *A Short Economic History of Japan*, 22.   [26] Horie, ..*Shihon Shugi*.., 32.

[27] Nomura, "Tokugawa Hōken Sei to Shōgyō," 133.   [28] *Ibid.*

[29] Cf. Norman, *Japan's Emergence as a Modern State*, 22, and footnote 27 on that page. Thomas C. Smith, in "The Japanese Village in the Seventeenth

The castle towns were the centers of the *han* economically as well as politically, and in principle, commerce was permitted in no other places in the *han*. However, with the spread of the money economy, retail markets and fairs were permitted in stipulated places in the countryside as well. There were four ways in which commercial goods reached the peasants:[30] (1) Peasants went to castle towns or other markets to shop, often on pilgrimages; (2) Small travelling fairs made regular circuits which included agricultural communities, and were expected at each point on a particular day of the month, such as 6–16–26; (3) Individual itinerant merchants were the most important suppliers of commercial goods to the peasants; (4) Despite prohibitions against merchants' living in agricultural communities, this became more and more common. They made trips to the nearest markets and brought back goods for sale. Peasants also did this on a part-time basis, some finding it profitable to carry on full-time trade, a tendency which the feudal lords and Confucian scholars denounced as disturbing the class lines which were the very basis of feudal society, but it was a practice which they found most difficult to prevent.

The undeveloped economy of Hokkaidō provided both a market and a source of raw materials which was first exploited by Ōmi merchants but which continued to be of importance as one of the very few new fields open for enterprising merchants. It is noteworthy that the enterprising merchants who made their fortunes in this field were provincial merchants. An example is Takadaya Kahei, who moved to Hyōgo (present Kōbe) in the Kansei period (1789–1800), and went into the shipping business. He became important in the Hokkaidō trade, opening a branch store in Hakodate in 1798. He established ten fisheries on the island and taught the native Ainu the best fishing methods. He gained such a reputation for honesty that merchants accepted goods from him without examining them, a most unusual practice in those times. He made Hakodate his headquarters, traded

Century, *Journal of Economic History*, XII, 1 (Winter, 1952), 1–20, has shown that these well-to-do "peasants" existed in pre-Tokugawa times, and in the remote countryside.

[30] Miyamoto, *Nihon Shōgyō Shi Gairon*, 180–1.

with the Russians — he was once captured and later released by them — and built up a considerable fortune.[31]

No doubt the most famous of the provincial merchants of the last years of the Tokugawa period was Zeniya Gohei (1773–1852). Since the rise of the provincial merchants in this period is little known in Western language literature and since Zeniya's career furnishes a good example of the scope of their activities and their methods of making money, we shall trace his career in some detail.[32] He was born in Miyakoshi, a port town in Kaga, the largest single *han* in Japan, under the powerful and conservative *daimyō* family of Maeda, and he made Miyakoshi the headquarters for all his far-flung commercial activities.[33] Gohei's father alternated between, and sometimes combined, a small shipping enterprise a money exchange and a usury business. However, in his later years the family fortunes were at a very low ebb and he abandoned the shipping business which he found full of danger and losses.[34]

In accordance with his father's desires, Gohei operated a pawn shop and a secondhand dry goods store, and also dealt in soy sauce and timber until he was 39, when his father died.[35] The next thirty years saw a most unusual commercial expansion from these humble beginnings.

---

[31] *NKSJ*, 525–6; 1003.

[32] The account which follows was included in my article, "Some Economic Reasons for the Marked Contrast in Japanese and Chinese Modernization..," *op. cit.*, 36–42.

[33] *NKSJ*, 916–17 has a good short summary of Zeniya's career, but has Zeniya embarking on the Hokkaidō trade at age 17, whereas he was actually 40. Miyakoshi functioned as the port for the important castle town of Kanazawa.

[34] *Ibid.*, 916.

[35] Shōfū Katei, *Zeniya Gohei Shinden*, op. cit., 43, 51. It is much less of a biography than a criticism of all previous biographies, with long quotations from correspondence and other documents written in the epistolary style (*sōrōbun*) which is, Shōfū admits, filled with errors and ambiguities. Honjō, in his bibliography of economic history (*Nihon Keizai Shi Bunken*), says: "This work is based on contemporary documents secretly stored by Zeniya's descendants. It attempts to correct and supplement the many writings on Zeniya Gohei, and should clarify the conditions of trade of the time." (Tokyo: 1933), 163.

Gohei was untraditional in not following his father's advice against new enterprises. It was usual to hold fast to the ancestral business and to avoid innovations. Family constitutions of rich merchants of the period often contain such phrases as: "Nothing other than the traditional business will be engaged in," "It is prohibited to change the business," "Continue without change."[36] Zeniya not only went into shipping, but he seems to have interested himself in any project which had some promise of profits.

It was somewhat by chance that Zeniya entered the shipping business. In 1813, when he was 40, three small boats were forfeited to his pawn shop. They had belonged to one of the pioneers in the Hokkaidō trade, and, armed with information from him and probably also from the writings of Honda Toshiaki and other "Dutch scholars" who were interested in expansion northward, Zeniya himself made the dangerous trip to Matsumae with a cargo of rice and returned to Miyakoshi with edible seaweed and dried herring, on which he realized a very good profit.[37] Gradually he expanded his business by these means, dispatching boats from Miyakoshi not only north to Hokkaidō but south to Kyūshū, and to the Osaka area. He established no fewer than 34 branch warehouses and stores in the key harbors, made contracts with the great commercial houses of Osaka and Edo, and arranged for reputable and successful merchants in other places to be his agents, on longterm contracts.[38]

As a shipper beginning with three small boats, he became an important boat owner, eventually building some of his own. His fleet reached a total of 13 vessels of between 1,000 and 2,500 koku capa-

---

[36] Horie Yasuzo, "The Life Structure of the Japanese People in its Historical Aspects," KUER XXI, 1 (April 1951), 3.

[37] Shōfū, op. cit., 51–2; NKSJ, 916. The information about Zeniya in Donald Keene, The Japanese Discovery of Europe (London: 1952), 76, seems to derive from inaccurate sources rather than from his cited source, Honjō's introduction to the collection of Honda's writings, Honda Toshiaki Shū (Tokyo: 1935), 9.

[38] Shōfū, 83–5. This type of commercial expansion was not unusual in his time, and his success was nearly paralleled by such men as Kongōya Jirōbei 金剛屋次郎兵衛 of Echizen, with whom Zeniya had close connections and with whom he cooperated on many transactions. Kongōya, a samurai turned merchant, tried to help Zeniya when he got in trouble at the end of his life with the Kaga authorities. Ibid., 84.

city, and some 110 of 1,000 *koku* capacity and less. Adding to this the small boats he maintained in various ports, "there is no knowing how many hundreds of boats he operated."[39] They ranged regularly as far as the Miyake and Hachijō Islands in the south and Etorofu in the Kuriles, and there are many stories of his boats "drifting," in happy compliance with unseasonable winds and in violation of the *Bakufu* prohibitions, to Korea, China, the South Sea Islands, and even to America. The last story has been proven to be the fabrication of one of Zeniya's captains who expanded a trading trip to Korea into a great and plausible story of adventure in America, but the accepted authority on Zeniya's life concludes that his boats did "drift" as far as the South Sea Islands.[40]

Zeniya's boats plied an illegal but profitable foreign trade on a regular basis both in the islands of the Satsunan-shotō south of Kagoshima and in the region of Etorofu in the Kuriles.[41] It was a secret trade, but had the tacit approval of the Maeda family. It was begun in the north when one of Zeniya's boats one day encountered a very large ship off Etorofu and the boat operator, summoning all his courage, approached it. Only after the Japanese captain went aboard and conferred with the foreign captain did he know it was a Russian trading ship. He made arrangements for regular meetings at sea for the purposes of trade, and Zeniya profited greatly from it. This was in 1825.[42]

Zeniya's precise relationship with the Maeda house must remain somewhat of a mystery, but it appears that he was considered a pro-tected merchant only in some of his activities, such as in trading monopolies in specific types of goods within the *han*. Shōfū, his latest biographer, emphasizes several times that his greatest activity as a shipper-trader was before he came under Maeda protection, and that his boats came under official protection only when Zeniya was 67 years of age. If this is true, Zeniya was quite different from most of the merchants of his time. When Zeniya was 54, he began building

[39] Shōfū, *Zeniya Gohei Shinden*, 83.
[40] *Ibid.*, 83, 138-9.
[41] *NKSJ*, 916; Shōfū, 83. Sources do not indicate with whom he traded in the south, but probably it was with Ryukyuans and perhaps Chinese.
[42] Shōfū, *Zeniya Gohei Shinden*, 83, 90, 97, 138.

his own boats to add to his already large fleet.[43] Ten years later, in 1837, the Kaga treasury was empty, and several prominent merchants, including the irrepressible Zeniya, were summoned to an audience with *han* officials, all expecting notice of forced loans. Before seating himself, Zeniya came forward and said with proper humility that he had not consulted the others, but was willing to provide 100,000 *ryō* himself if one request were granted. The officials were much surprised at such magnificent beneficence, and the presiding official inquired what the request was. The conversation went something like this:

Zeniya:	"I have only a simple request, that you lend me two large ships."
Presiding official:	"What a strange request! How large?
Zeniya:	"I have eight or nine ships of 1,900 *koku* capacity, but what a *chōnin* finds very difficult to obtain are ships of 2,000 *koku* or more. For this I would like to borrow your influence."
Presiding official:	"If so, how many would you build?"
Zeniya:	"At first, two. Two would be quite sufficient."

Thus, he was given permission to build large ships which would nominally belong to the *daimyō* of Kaga but which were in fact the property of Zeniya. He built one of 2,500 *koku* capacity, at a cost of 2,000 *ryō*, in Osaka, and one of 2,000 *koku* capacity in Miyakoshi, marked as official ships of the *daimyō* and able to sail anywhere.[44]

Soon after Zeniya received permission to build these large ships, all his boats were placed "at the service of, and under the protection of, the *daimyō*."[45] His resourcefulness was apparent to the Kaga authorities, they treated him with care, and "to a certain extent" had Zeniya act for them, but Zeniya did not take undue advantage of this

[43] Shōfū, *Zeniya Gohei Shinden*, 48, 51.

[44] *Ibid.*, 49–50, 64. The conversation is from a historical novel, *Zeniya Gohei*, by Watanabe Katei 渡邊霞亭, which is generally far from accurate, but this story has been documented, according to Shōfū. The ship built in Miyakoshi aroused such interest that people came for miles to see it. Characteristically, Zeniya postponed launching for four months, built no less than 54 small temporary tea houses for visitors, and charged a small fee to inspect the ship. Unfortunately, it was blown onto a reef and broken in two during a typhoon in 1848. *Ibid.*, 75, 51.   [45] *Ibid.*, 118.

protection, and the Maeda kept secret his association with them in most things.[46]

Information is similarly scanty in regard to Zeniya's methods of organization and operation, and many questions must go unanswered, such as how his ship captains and agents scattered throughout Japan were paid or obtained profits. Their correspondence with Zeniya is voluminous, and extracts from it make up most of Shōfū's book, but it leaves much unsaid. It has a conspiratorial tone, and the poor *sōrōbun* (epistolary style) in which it is written is not conducive to precision. However, some of the descriptions of the actual trading are very detailed, filled with statistics and frank enough to describe, for instance, the illegal trade with the Russians. Zeniya must have trusted his men, and the fact that he accumulated such capital in such a short time would suggest that his trust was not misplaced. In Miyakoshi, he carried on his usury business and directed his multifarious trading activities. He had close relations with other merchants and often shipped their goods for them, and no doubt participated in the contract business of shipping tax rice, but his fleet was mainly used in his own trading operations. In his branch warehouses he laid in large stocks of paper, cotton and silk goods, raw silk, wax, candles, sugar, salt, honey, rice and innumerable other items. These goods were purchased throughout Japan, but particularly in Osaka and Chūgoku (the southwest area of Honshū). In Hokkaidō his principal purchases were dried herring, seaweed and soybeans, and in Kyūshū his major purchase was lumber. He followed the common practice of charging samurai higher prices.[47]

Zeniya's great wealth was not attained without treading on a number of toes. There were two major merchant families in Kaga who were well established before him and whom he soon outstripped. However, although a *nouveau riche*, he seems to have remained on fairly good terms with them, mainly by dealing them in on some of

---

[46] Shōfū, *Zeniya Gohei Shinden*, 117. In 1828, at the age of 55, Zeniya went into nominal retirement (as his father had when Gohei was 17) and let his three sons handle the details of the business, but he continued to direct activities from a small and quiet village near Miyakoshi. *Ibid.*, 85.

[47] *Ibid.*, 84, 97–8.

his schemes.[48] But his activities were bound to bring him into conflict with the established monopolists. The Maeda were conservatives in economic policy, and followed *Bakufu* policies generally. One of the traditional Kaga monopolies was the candle guild (*rōsoku-za*), with 29 shareholding members and headquarters in Kanazawa. It held a long-standing monopoly of sale (at very high prices) for Kaga and the two neighboring provinces of Noto and Etchū. Zeniya had a flourishing trade with Aizu, north of Edo, where candles were a major product, and in the 1820's his stocks of candles were piling up while he looked feverishly for new outlets. He decided to use his influence with the *han* authorities to break into the candle markets closest to home.[49]

Zeniya first memorialized the *han* authorities, explaining that he had a large stock of Aizu candles which were much superior in quality and lower in price than those of the Kanazawa candle guild. Therefore, he proposed to sell Aizu candles at a low price, bringing in new stocks with his own boats and remitting "the larger part of the profits" to the *han* as a voluntary contribution. He justified it as being in the interest of the majority of the people as well as a benefit to the *han* finances, and added that at a private discussion with the members of the candle guild, he had urged them to handle his Aizu candles, but "on one pretext or another" they had turned a deaf ear. This refusal is understandable because the guild's own product could not possibly compete with the low-priced Aizu candles. Zeniya then asked the authorities to constitute him as a special guild, to share the market with the existing guild, no doubt knowing that this would cause the eventual failure of the guild.[50]

Zeniya's proposal was well calculated to interest the *han* authorities who in the 1820's were having grave financial troubles. However, they decided to let the candle guild have a hearing. The guild members

[48] *NKSJ*, 916-17.

[49] Endō Masao, "Zeniya Gohei no Kaga Ryōnai Rōsoku-za Appaku Jiken 錢屋五兵衛の加賀領內蠟燭座厭迫事件 [The Incident of Zeniya Gohei's Pressure on the Candle Guild in the Domain of Kaga] *KSK*, XLVI (Aug. 1933), 46-7. This article is reprinted in Endō's *Nihon Kinsei Shōgyō Shihon Hattatsu Shiron*, op. cit., 58-104.

[50] Endō, "Zeniya Gohei..," 165-6, 169.

insisted that Zeniya had made unfair and inaccurate statements due to his own greed, and they presented a spirited defense of the high price of candles in Kaga in terms of costs which Zeniya had omitted from his detailed memorial, pointing out the inconvenience of depending upon a distant supply, with no means to deal with emergency needs, and branding Zeniya's proposal as a paper scheme overlooking present and future difficulties.[51]

The outcome was in doubt and Zeniya expressed pessimism, but the decision finally went in his favor, not because the authorities decided it would profit the people, and not primarily because it promised more benefit to the *han* finances, but, according to Endō, simply because the pro-Zeniya party was larger among the officials due ultimately to Zeniya's greater financial power.[52] The result was, as might have been predicted, no great triumph for free trade. Zeniya soon came to monopolize the entire candle trade of the three provinces.[53]

In this conflict Zeniya earned the hatred and fear of the entrenched guilds, and he even stepped on the toe of one of his colleagues. Kubo Kihei, another Kaga merchant, who acted as a go-between for Zeniya, wrote the memorial for him, and contributed 500 *ryō* towards the proposed special candle guild. When the result was in their favor, he expected Zeniya to share profits with him. After a long silence, he asked Zeniya about how the business was going, and Zeniya replied that he had been silent because the business was running at a loss, and that he had only refrained from asking Kubo to contribute more capital. Kubo was suspicious and procured information from one of Zeniya's employees that the enterprise was making a fair profit. Kubo then brought the matter to litigation, whereupon Zeniya offered as evidence records which showed a steady loss. Kubo attacked the records as having been falsified, but lost the suit. Endō concludes that the records were in fact falsified, but points out also that Kubo's figures were fixed in his own favor. Litigation of this kind added to the suspicion of Zeniya's methods and contributed to his fall.[54]

[51] Endō, "Zeniya Gohei..," 50, 174, 286–90.
[52] *Ibid.*, 291. Endō believes bribes may have been used by Zeniya, distributed by go-betweens. *Ibid.*   [53] *Ibid.*
[54] *Ibid.*, 292–8. The summary of the incident given here is much compressed.

Zeniya died at the age of 80 after a few weeks in prison, presumably from old age and shock, awaiting trial on a rather strange charge, namely, that he had been responsible for the poisoning of fish which in turn poisoned some people, some of whom died. It all began when his third (and favorite) son, Yōzō, a chip off the old block, conceived a grandiose scheme of draining a large marshy lake near Miyakoshi to reclaim the land for agriculture. It was a difficult engineering problem, but Zeniya approved the plan and quickly gained the assent of Maeda, Tosa no Kami, a high official of the *han*. Formal permission was gained in 1851 despite considerable opposition from the fishermen who fished on the lake. Yōzō immediately went to work, hiring coolies to dig a large drainage ditch, but had quarrels with fishermen who broke the timbers being used for the ditch as they stood on them to catch fish. The fish, attracted by the new timbers in the water, swarmed around the ditch. Yōzō replied to this by having lime, coal and oil thrown into the water to keep the fish away. One morning the fisherman found a large number of fish lying on top of the water, and "joyous at having such a big catch," quickly gathered them up and sold them in Miyakoshi. The unfortunate people who ate the fish became desperately ill, and some even died. The result was a great cry against Zeniya in which his enemies joined with gusto, and the *han* authorities arrested him and his three sons.[55] The incident furnished them with a good pretext to confiscate Zeniya's wealth in Kaga. It was an excellent haul, estimated at 365,800 *ryō* in gold and silver alone, and numerous treasures as well as large stocks of goods.[56]

Zeniya's career demonstrates both the great opportunities which still existed for a commercial career and its limitations — in Zeniya's

[55] Shōfū, *Zeniya Gohei Shinden*, 171, 184–7. Takigawa's acceptance (*Nihon Shakai Shi*, 323) of the popular tradition that Zeniya was crucified for his participation in foreign trade illustrates one of the pitfalls of treating historical figures whose lives have become encrusted with legends.

[56] Shōfū, *Zeniya Gohei Shinden*, 232–44. Shōfū is not quite certain that this is the correct explanation for the confiscation (*kessho*), and believes the real reason for it may have been another offense which will probably remain a secret to history. He rejects entirely the usual explanation, that Zeniya was punished for participating in illegal foreign trade. The Zeniya confiscation is probably as famous as that of Yodoya.

case, its tragic limitations. Only a comparatively few provincial merchants could participate in the Hokkaidō trade and in illegal foreign trade. Since the provincial markets were rather limited ones, and the city markets, still by far the most important, were monopolized by city merchants, it is understandable that provincial merchants desired to have access to these markets without being at the mercy of the city monopolists. One method used was to intercept boats bound for the Osaka market. Provincial merchants, especially from Owari (whose castle town was Nagoya) stationed boats in the Inland Sea to intercept and buy goods destined for Osaka "using money lent them by their customers," rather than to buy in Osaka at monopoly prices. In the Tempō period (1830–43) there were as many as two hundred Owari boats of this kind.[57]

Anyone by-passing a city *nakama* or *ton'ya* was blacklisted. The special privileges permitted by charter to *kabu nakama* and *ton'ya* were geographical, and routes were fixed so that they would not be by-passed.[58] However, with the decline of the *kabu nakama* in the late Tokugawa, they were often by-passed. Merchants appeared to carry on more direct trade. An example of this is when cotton merchants from Echizen (on the Japan Sea coast) and Ōzu, Iyo Province (Shikoku) would go to Nagoya, obtain lodging where they could auction off their goods, and sell directly to middlemen without going through the *ton'ya*, on the pretext that the goods had been ordered. Also, the *daimyō* who had monopolies of goods which they sold in markets outside their *han* were in effect powerful merchants who did not have always to go through the established *ton'ya* and *nakama*, another factor in their decline.[59] Provincial merchants began to avoid Osaka and brought their goods in to other harbors like Hyōgo, where they could market them on their own terms. As a result of this practice, receipts of cotton goods in Osaka dropped off to half.[60] Even the monopoly in Kyoto of the famous Kyoto Nishijin silks was in

[57] Smith, "Materials..," *op. cit.*, 87.
[58] This was generally true in the provinces as well. Miyamoto, *Nihon Shogyo Shi*, 172–3.
[59] *Ibid.*, 173–5.
[60] Kobata, *Kinsei Keizai no Hattatsu*, op. cit., 272.

danger of competition from provincial production, and three merchants of Ōmi finally broke the monopoly. They gained entry to the
Kyoto market through bribing the Nijō magistrate (bugyō) of Kyoto.[61]
Many more examples could be cited to show how provincial merchants
by-passed and broke many of the existing city monopolies in the
period from about 1818 to the Tempō reform.[62]

While the monopolistic privileges of the city merchant organizations were being successfully challenged from without, there was
an internal breakup in process. From their beginnings, the desire of
nakama members to increase their profits always pushed against the
restraints of the organization.[63] The merchants who had banded together in the interests of corporate security underwent years of feudalistic discipline, but finally violations of kabu nakama restrictions
became more and more common. The many examples of violations
of these self-imposed regulations in the years preceding the Tempō
reform are indicative, according to Professor Miyamoto, of the assertion of individualism and the idea that "in a profit society, profits
should come first."[64] The kabu nakama lost the power to stop the
struggle both inside and outside the organization. By the time of the
dissolution in the Tempō reform, despite encroachment from without
and the inner process of self-destruction, however, they still appeared
from the outside to be strong. Tadakuni's dissolution seems to have
been carried out without the knowledge that the kabu nakama were
already approaching dissolution.[65]

The period from 1843 to 1851, when the kabu nakama and ton'ya
were officially illegal, gave an opportunity for new merchants. Although economic conditions were chaotic, or perhaps because they
were, enterprising merchants who were not tied to the restrictions
of the city monopolies made progress. Even after the kabu nakama
were revived in 1851, official policy did not revert to the Yoshimune
policy. New kabu nakama were encouraged to form, and new members

---

[61] Miyamoto, Kabu Nakama no Kenkyū, op. cit., 280.

[62] See ibid., 277–82.   [63] See above, p. 57.

[64] Miyamoto, Kabu Nakama no Kenkyū, 272. For examples of violations and
non-attendance at kabu nakama meetings, failure to pay dues, etc., see
ibid., 272-7.

[65] Nomura, "Tokugawa Hōken Sei to Shōgyō," 132, 130.

permitted entry. The *Bakufu* authorities saw that the revival of the *kabu nakama* was necessary, but they did not want monopolistic *kabu nakama*.[66] It would seem highly doubtful if the *kabu nakama* could have retrieved their former monopolistic position, in any case.

The opening of the country to foreign trade in 1858 worsened the already chaotic economic conditions of the time, and dealt an additional blow to the traditional merchant organizations. One of the conditions under which trade was opened was that it would be open to all comers.[67] The provincial merchants and small rural industrialists swarmed into the treaty ports. They learned what goods were in demand, and went through the country rounding them up, and especially buying up raw silk.[68] The *daimyō* with monopolies also took advantage of this opportunity and were among those most active in foreign trade, represented by the provincial merchants who collaborated with them.[69] Besides the military industries introduced in *Bakufu*, Mito, Kagoshima and Saga domains during this pre-Restoration period, a Western type cotton factory was built in Akita about 1858 or 1859, and in 1867 a cotton-spinning factory was set up in Kagoshima, under *han* sponsorship.[70]

The reaction of the old-style city merchants is almost predictable. They petitioned the *Bakufu* to cut off all foreign trade, blaming it as the source of the shortage of goods and the rising prices. This did

[66] Nomura, *Tokugawa Jidai no Keizai Shisō*, op. cit., 74. The proclamation restoring the *kabu nakama* included this plea: "We trust that people will make no attempt to monopolize supplies, nor to supply goods of inferior quality, undersized or underweight. Prices should be as low as possible and business done fairly." Smith, "Materials..," *op. cit.*, 105.

[67] See M. Paske-Smith, *Western Barbarians in Japan and Formosa, 1603–1868* (Kobe: 1930), 201, for a translation of the decree allowing free participation in the trade.

[68] Nobutaka Ike, *The Beginnings of Political Democracy in Japan* (Baltimore: 1950), 16. This excellent study is the first in a Western language to bring out clearly the important role of the provincial merchants in the last years of the Tokugawa period, the Restoration and the political movements of the time.

[69] Horie, ..*Shihon Shugi*.., 41.

[70] Kobata, *Kinsei Keizai no Hattatsu*, 273. See Thomas C. Smith, "The Introduction of Western Industry to Japan during the Last Years of the Tokugawa Period," *Harvard Journal of Asiatic Studies* II, 1 & 2 (June 1948), 130–52.

not go unchallenged by the provincial merchants, who insisted correctly that it was not foreign trade but the disparity between supply and demand that was to blame for higher prices. This point was made in a memorial to the Shogun. "Moreover, as if to put teeth into their arguments, they hired *rōnin* to terrorize the guild merchants."[71] This was a struggle between the new and the old in the economic field which was paralleled in the political field in the anti-*Bakufu* movement. The outcome was in doubt until the Restoration was achieved.

The protected merchants and merchant organizations in the provinces bear many resemblances to their city counterparts. They were perhaps as dependent upon feudal protection and privilege. But, with the exception of the city *ton'ya* which reached out into the countryside for their goods, the provincial merchants were less dependent upon the feudal relationships for their sources of materials and for their markets. Most of the commercial commodities which were marketed in the cities came in the form of goods collected as taxes by the feudal lords and the *Bakufu*. The most dependent merchants were those of Edo. The provincial merchants were freer to develop their own markets and sources of commodities. It is true that they were under many restrictions due to the mercantilistic policies of the various *han*, but so long as they conformed with *han* regulations, paying their tariffs or license fees, they were able to push their trade farther and farther and, as the amazing career of Zeniya Gohei demonstrates, they sometimes could try anything that held promise of profit. Perhaps their most important source of commercial freedom was the fact that their activities were not sedentary nor so minutely specialized as they were in the cities. They carried on trade more as individual enterprisers than as members of organizations where conformance to feudalistic regulations had become a habit and was considered a moral obligation. The provincial merchants injected a definitely new and more enterprising note into the commercial history of the period.

It is very likely that the inner decline of the *kabu nakama*, which was due to the rise of individual interests over corporate interests, was influenced by the individualistic element in the provincial mer-

[71] Ike, *The Beginnings of Political Democracy in Japan*, 16.

chants. If this is true, it can be said that the decline of the *kabu na-kama* and the old guilds like the Kaga candle guild as well was due indirectly to the rise of new provincial merchants. The by-passing of the city monopolists by the provincial merchants was a direct cause of the decline of the city merchant organizations. The *nakama* represented a voluntary self-restriction by the merchants in order to fit into the feudal society and not disturb it enough to damage their peculiarly advantageous economic position. Its decline meant the decline of an economic structure which had permitted the coexistence of feudal and mercantile power. The Tempō dissolution and the failure of the feudal authorities to provide an alternative meant that the economic system had crumbled before the political revolt had begun.

CHAPTER IX

CONCLUSION
THE SIGNIFICANCE OF THE RISE OF THE MERCHANT CLASS

THE LATE Ashikaga period was one of major economic and social change in which the merchant class made great strides and gained for the first time in Japanese history a degree of political as well as economic power. This is seen in the emergence of such autonomous merchant cities as Sakai. With the unification of the country by Nobunaga and Hideyoshi and the restoration of peace, there was a significant development of overseas trade by Japanese merchant ships, but this vigorous activity was dealt a death blow by the exclusion edicts, completing the process of bringing the merchants under the political domination of the feudal rulers, and channeling economic energies into the narrower stream of domestic commerce. Both *Bakufu* and *daimyō* viewed the merchant class as a useful tool which, deprived of political influence, they did not expect ever to become a danger to the feudal system.

In the Tokugawa period, the rise of the merchant class went on almost unnoticed in the first hundred years. During this period of expanding economy, merchants were successful in ingratiating themselves with the feudal authorities, and while the samurai class was enjoying the fruits of peace and gradually losing its taste for the stern frugality of the military code, the merchants were silently and industriously creating and elaborating the most ingenious commercial and financial institutions. At the same time they were evolving from their experience a code of their own which fostered mutual honesty and loyalty among members of trade associations which sought to take advantage of the merchants' monopoly of commercial activities while avoiding friction with the feudal authorities.

It was not until after the Genroku period, when the economic expansion slowed to a virtual halt, that the feudal rulers began to realize that the merchant class was a serious menace to the feudal system. The Yodoya confiscation began a long struggle which ended in complete failure on the part of the feudal authorities either to use or to suppress the merchants.[1] The one exception to this general failure was the *han* monopoly system which was successful in restoring solvency through the use of commerce, but it had its limitations and could not be adapted to the needs of the *Bakufu*. As evidence of the growing strength of the merchant class in this period could be cited first the fact that, unlike the many general cancellations of debts (*tokusei*) in earlier times, there were only two *kien* during the Tokugawa period, both greatly limited in scope, indicating the progress of the money economy and the increased strength of the merchant class. Also one could cite the refusal of merchant money lenders to lend money except on their own terms, a refusal which was made effective by the solidarity of the merchant organizations; the increasing degree of failure of each of the three "great reforms," and the ability of the merchants to modify in practice the impositions of *unjō*, *myōga-kin* and *goyō-kin*, and to oppose price regulations passively by getting around them, as in the attempted price reductions in the Tempō reforms.

The inherent strength of the merchants' position lay in their monopoly of commercial and financial activities and the consequent dependence of the samurai class on the merchants for the distribution of food and all types of commercial commodities, and for the essential financial services, especially lending services, which became more and more necessary to them because of their deepening indebtedness. The large non-productive samurai population in the cities and castle towns whose livelihood constituted the basic feudal financial problem had to rely for their very existence on a distribution system whose transport inefficiencies gave the merchants an opportunity for monopoly profits. The inefficiencies in the monetary system gave the money exchanges and financial agents (especially the *kakeya*) an equally advantageous position. The degree of interdependence of the

---

[1] In China, even up to recent years, the success of the officials in utilizing commerce for their own enrichment was a far greater obstacle to modernization than any factor to be found in pre-modern Japan. Cf. my article, "Some Economic Reasons for the Marked Contrast in Japanese and Chinese Modernization..," *op. cit.*, 49–60.

merchants and the feudal lords in Japan furnishes a significant contrast to European conditions. In western Europe of the middle ages, the city and town economy revolved around relations of direct exchange between peasants in the countryside and handicraft workers in the towns. In Japan, however, the merchants had far closer relations of exchange with the feudal ruling classes.

The reasons why the samurai class continued to live under an economic system which became more and more disadvantageous to them are many. The dead hand of bureaucratic lethargy can be counted as one. The individual samurai was an essential part of this rather unimaginative bureaucracy. With a regular stipend, often increased by allowances for official duties, the samurai seldom felt a real need for the essentials of life, and the comparative decline in the samurai's standard of living was not sudden enough to stimulate any real desire for change, especially if such a change meant forfeiting his status as samurai. One reason that Japanese writers usually emphasize is the moral principle, based on Japanese Confucian-feudal theory and reinforced by law, that the handling of money, the calculation of profits, in short, commercial conduct, was beneath the samurai. Avoidance of commercialism was one of their claims to pride in being samurai. However, this way of thinking alone was by no means decisive. Some of the most important of the merchant houses were established in the early Tokugawa period by samurai who relinquished their status to become merchants. But those early years were filled with commercial opportunities. This was before commerce was tightly organized into monopolistic groups jealous of their privileges and watchful to keep outsiders out. In addition, the extraordinary complexity and minute specialization of financial functions which were fully developed by about the Genroku period must have been strong deterrents to samurai who were expected to pride themselves on their lack of knowledge of such things, and who would hardly have welcomed a long commercial apprenticeship.

The evolution of merchant organization went through three general phases. In the first phase, the merchants built up a body of ingenious commercial and financial techniques and succeeded in forging a new class solidarity and class consciousness within the feudal system and under an ever-present threat to their security. During this first phase, the merchants relied to a large extent upon borrowed strength — the protection of feudal lords or *Bakufu*. An example is the dependence of merchant money lenders in *Bakufu* territories upon the *Bakufu* courts to uphold their claims against the *daimyō*. The second phase was the achievement of a degree of security through organization. Although still dependent upon feudal protection, the merchants were finally able to wield a certain power of their own. Their refusal to lend money except on their own conditions and their boycotting of recalcitrant debtors, both impossible without effective organization, are examples of this newfound power. The third phase was the gradual breakdown of their own feudalistic organizations and the decline of the uneasy coexistence which began in the time of Yoshimune. This phase saw the rise of provincial merchants who were less dependent upon feudal protection, and it also saw the inner decline of the *kabu nakama* whose members now felt safe enough to put their individual interest before the group interest. The decline of the economic organization which was adapted to Tokugawa feudalism left a chaotic situation which was ready for the reforms of the Meiji period at least fifteen years before the Restoration.

It can be said that two kinds of economy existed during the Tokugawa period: the feudal economy based directly on the land, and the rising money and commercial economy. The latter was gradually taking precedence over the former, and the merchants benefited from this historical transition because they controlled the money and commercial economy completely. Some Japanese scholars speak of the contradiction between the land and the money economy in Tokugawa times. However, in actuality, there was no such contradiction unless the term "land economy" is defined to mean a typical natural or self-sufficient economy. In fact, the money economy developed through a dependence upon the feudal land economy. This was the cause for its feudal character. However, there was an incompatibility in power relationships between the land economy and the money economy. The feudal lords, for example, were entirely involved in the money economy for their consumption and daily existence, whereas their source of income was the land. Although collections were definitely limited, expenditures were not, and this was the basic reason for their financial bankruptcy. Into this financial gap, commercial capital and capital from usury encroached, and caused an ever-increasing impoverishment, especially when merchants and usurers became landowners and creditors and siphoned off feudal revenues. It was the same for the samurai on their fixed stipends. The feudal rulers depended economically on the production of the peasants, and for this reason, when their finances were pinched, they had no alternative but to reduce their samurai's stipends and — more important — they were forced to squeeze the peasants. To make matters worse, the money economy, through commercial transactions and the lending of capital, penetrated directly into the agricultural communities and became a direct cause of further discontent. The relative impoverishment of the lower peasants disturbed the foundations of the feudal social and political order. In this way, the merchants touched off a series of chain reactions which became really serious to the feudal ruling classes when the squeezing of the peasants reached a point of diminishing returns and resulted in a decline in productivity through peasants' leaving their land and resorting to rebellion and restriction of population. The policy of squeezing the peasants thus ultimately defeated its own purpose.[2]

The rise of the merchant class is significant not only because it exercised a profound and destructive influence on the feudal economy. Growing in numbers and in economic power, merchants exerted tremendous influence on Japanese culture and society. Although traditional literary and artistic schools continued to exist, they were influenced by and far overshadowed by the new forms created by the merchant culture of the cities. Leisure, the prestige which culture enjoyed among merchants, and a desire to get ahead gave rise to an insistent demand for education. Ishida's *shingaku* school and the Kaitokudō of Osaka were established in response to this demand. The number of temple schools (*terakoya*) 寺小屋 for commoners in the towns and cities increased from 94 at the beginning of the Tokugawa period to 5,867 at the end.[3] Merchant Confucianists gained

[2] Cf. Horie, . .*Keizai Seisaku*, 76–7, and Horie, . .*Shihon Shugi*. ., 43–4.
[3] *NKSJ*, 1121.

a hearing from feudal lords and they aspired to become the intellectual leaders of the nation.[4] Knowledge, culture, and power were spread over a larger area of population than ever before in Japanese history.

Merchant scholars were primarily concerned with the problem of integrating the merchant more completely into the feudal society, and there appears to have been no antifeudal thought sponsored by merchants. However, the new social conditions which the merchant class was instrumental in creating in the cities gave rise to intellectual discontent and a questioning of tradition. The nationalist (or nativist) school (*kokugaku*) had its point of origin in the consciousness of a way of life on the part of townspeople, and looked back to pre-feudal Japan as its ideal. *Kokugaku* began as a city literary movement, arising from an emotional revulsion against the feudal elements in city life. From the denial of the restrictions of medieval life to the denial of the literature it produced, it went back to early literature. Although there were men of merchant background who were leaders in the movement,[5] its nucleus was the stipended samurai of the cities, especially Edo, as the discontented intellectual group in the cities.[6]

The development of city culture included a new humanism and realism and a degree of receptivity to Western natural sciences which contrasts strongly with the history of Western ideas in China.[7] This new spirit had its roots in the cities, and was opposed by the feudal psychology which criticized European natural sciences as lacking the true characteristics of abstract learning. The prevailing feudal mentality tried to incorporate Western natural sciences into the spirit of Chu Hsi's "investigation of nature" whose object was not to conquer and use nature but to know its fixed laws in order to be in har-

---

[4] Takigawa, *Nihon Shakai Shi*, 246.

[5] Kamo Mabuchi once managed an inn in Hamamatsu, and Motoori Norinaga was also of merchant stock.

[6] Yamamoto and Watanabe, *Kokugaku Ron*, op. cit., 9 –10; 53.

[7] Ishida, *Kinsei Bunka no Tenkai*, op. cit., 412. Realism is seen in such writers as Saikaku. Realism in the arts can be seen in the important influence of Western art which moved from Nagasaki to Kyoto, Osaka and Edo. Ishida characterizes this new spirit as "positivism." *Ibid.*, 391.

mony with them.[8] These new currents of thought were unable to shake the foundations of the Chu Hsi feudal morality, but the isolated scholars who devoted themselves enthusiastically but with great sacrifice and under difficult conditions to the study of Dutch and Western sciences were to be of great service in the modernization of their country.

The hostility between the samurai and merchant classes never appears to have been very active or profound. This was no doubt due to the consciousness of their interdependence. At any rate, towards the nineteenth century this hostility came under the modifying influence of more official collaboration with merchants and more social mobility with the sale of samurai rank and the linking of wealth and status by merchant-samurai marriage alliances and adoptions.[9] The closest working merchant-official collaboration was in the *han* monopolies. The merchants were used, closely supervised and not given much freedom of action, because the monopolies were created by means of the political prerogatives of the feudal lords and they were meant to serve a feudal purpose. However, the feudal lords themselves became capitalistic entrepreneurs willing to learn from the merchants and were in no position to look down at them in the traditional manner. The samurai who were in close collaboration with the merchants sometimes became important industrialists themselves in the Meiji period.[10]

The breakdown in the rigid social structure through the intermingling of the classes which began as early as Yoshimune's time and accelerated towards the end of the Tokugawa period has been amply and skillfully described elsewhere.[11] The substitution of a

[8] Ishida, *Kinsei Bunka no Tenkai*, 414, 390. [9] Endō, . . *Shōgyō Shihon* . ., 15.
[10] Horie, . . *Shihon Shugi* . ., 40. Mitsubishi, second only to Mitsui among the zaibatsu, was founded by Iwasaki Yatarō, a country samurai (*gōshi* 郷士) who got his start working for the Tosa trading organ, the Tosa Shōkai, eventually becoming its head. Later he was put in charge of Tosa finances. When *han*-controlled enterprises were prohibited in 1870, the Tosa enterprise continued under another name, with Iwasaki as president. *NKSJ*, 1565.
[11] Especially in Sansom, *Japan, a Short Cultural History*, 520–22, the best summary, which seems to be based on Honjo's *The Social and Economic History of Japan*. Also see Norman, *Japan's Emergence as a Modern State*, 56, 61. For more details, see Honjo, 85, 127–8, 204–6, 226–7.

"cash nexus"[12] for the feudal relations based on loyalty and service on the one hand and paternalism on the other was seen more and more in such practices as the replacement of hereditary retainers by hired men on a yearly basis. This long process of dissolution of feudal relationships and replacement by more impersonal and economically rationalized relationships was of inestimable value to the Meiji reformers in their abolishment of the political structure of feudalism and encouragement of capitalism.

To analyze the role of the merchant class in the modernization of the Meiji period would be to go beyond the scope of the present study. Such an analysis, with this study of the merchant in the Tokugawa period as the point of departure, is one which could be of much value in understanding the complicated forces which combined to achieve the Meiji reforms. For our purposes, a preliminary sketch of the outlines of such an analysis will have to suffice. It is the general consensus that the role of the merchants in the Meiji modernization was, with certain exceptions, not a very active one.[13] In a general way, this can be understood from our description of the nature of the Tokugawa

----

[12] A term often used by writers on European economic history to describe the same phenomenon in Europe.

[13] In the maneuverings and struggles of the Restoration period, the Mitsui appear to have been on both sides, but they point to their large-scale support of the Imperial forces as evidence of their patriotism, although foresight might be a better word. Their precise position, as well as that of other major commercial and financial houses, is a difficult subject but one well worth further study. The Restoration movement was led by samurai and supported financially by prominent city and provincial merchants, thereby establishing close and lasting ties. A study of the nature of these ties, and the origins and lives of prominent Meiji businessmen, would be of much interest. Although a large number of able samurai entered business and injected a new and often dynamic influence, many leaders of Japanese business in this period of feverish modernization of the economy were of strictly merchant class background. For example, one of the foremost financial geniuses who emerged in the Meiji period was Hirose Saihei, who started in Tokugawa times as an apprentice for Sumitomo at the age of ten. He worked his way up to be in charge of the Besshi mines at the time of the Restoration. After the Restoration, he was put in charge of all Sumitomo interests and saw them very successfully through the difficult transitional period during which many enterprises failed, whether directed by merchants or samurai.

merchants and their "built-in" dependence upon the feudal ruling class. It is also a function of the limitations on the development of industrial capital, a subject which deserves some elaboration, and which will serve to summarize the position of the merchant class as an economic force for change at the end of the Tokugawa period.

Professor Horie enumerates five obstacles to the development of industrial capital in Tokugawa Japan:[14]

(1) Narrowness of the market. The circulation of commercial goods was becoming nation-wide, the provincial economies were developing and becoming part of the national economy. However, the policy of the *han* to maintain as much as possible their economic autonomy ran counter to the trend towards a nation-wide economy. Also, the agricultural products collected by the feudal lords reached the market through the feudal lords themselves, preventing the peasants from an active participation in trade which would have meant a direct transition from a self-sufficient peasant economy to a commercial economy. In addition, the insistence upon feudal frugality (to the extent that it was effective) and, more important, the squeezing of the peasants, hampered greatly the increase in the standard of living, and made impossible any rapid extension of the domestic market.

In the case of Western nations, the narrowness of domestic markets was remedied by the opening up of foreign markets, especially the new colonial markets of undeveloped areas. In the case of Japan, however, this course was not open to her because of the exclusion policy. The small volume of foreign trade with China and Holland (both more highly developed countries than Japan) permitted at Nagasaki was wholly passive in nature.

(2) The lack of the technical means of manufacture (i.e., implements and machinery) which would attract and utilize industrial capital. This technical inadequacy was due in part to the narrowness of the market and to the undeveloped state of natural sciences in Japan.

(3) The lack of a labor market sufficient to meet the needs of large scale industrial enterprises. Agriculture was highly intensive and required even the labor of women and children. The peasant economy was a self-sufficient one, and as handicraft production was mainly

[14] Condensed from Horie, *..Shihon Shugi..*, 46–8.

by peasants, there was in actuality no real social division of labor between agriculture and industry. Also, because of the employment conditions in the cities, the exclusivism of organized artisans and merchants, and the restraints of status due to tradition and law, there were many difficulties for the propertyless peasant in leaving his village.

(4) The lack of progressiveness in commercial capital itself. Commercial capital was accumulated mainly due to special relationships with feudal lords and common samurai, and was made possible through the heavy exactions squeezed by the ruling classes from the peasants. Therefore, to destroy the feudal system and change over to a new economic system meant the death of the old type merchant.[15] In addition, due to the obstacles already discussed, commercial capital tended to go into usury rather than into industrial capital.

(5) The *kabu nakama* system was an obstacle because it prohibited free competition. Economic liberalism is a principle of the capitalist economy which could not exist under the *kabu nakama* system. Members of *kabu nakama* were unable to advance to the stage of free competition for subjective as well as objective reasons. Subjectively, their aggressive and enterprising spirit was almost non-existent. Their efforts were spent in preserving the family enterprise intact and essentially unchanged. They knew their place and kept it. In addition, for wealthy merchants there was no greater honor than to wear the two swords of the specially protected merchant and to consider themselves equal to the samurai in status. They wanted nothing more.

Professor Horie concludes, "There were fixed bounds to the development of commercial capital during the Edo period due to the feudal character of its accumulation and related reasons. Of course, it can be well imagined that in time these limitations could have been broken down and the way cleared for a general development of industrial capital. However, as far as can be seen from the stage of economic development reached by the end of the Tokugawa period, it must be concluded that it had reached a point where industrial capital was only in its infancy. This is definitely not to say, however, that this stage had no influence on the formation of Japanese capitalism. On

[15] Cf. Takahashi Kamekichi, *Nihon Shihon Shugi Hattatsu Shi*, op. cit., 36, and Norman, *Japan's Emergence as a Modern State*, 51, ftnte. 7.

the contrary, the total of the elements put together meant the existence of the potential for industrial capital development."[16]

Thus, the merchants — especially the city merchants — entered the period of modern Meiji capitalism under serious disadvantages. Some, like the Mitsui, Kōnoike and Sumitomo who financed the beginnings of the new government were able to adjust to the times and with government collaboration, succeeded in reaching new heights of power and activity. This was made possible by the continuation of government protection, even though it took new forms. The *kabu nakama* system, although abolished, was adapted to the needs of government-controlled foreign trade and was found helpful for this purpose.[17] But Sir George Sansom is probably correct in his judgment of the old type merchants: "Their outlook was too narrow, they had thrived on protection, and with a few exceptions they fell back to huckstering, while ambitious samurai of low and middle rank became bankers, merchants and manufacturers."[18] The unusual ingenuity and enterprise which the merchants demonstrated in the early years of the Tokugawa period was dulled by the need to settle down comfortably within the feudal system, content with monopolizing their respective shares of a static economy. However, ingenuity and enterprise were not dead by any means, as we have seen in the examples of provincial merchants. Provincial merchants, just beginning to rise and to break down the old monopolies, were active in the Restoration movement[19] because they welcomed a change which would give them new opportunities. But their potential power was limited, and the majority of the merchants, passive, cautious, and conservative, clung to their old comfortable ways, and it was the ambitious young samurai in government and business who took the active lead in the economic modernization of the Meiji period, although making use of the mercantile community and drawing upon its wide and valuable experience and techniques.

[16] Horie, ..*Shihon Shugi*.., 48.
[17] According to Honjō, "The necessity for promoting cooperative advantages still existed, particularly in foreign trade. Therefore, a system of trade associations was carried out." *NKSJ*, 262.
[18] *Japan, a Short Cultural History*, 509.
[19] Cf. Ike, *The Beginnings of Political Democracy in Japan*, 18–23.

LIST OF NAMES
OF PERSONS WITH DATES WHEN KNOWN

Andō Shōeki	安藤昌益	c.	1700–
Buyō Inshi	武陽隠士		
Chikamatsu Monzaemon	近松門左衛門		1653–1724
Chu Hsi	朱熹		1130–1200
Dazai Shundai	太宰春臺		1680–1747
Gamō Kumpei	蒲生君平		1768–1813
Hayashi Shihei	林子平		1754–1793
Hiranoya	平野屋		
Honda Toshiaki	本多利明		1744–1821
Ibara Saikaku	井原西鶴		1642–1693
Ishida Baigan	石田梅巖		1685–1744
Itō Jinsai	伊藤仁齋		1627–1705
Kaiho Seiryō	海保青陵		1755–1818
Kamo Mabuchi	賀茂眞淵		1697–1769
Kanda Takahira	神田孝平		1830–1898
Kawamura Zuiken	河村瑞軒		1618–1700
Kawashima Matahei	川島又兵衛		
Kinokuniya Bunzaemon	紀の國屋文左衛門		
Kōnoike Shinroku	鴻池新六		
Kubo Kihei	久保喜兵衛		
Kumazawa Banzan	熊澤蕃山		1619–1691
Kusama Naokata	草間直方		1753–1831
Matsudaira Sadanobu	松平定信		1758–1829
Mitsui Hachirobei	三井八郎兵衛	d.	1694
Miura Baien	三浦梅園		1725–1789
Mizuno Tadakuni	水野忠邦		1794–1851
Motoori Norinaga	本居宣長		1730–1801
Muro Kyusō	室鳩巣		1658–1734
Nakae Tōju	中江藤樹		1608–1648
Nakai Chikuzan	中井竹山		1730–1804
Naraya Mōzaemon	奈良屋茂左衛門		
Nishikawa Joken	西川如見		1648–1724
Oda Nobunaga	織田信長		1534–1582
Ogyū Sorai	荻生徂徠		1666–1728
Ōshima Kōnin	大島高任		1826–1901
Sakurada Tada	櫻田迪		
Satō Shin'en	佐藤信淵		1769–1850
Shimomura	下村		
Shingū Ryōtei	新宮凉庭		1787–1854
Sumitomo Masatomo	住友正友	c.	1585–1652

Takadaya Kahei	高田屋嘉兵衛	1769–
Tanuma Okitsugu	田沼意次	1719–1788
Tennōjiya Gohei	天王寺屋五兵衞	
Tokugawa Hidetada	德川秀忠	1579–1632
Tokugawa Iemitsu	家光	1603–1651
Tokugawa Ieyasu	家康	1542–1616
Tokugawa Tsunayoshi	綱吉	1646–1709
Tokugawa Yoshimune	吉宗	1677–1751
Toyotomi Hideyoshi	豊臣秀吉	1536–1598
Yamaga Sokō	山鹿素行	1622–1685
Yamagata Bantō	山片蟠桃	1789–1821
Yodoya Keian	淀屋个庵	
Yodoya Saburoemon	三郎右衞門	c. 1667–?
Zeniya Gohei	錢屋五兵衞	1773–1852

Bakufu	幕府	Literally, "tent government": the Tokugawa bureaucracy.
chishi-sen	地子錢	A tax on houses and lots upon which they were built.
chōnin	町人	Townspeople. Literally, the residents of the commercial streets or districts, as distinct from the residents of the samurai quarters. They comprised two classes, the artisans and the merchants.
daimyō	大名	Literally, "great names": feudal lords. During the Tokugawa period, those holding fiefs (*han*) whose annual rice production was assessed at more than 10,000 *koku*.
Eiraku-sen	永樂錢	Chinese coins of the Ming period, Yung-lo 永樂 reign (1403–1424), used as a standard coin in Japan until prohibited in 1608.
fudasashi	札差	The *kakeya* of Edo. See *kakeya*.
go-kenin	御家人	Literally, "housemen": samurai of low rank who were direct vassals of the Tokugawa house.
gonin-gumi	五人組	Five-family associations, the basic unit in administrative organization of the people.
goyō-kin	御用金	Forced loans. In principle they were to be repaid, but seldom were. The term means literally, "money for government use."
han	藩	Feudal domains or fiefs. In Tokugawa times, those fiefs of more than 10,000 *koku* assessed annual rice production. Sometimes translated "clan."
hatamoto	旗本	Banner knights, immediate vassals of the Tokugawa house whose domains

were assessed at less than 10,000 *koku* annual rice production and were administered directly by the *Bakufu*.

kabu	株	Membership privileges in *nakama, kabu nakama,* or *ton'ya.*
kabu nakama	株仲間	A chartered guild (or trade association) with a legal limitation of the number of *kabu.*
Kaitokudō	懷德堂	The Confucian school in Osaka where the Nakai family taught.
kakeya	掛屋	Merchant appointed to handle financial services connected with the sale of tax rice and other commodities by the fendal lords. Sometimes included the functions of *kuramoto.*
kessho	闕所	Confiscation of property, a part of most criminal punishments, always when a person was exiled. Used against merchants who exceeded the bounds of what the authorities could claim was permissible in the way of luxury and ostentation.
kien	棄捐	A modified type of debt cancellation.
koku	石	A unit of capacity measurement standardized at 5.12 bushels.
kogaku-ha	古學派	The school of ancient learning, a Confucian school of Japanese origin.
kokugaku-ha	國學派	The nationalist (or nativist) school, an anti-Confucian school.
kumi	組	(1) Groups, either made up of *ton'ya,* or, in some cases, *nakama.* (2) Divisions of a *nakama.* Variant form: *gumi.*
kuramoto	藏元	Merchant appointed as warehouse keeper, usually took care of the sale of tax rice for the feudal lords, sometimes also handled the financial services ordinarily carried out by a *kakeya.*
kurayashiki	藏屋藏	Warehouses used by *daimyō* and other feudatories for the storage of tax rice and other commodities.
machi bugyō	町奉行	Town magistrate. A samurai official

who held administrative, judicial and police powers.

machi doshiyori	町年寄	Semi-official councils of city elders of either merchant or artisan class through whom the feudal authorities administered towns and cities.
myōga-kin	冥加金	Ordinarily an enterprise fee paid each year to the feudal authorities, in many cases fixed for a number of years but always subject to re-negotiation. Sometimes called simply *myōga*.
nakagai	仲買	Intermediary trader. Either a broker or a middleman.
nakama	仲間	Trade associations or guilds (unchartered) of the Tokugawa period.
nanushi	名主	Commoners appointed as semi-officials, of some cities, towns and villages, charged with the transmittal and enforcement of orders. A term used mainly in Edo and Eastern Japan. In Kansai and the west, *shōya* was the common term.
rakuichi	樂市	Free markets.
rakuza	樂座	Free guilds.
ryō	兩	The numerical unit of the gold currency, derived originally from a weight unit equal to 10 *momme* (or 37.5 grams). Gold *ryō* differed from this in actual weight.
ryōgae-ya	兩替屋	Money exchanges, which came to carry on most of the functions of a modern bank.
sankin kōtai	參覲交代	The system requiring all feudal lords to attend the Shogun's court at periodical intervals, and to leave their wives and children in Edo as hostages while they were in their own domains. Regularized and made compulsory in 1634.
sekisho	關所	Barriers maintained by feudal authorities on roads and waterways for military, economic and policing purposes. Also called *seki*.

shingaku	心 學	The Confucian school of Ishida Baigan, also called *Sekimon shingaku* 石 門 心 學 to differentiate it from the Ōyōmei (Wang Yang-ming) school.
sōrōbun	候 文	Epistolary style.
sō toshiyori	惣 年 寄	Osaka council corresponding to the *machi doshiyori* of most cities and towns.
toiya	問 屋	Wholesale houses. *Doiya* is a variant form.
ton'ya		Edo dialect for *toiya*. *Don'ya* is a variant form.
unjō-kin	運 上 金	"Thank money," a type of enterprise tax paid on occasion of chartering and on certain other occasions. Usually called simply *unjō*.
za	座	Guilds.

BIBLIOGRAPHY*

I. Source Materials
  A. In Japanese
    1. Collections.

Dai Nihon Shiryō 大日本史料 [Historical Materials of Japan.] Tokyo: Imperial University, 1903–53. 172 Vols.

Honjō Eijirō 本庄榮治郎, ed., *Kinsei Shakai Keizai Gakusetsu Taikei* 近世社會經濟學說大系 [A Compendium of Socio-economic Theories of the Early Modern Period]. Tokyo: Seibundō Shinkōsha, 1935, 10 Vols.

Honjō, ed., *Kinsei Shakai Keizai Sōsho* 近世社會經濟史 [Early Modern Socio-Economic Series]. Tokyo: Kaizōsha, 1926–7, 12 Vols.

Nihon Rinri Ihen 日本倫理彙編 [A Compilation of Japanese Works of Moral Philosophy]. Tokyo: Ikuseikai, 1901–1920. 10 Vols.

Satō Shin'en-ka Gaku Zenshū 佐藤信淵家學全集 [Complete Scholarly Works of the Family of Satō Shin'en]. Tokyo: Iwanami Shoten, 1924–6. 3 Vols.

Takimoto Seiichi 瀧本誠一, ed., *Nihon Keizai Sōsho* 日本經濟叢書 [Japanese Economic Series]. Tokyo: Nihon Keizai Sōsho Kankō Kai, 1914–17. 36 Vols.

Takimoto, ed., *Nihon Keizai Taiten* 日本經濟大典 [A Cyclopedia of Japanese Political Economy]. Tokyo: Shishi Shuppansha, Keimeisha, 1928–30. 54 Vols.

Tokugawa Jidai Shōgyō Sōsho 德川時代商業叢書 [Tokugawa Period Commercial Series]. Tokyo: Kokusho Kankōkai, 1913–14. 3 Vols.

    2. Individual Works.

Anonymous, *Seji Kemmon Roku* 世事見聞錄 [A Record of Wordly Affairs], with a preface written by Buyō Inshi in 1816. Vol. I of *Kinsei Shakai Keizai Sōsho*.

---

* Items with asterisks are works which have been consulted but to which reference has not been made. For those who wish to know the Japanese characters for publishers, see the list of publishers on pages 159–165 of John W. Hall, *Japanese History: A Guide to Japanese Reference and Research Materials*. (Ann Arbor: 1954).

182

Hayashi Shihei 林子平, *Jōsho* 上書 [Memorials], in *Nihon Keizai Sōsho*, XII, 5–50.

Honda Toshiaki 本多利明, *Keisei Hisaku* 經世秘策 [A Secret Plan of Government], in *Kinsei Shakai Keizai Gakusetsu Taikei*, X, 5–85.

Koji Ruien 古事類苑 [An Encyclopedic Collection of Historical Materials]. Tokyo: Koji Ruien Kankōkai, 1935–38 ed. 60 Vols.

Kumazawa Banzan 熊澤蕃山, *Shūgi Gesho* 集議外書, in *Nihon Rinri Ihen*, II, 9–332.

Kumazawa Banzan, *Shūgi Washo* 集義和書, in *Nihon Rinri Ihen*, I, 255–560.

Mitsui Takafusa 三井高房, *Chōnin Kōken Roku* 町人考見録 [A Record of Observations of Townsmen], in *Tokugawa Jidai Shōgyō Sōsho*, I, 155–194.

Ogyū Sorai 荻生徂徠, *Taiheisaku* 太平策, in *Nihon Keizai Sōsho*, II, 531–563.

Ogyū Sorai, *Seidan* 政談 [Talks on Political Economy], in *Nihon Keizai Sōsho*, III, 339–530. (Also found in *Kinsei Shakai Keizai Gakusetsu Taikei*, VI.)

Satō Shin'en, *Kaibō Saku* 海防策 [A Policy for Coastal Defense], in *Satō Shin'en-ka Gaku Zenshū*, III, 819–829.

Satō Shin'en, *Keizai Teiyō* 經濟提要 [A Manual of Political Economy], in *Satō Shin'en-ka Gaku Zenshū*, II, 549–89.

Tanaka Kyūgū 田中丘隅, *Minkan Seiyō* 民間省要 [Essentials of Civic Life], in *Nihon Keizai Sōsho*, I, 229–740.

Tokugawa Kinrei Kō 德川禁令考 [A Commentary on Tokugawa Prohibitory Regulations]. Tokyo: Yoshikawa Kōbunkan, 1932 Edition. 6 Vols.

Yamaga Sokō 山鹿素行, *Yamaga Gorui* 山鹿語類, in *Kinsei Shakai Keizai Gakusetsu Taikai*, II, 171–376.

Yamagata Bantō 山片蟠桃, *Yume no Shiro* 夢の代, Vol. XXXVII of *Nihon Keizai Taiten*.

B. In Western Languages.

*Caron, François, *A True Description of the Mighty Kingdomes of Japan and Siam*. Reprinted from the English edition of 1663 with notes by C. R. Boxer. London: Argonaut, 1935. 197 pp.

Kaempfer, Engelbert, *The History of Japan*, 1690–1692. (Translated by J. G. Schenzer). New York: The Macmillan Co., 1906. 3 Vols.

*Thunberg, Charles Peter, *Voyages de C. P. Thunberg, au Japon, etc*. Paris: Dandre, 1796. 4. Vols.

*Siebold, Philipp Franz von, *Nippon*. London: 1841 (The English edition of the original 1832 edition in German). 5. Vols.

II. Special Studies
  A. In Japanese.
    1. Books.

Akabori Matajirō 赤堀又次郎, *Tokugawa Jidai no Shōnin* 徳川時代の商人 [Merchants of the Tokugawa Period], in *Nihon Shōnin Shi* 日本商人史 [A History of Japanese Merchants]. Tokyo: Nihon Rekishi Chiri Gakkai, 1935, 187–234.

Bamba Masatomo 萬羽正朋, *Nihon Jukyō Ron* 日本儒教論 [An Essay on Japanese Confucianism]. Tokyo: Mikasa Shoin, 1939. (Vol. XVIII of *Nihon Rekishi Zensho*). 328 pp.

Endō Masao 遠藤正男, *Nihon Kinsei Shōgyō Shihon Hattatsu Shi Ron* 日本近世商業資本發達史論 [An Essay on the History of the Development of Commercial Capital in Japan in the Early Modern Period]. Tokyo: Nihon Hyōronsha, 1936. 354 pp.

*Honjō Eijirō, *Bakumatsu no Shinseisaku* 幕末の新政策 [The New Policies of the Last Years of the Bakufu]. Tokyo: Yūhikaku, 1940, rev. ed. 335 pp.

Honjō, *Jinkō oyobi Jinkō Mondai* 人口及び人口問題 [Population and Population Problems]. Tokyo: Nihon Hyōronsha, 1930. 158 pp.

*Honjō, *Nihon Keizai Shisō Shi Kenkyū* 日本經濟思想史研究 [Studies in the History of Japanese Economic Thought]. Tokyo: Nihon Hyōronsha, 1942. 466 pp.; supplementary volume, same title, 1947. 270 pp.

Honjō, *Nihon Shakai Keizai Shi* 日本社會經濟史 [A Socio-Economic History of Japan]. Tokyo: Kaizōsha, 1928. 631 pp.

Honjō, *Tokugawa Bakufu no Beika Chōsetsu* 徳川幕府の米價調節 [The Regulation of the Price of Rice by the Tokugawa *Bakufu*]. Kyoto: Kobundō Shobō, 1924. 415 pp.

Horie Yasuzō 堀江保藏, *Nihon Keizai Shi* 日本經濟史 [An Economic History of Japan]. Tokyo: Tōyō Shokan, 1949. 322 pp.

Horie, *Kinsei Nihon no Keizai Seisaku* 近世日本の經濟政策 [Economic Policies of Japan in the Early Modern Period]. Tokyo: Yūhikaku, 1942. 396 pp.

Horie, *Nihon Shihon Shugi no Seiritsu* 日本資本主義の成立 [The Formation of Capitalism in Japan]. Tokyo: Yūhikaku, 2nd ed., 1948. 292 pp.

Horie, *Waga Kuni Kinsei no Sembai Seido* 我國近世の專賣制度 [The Monopoly System in our Country in the Early Modern Period]. Tokyo: Nihon Hyōronsha, 1933. 280 pp.

Ishida Ichirō 石田一良, *Kinsei Bunka no Tenkai* 近世文化の展開 [The Unfolding of the Early Modern Culture], in *Kinsei Shakai* (q.v.), Kobata Jun, ed., 308–415.

Kanno Watarō 菅野和太郎, *Nihon Kaisha Kigyō Hassei Shi*

no Kenkyū 日本會社企業發生史の研究 [Studies in the History of the Origination of Company Enterprises in Japan]. Tokyo: Iwanami Shoten, 1931. 726 pp.

Kanno, *Nihon Shōgyō Shi* 日本商業史 [Commercial History of Japan]. Tokyo: Nihon Hyōronsha, 1930. 352 pp.

Kanno, *Ōmi Shōnin no Kenkyū* 近江商人の研究 [A Study of Ōmi Merchants]. Tokyo: Yūhikaku, 1941. 329 pp.

Kobata Jun 小葉田淳 ed., *Kinsei Shakai* 近世社會 [Early Modern Society]. Tokyo: Asakura Shoten, 1952. (Vol. IV of *Shin Nihon Shi Taikei*). 429 pp.

Kobata Jun, *Kinsei Keizai no Hattatsu* 近世經濟の發達 [Economic Development of the Early Modern Period], in *Kinsei Shakai*, 215–307.

Kōda Shigetomo 幸田成友, *Edo to Ōsaka* 江戶と大阪 [Edo and Osaka]. Tokyo: Fuzambo, 1934. 333 pp.

Kōda, *Nihon Keizai Shi Kenkyū* 日本經濟史研究 [Studies in Japanese Economic History]. Tokyo: Ōokayama Shoten, 1928. 854 pp.

Matsuyoshi Sadao 松好貞夫 *Nihon Ryōgae Kin'yū Shi Ron* 日本兩替金融史論 [History of Japanese Money Exchange and Money Market]. Tokyo: Bungei Shunjūsha, 1932. 447 pp.

*Matsuyoshi, *Shinden no Kenkyū* 新田の研究 [A Study of Reclaimed Fields]. Tokyo: Yūhikaku, 1936. 311 pp.

Miyamoto Mataji 宮本又次, *Kabu Nakama no Kenkyū* 株仲間の研究 [Studies in Chartered Guilds and Trade Associations]. Tokyo: Yūhikaku, 1938. 434 pp.

Miyamoto, *Kinsei Shōgyō Keiei no Kenkyū* 近世商業經營の研究 [Studies in the Commercial Operations of the Early Modern Period]. Kyoto: Dai Hassu, 1948. 389 pp.

Miyamoto, *Kinsei Shōgyō Soshiki no Kenkyū* 近世商業組織の研究 [Studies in the Commercial Organization of the Early Modern Period]. Tokyo: Yūhikaku, 1939. 293 pp.

Miyamoto, *Kinsei Shōnin Ishiki no Kenkyū* 近世商人意織の研究 [Studies in the Merchant Mentality of the Early Modern Period]. Tokyo: Yūhikaku, 1941. 320 pp.

Miyamoto, *Nihon Kinsei Ton'ya Sei no Kenkyū* 日本近世問屋制の研究 [Studies in the Ton'ya System in Japan in the Early Modern Period]. Tokyo: Tōkōshoin, 1951. 426 pp.

Miyamoto, *Nihon Shōgyō Shi* 日本商業史 [Commercial History of Japan]. Tokyo: Ryūginsha, 1943. 423 pp.

Miyamoto, *Nihon Shōgyō Shi Gairon* 日本商業史概論 [An Outline of Japanese Commercial History]. Kyoto: Sekai Shisōsha, 1954. 367 pp.

*Miyamoto, *Zoku Nihon Kinsei Ton'ya Sei no Kenkyū* 續日本近問屋制の研究 [Continuation of Studies in the Ton'ya System in Japan in the Early Modern Period]. Kyoto: Sanwa Shoin, 1954. 366 pp.

*Nomura Kanetarō 野村兼太郎, *Nihon Keizai Shisō* 日本經濟思想 [Japanese Economic Thought]. Tokyo: Keiō, 1914. 163 pp.

Nomura, *Tokugawa Hōken Shakai no Kenkyū* 德川封建社會の研究 [Studies in the Tokugawa Feudal Society]. Tokyo: Nikkō Shoin, 1941. 572 pp.

Nomura, *Tokugawa Jidai no Keizai Shisō* 德川時代の經濟思想 [The Economic Thought of the Tokugawa Period]. Tokyo: Nihon Hyōronsha, 1939. 562 pp.

Ono Kin 小野均, *Kinsei Jōka-machi no Kenkyū* 近世城下町の研究 [A Study of Castle Towns in the Early Modern Period]. Tokyo: Shibundō, 1928. 298 pp.

Ono Takeo 小野武夫, *Nōson Shakai Shi Ronkō* 農村社會史論講 [Discussions on the Social History of Peasant Villages]. Tokyo: Ganshōdō, 1935. 422 pp.

Osaka Municipal Council 大阪參事會, comp., *Ōsaka Shi Shi* 大阪市史 [History of the City of Osaka]. Osaka: 1911–15. 8 Vols.

Sakata Yoshio 坂田吉雄, *Chōnin* 町人 [The Townsmen]. Tokyo: Kōbundō Shobō, 1939. 158 pp.

Shōfū Katei 松風嘉定, *Zeniya Gohei Shinden* 錢屋五兵衛眞傳 [A True Biography of Zeniya Gohei]. Kyoto: Fujioka Kōji, 1930. 264 pp.

*Suzuki Naoji 鈴木直二, *Tokugawa Jidai no Beikoku Haikyū Soshiki* 德川時代の米穀配給組織 [The Organization of the Distribution of Rice in the Tokugawa Period]. Tokyo: Ganshōdō, 1938. 728 pp.

Takahashi Kamekichi 高橋龜吉, *Nihon Shihon Shugi Hattatsu Shi* 日本資本主義發達史 [History of the Development of Capitalism in Japan]. Tokyo: Nihon Hyōronsha, 6th ed., 1939. 412 pp.

*Takahashi, *Tokugawa Hōken Keizai no Kenkyū* 德川封建經濟の研究 [Studies in Tokugawa Feudal Economy]. Tokyo: Tōyō Shokan, 1941. 452 pp.

Takigawa Masajirō 瀧川正次郎, *Nihon Shakai Shi* 日本社會史 [A Social History of Japan]. Tokyo: Kangensha, 3rd ed., 1948. 377 pp.

Takimoto Seichii 瀧本誠一, *Nihon Kahei Shi* 日本貨幣史 [A Monetary History of Japan]. Tokyo: Shunjūsha. 1929. 172 pp.

Toyoda Shirō 豐田四郎, *Nihon Shihon Shugi Hattatsu Shi* 日本資本主義發達史 [History of the Development of Capitalism in Japan]. Tokyo: Rōdō Bunkasha, 1950. 195 pp.

Tsuji Zennosuke 辻善之助, *Tanuma Jidai* 田沼時代 [The Tanuma Period]. Tokyo: Nihon Gakujitsu Fukyūkai, 1936. 346 pp.

*Tsuchiya Takao 土屋喬雄, *Hōken Shakai Hōkai Katei no Kenkyū* 封建社會崩壞過程の研究 [A Study of the Process of Disintegration of the Feudal Society]. Tokyo: Kōbundō, 1927. 729 pp.

Tsuchiya Takao, *Nihon no Seishō* 日本の政商 [Political Merchants of Japan]. Tokyo: Keizai Ōrai Sha, 1956. 287 pp.

Wada Atsunori 和田篤憲, *Bansen to Seishu Torihiki no Kanrei* 番船と清酒取引の慣例 [The Customs of Bansen and Transactions in Refined Sake], in *Nihon Kōtsū Shi no Kenkyū* 日本交通史の研究 [Studies in the History of Japanese Transportation]. Honjō, ed., Tokyo: Kaizōsha, 1929, 417–448.

Yamamoto Masahide 山本正季 and Watanabe Shū 渡邊季, *Kokugaku Ron* 國學論 [An Essay on Kokugaku]. (Vol. XIX of *Nihon Rekishi Zensho*), Tokyo: Mikasa Shobō, 1939. 208 pp.

Yokoi Tokifuyu 横井時冬, *Nihon Shōgyō Shi* 日本商業史 [Commercial History of Japan]. Tokyo: Hakuyōsha, 1926 ed. 445 pp.

2. Periodical Articles.

Endō Masao 遠藤正男, "Zeniya Gohei no Kaga Ryōnai Rōsokuza Appaku Jiken 錢屋五兵衛の加賀領内蠟燭座壓迫事件" [The Incident of Zeniya Gohei's Pressure on the Candle Guild in the Domain of Kaga], *Keizai Shi Kenkyū* (henceforth cited as *KSK*), XLVI (Aug. 1933), 38–54; XLVII (Sept. 1933), 162–174; XLIX (Nov. 1933), 286–302.

Hamamura Shōzaburō 濱村正三郎, "Eiraku-sen no Kinshi wo Ronzu 永樂錢の禁止を論ず" [Comments on the Prohibition of Eiraku-sen], *KSK*, XXVII (1942), 362–78.

Honjō Eijirō, "Sankin Kōtai Seido no Keizai Kan 參觀交代制度の經濟觀" [An Economic View of the Sankin Kōtai System], *Keizai Ronsō*, II, 6 (Dec. 1916), 828–41; IV, 4 (Oct. 1917), 55–74.

Honjō, "Tokugawa Jidai no Kin'yū Seido Gaisetsu 德川時代の金融制度概説" [An Outline of the Credit System in the Tokugawa Period]. *KSK*, XI–X (Aug.–Sept., 1930), 47–57; 57–68.

*Horie Yasuzō, "Bakumatsu ni Okeru Shihon Shugi Keizai no Hōga 幕末に於ける資本主義の萌芽" [The Germination of Capitalist Economy in the Last Years of the Bakufu], *KSK*, XIX, 2 (Feb. 1928), 50–74.

Horie, "Edo Jidai no Ōsaka no Kōgyō 江戸時代の大阪の工業" [Osaka Industry in the Edo Period], *Keizai Ronsō*, LI, 5 (Nov. 1940), 128–147.

Horie, "San Dai Kaikaku to Zaisei 三大改革と財政" [The Three Great Reforms and Finances], *KSK*, XV, 1 (Jan. 1936), 23–41.

Horie, "Tokugawa Jidai no Rikujō Kōtsū 德川時代の陸上交通" [Overland Transportation of the Tokugawa Period], *KSK*, XI, 2 (Feb. 1934), 73–86.

Horie, "Tokugawa Jidai no Suijō Kōtsū 德川時の水上交通" [Water Transportation of the Tokugawa Period], *KSK*, XIV, 1 (July, 1935), 74–87.

Kanno Watarō, "Tokugawa Jidai no Tokumei Kumiai 德川時代の匿名組合" [The Anonymous Combinations of the Tokugawa Period], *KSK*, IX (July, 1930), 38–46.

Kanno, "Tokugawa Jidai Shōnin no Chifu 德川時代商人の致富" [The Accumulation of Wealth by Merchants of the Tokugawa Period], *Hikone Kōshō Ronsō* VIII (Dec., 1930), 15–64.

Matsuyoshi Sadao, "Tokugawa Bakufu no Kaikon Seisaku Kanken 德川幕府の開墾政策管見" [A Personal Interpretation of the Policy of the Tokugawa Bakufu for the increase of Arable Land], *KSK*, XIII, 3 (Mar. 1935), 13–26.

Mitsui Takakore 三井高維, "Edo Jidai ni Okeru Tokushu Shōgyō to shite no Gofuku-ya to Ryōgae-ya 江戸時代に於ける特殊商業としての呉服屋と両替屋" [The Dry Goods Business as a Special Type of Commerce in the Edo Period, and Money Exchanges], *Shakai Keizai Shi Gaku*, II, 9 (Sept. 1932), 57–62.

Miyamoto Mataji, "Kinsei no Sonraku to Shōgyō 近世の村落と商業" [Villages and Commerce in the Early Modern Period], *Hikone Kōshō Ronsō*, XXIV (June, 1941), 147–177.

Miyamoto, "Tempō Kaikaku to Kabu Nakama 天保改革と株仲間" [The Tempō Reform and Kabu Nakama], *KSK*, XV, 1 (Jan. 1936), 85–111.

Miyamoto, "Waga Kuni Kinsei ni Okeru Shōgyō Rijun no Tokushitsu 我國近世に於ける商業利潤の特質" [The Special Characteristics of Commercial Profits in Our Country in the Early Modern Period], *KSK*, XVII, 1 (Jan. 1937), 137–156.

Nomura Kanetarō, "Tokugawa Hōken Sei to Shōgyō 德川封建制と商業" [The Tokugawa Feudal System and Commerce], *Shakai Keizai Shi Gaku*, VI, 10 (Jan. 1937), 113–133.

Sakata Yoshio, "Meiji Ishin to Tempō Kaikaku 明治維新と天保改革" [The Meiji Restoration and the Tempō Reform], *Jimbun Gakuhō*, II (1952), 1–26.

Shiba Kentarō 柴謙太郎, "Nagegane to wa Nani, Kaijō Kashitsuke ka, Kommenda Tōshi ka 投銀とは何海上貸附ガコンメンダ投資ガ" [What was 'Nagegane'? A Marine Loan, or Commenda Investment?], *KSK*, 45–7 (July–Sept., 1933), 617–634; 14–27; 123–145.

Yoshimura Miyao 吉村宮男, "Edo Jidai ni Okeru Shōgyō no Seishitsu 江戸時代に於ける商業の性質" [The Nature of Commerce in the Edo Period], *Rekishi Kyōiku*, XI, 3 (1936), 195–204.

B. In Western Languages.

1. Theses.

*Burks, Ardath Waller, *Economics in Japanese Thought* (Unpublished Ph. D. Dissertation, School of Advanced International Studies, Johns Hopkins: 1948). 318 pp.

*Fredman, Herman Bernard, *The Monetary Theory of Arai Hakuseki*. (Unpublished M.A. Thesis, University of California: 1948), 89 pp.

Manchester, Curtis A., *The Development and Distribution of Sekisho in Japan*. (Unpublished Ph. D. Dissertation, University of Michigan: 1946), 224 pp.

Sheldon, Charles David, *Monetary Problems of Seventeenth Century Japan*. (Unpublished M.A. Thesis, University of California: 1951). 117 pp.

*Spencer, Daniel L., *Transition from Tokugawa to Meiji*: *A Study in Economic Development*. (Unpublished M.A. Thesis, University of California: 1950). 143 pp.

Tsukahira, Toshio George, *The Sankin Kōtai System of Tokugawa Japan*. (Unpublished Ph. D. Dissertation, Harvard University: June, 1951). 241 pp.

Wald, Royal, *Development of Ōsaka during the Sixteenth Century*. (Unpublished M.A. Thesis, University of California: 1947), 76 pp.

2. Books.

Allen, George C., *A Short Economic History of Modern Japan, 1867–1937*. London: Allen & Unwin, 1946. 200 pp.

*Barret, F., *L'évolution du capitalisme japonais*. Paris: Editions Sociales, 1945–7. 3 Vols.

Bellah, Robert N., *Tokugawa Religion, The Values of Pre-Industrial Japan*. Glencoe, Ill.: Free Press, 1957. 249 pp.

*Boxer, Charles Ralph, *The Christian Century in Japan*, 1549–1650. Berkeley and Los Angeles: Univ. of Calif. Press, 1951. 535 pp.

Brown, Delmer M., *Money Economy in Medieval Japan. A Study in the Use of Coins*. New Haven: Yale University, 1951. 128 pp.

Hall, John W. *Tanuma Okitsugu, Forerunner of Modern Japan* (Harvard University Press: 1955). 208 pp.

Honjo, Eijiro, *Economic Theory and History of Japan in the Tokugawa Period*. Tokyo: Maruzen, 1943. 350 pp.

Ike, Nobutaka, *The Beginnings of Political Democracy in Japan*. Baltimore: Johns Hopkins Press, 1950. 246 pp.

Ishii, Ryoichi, *Population Pressure and Economic Life in Japan*. London: P. S. King, 1937. 159 pp.

Keene, Donald, *The Japanese Discovery of Europe*: *Honda Toshiaki and Other Discoverers, 1720–1798*. London: Kegan Paul, 1952. 246 pp.

*Kinosita, Yetaro, *The Past and Present of Japanese Commerce*. New York: Columbia Univ. Press. 1902. 164 pp.

Norman, E. Herbert, *Japan's Emergence as a Modern State*. New York: Institute of Pacific Relations, 1946. 254 pp.

Paske-Smith, M., *Western Barbarians in Japan and Formosa, 1603–1868*. Kobe: J. L. Thomson & Co., 1930. 431 pp.

*Rein, Johann Justus, *The Industries of Japan*. London: Hodder and Stoughton, 1889. 554 pp.

Russell, Oland D., *The House of Mitsui*. Boston: Little, Brown, 1939. 328 pp.

Smith, Thomas C., *Political Change and Industrial Development in Japan: Government Enterprise, 1868–1880*. (Stanford Univ. Press: 1955). 126 pp.

*Soyeda, Juichi, *Banking and Money in Japan*, in *A History of Banking in All the Leading Nations*. New York: Journal of Commerce and Commercial Bulletin, 1896. Pp. 409–544.

*Spae, Joseph John, *Itō Jinsai, A Philosopher, Educator and Sinologist of the Tokugawa Period*. Peiping: Cath. Univ. of Peking, Monumenta Serica Monograph XII, 1948, 278 pp.

Takizawa, Matsuyo, *The Penetration of Money Economy in Japan*. New York: Columbia University Studies in History, Economics and Law 285, 1927. 159 pp.

*Thomas, A. F., and S. Koyama, *Commercial History of Japan*. Tokyo: Yuhodo, 1936. 168 pp.

*Tsuchiya, Takao, *The Development of Economic Life in Japan (Dealing Principally with the Tokugawa and Meiji Periods)*. Tokyo: Kokusai Bunka Shinkōkai, 1936. 33 pp.

Tsuchiya, Takao, *Economic History of Japan*. Transactions of the Asiatic Society of Japan. Tokyo, Vol. XV (Second Series), Dec., 1937. 269 pp.

Tsukamoto, T., *The Old and New Coins of Japan*. Osaka: Tōyō Kahei Kyōkai, 1930. 205 pp.

3. Periodical Articles.

*Asakawa, K., "Notes on Village Government in Japan after 1600," *Journal of the American Oriental Society*. (1910), Part II, 259–300; (1911), Part II, 151–216.

Borton, Hugh, "Peasant Uprisings in Japan of the Tokugawa Period," *Transactions of the Asiatic Society of Japan* (hereafter, *TASJ*), 2nd Series 16 (1938), 1–120.

*Brown, Delmer M., "Importation of Gold into Japan by the Portuguese during the Sixteenth Century," *Pacific Historical Review*, XVI, 2 (May, 1947), 125–33.

Droppers, Garrett, "The Population of Japan in the Tokugawa Period," *TASJ* 22, 2 (1894), 253–84.

*Fisher, Galen M., "Kumazawa Banzan, His Life and Ideas," *TASJ*, 2nd Series 16 (1938), 222–58.

Fisher, Galen M., "Dai Gaku Wakumon, a Discussion of Public Questions in the Light of the Great Learning, by Kumazawa Banzan," *TASJ*, 2nd Series 16 (May 1938), 259–356.

Hall, John W., "The Castle Town and Japan's Modern Urbanization," *Far Eastern Quarterly*, XV, 1 (Nov. 1955), 37–56.

Hall, John W., "Notes on the Early Ch'ing Copper Trade with Japan," *Harvard Journal of Asiatic Studies*, 12 (1949), 444–61.

Hall, John W., "The Tokugawa Bakufu and the Merchant Class," *Occasional Papers*, Center for Japanese Studies, University of Michigan, 1 (1951), 26–33.

Henderson, Dan F., "Some Aspects of Tokugawa Law," *Washington Law Review*, 27, 1 (Feb., 1952), 85–109.

Hibbett, Howard S., "Saikaku as a Realist," *Harvard Journal of Asiatic Studies*, 15, 3–4 (Dec. 1952), 408–18.

*Honjo, Eijiro, "Changes of Social Classes during the Tokugawa Period," *Kyoto University Economic Review* (hereafter *KUER*), I (July 1928), 56–75.

*Honjo, Eijiro, "Economic Thought in Tokugawa Days," *KUER*, XIII, 1 (July, 1938), 1–22.

*Honjo, Eijiro, "Facts and Ideas of Japan's Over-sea Development prior to the Meiji Restoration," *KUER*, XVII, 1 (Jan. 1942), 1–13.

*Honjo, Eijiro, "Financial Development of Japan," *KUER*, V, 2 (Dec. 1930), 66–80; VI, 1 (July 1931), 14–28.

*Honjo, Eijiro, "From the Tokugawa Period to the Meiji Restoration," *KUER*, VII (July 1932), 32–51.

*Honjo, Eijiro, "Japan's Overseas Trade in the Closing Days of the Tokugawa Shogunate," *KUER*, XIV, 2 (April, 1939), 1–23.

*Honjo, Eijiro, "On the Finance of the Tokugawa Government," *KUER*, VI, 2 (Dec. 1932), 16–33.

*Honjo, Eijiro, "Population Problems in the Tokugawa Era," *KUER*, II, 2 (Dec. 1927), 42–63.

*Honjo, Eijiro, "A Short History of Social Problems in Japan before the Restoration," *KUER*, VIII, 2 (Dec. 1928), 41–85.

*Honjo, Eijiro, "A Survey of Economic Thought in the Closing Days of the Tokugawa Period," *KUER*, XIII, 2 (Oct. 1938), 21–39.

*Honjo, Eijiro, "Views in (sic) the Taxation on Commerce in the Closing Days of the Tokugawa Age," *KUER*, XVI, 3 (July, 1941), 1–15.

Horie, Yasuzo, "Clan Monopoly Policy in the Tokugawa Period," *KUER*, XVII, 1 (Jan. 1942), 31–52.

*Horie, Yasuzo, "Development of Economic Policy during the Later Tokugawa Period," *KUER*, 4 (Oct. 1942), 48–63.

Horie, Yasuzo, "The Life Structure of the Japanese People in Its Historical Aspects," *KUER*, XXI, 1 (April 1951), 1–22.

Horie, Yasuzo, "An Outline of Economic Policy in the Tokugawa Period," *KUER*, XV, 4 (Oct. 1940), 44–65.

*Horie, Yasuzo, "An Outline of the Rise of Modern Capitalism in Japan," *KUER*, XI, 1 (July, 1936), 99–115.

Ike, Nobutaka, "The Development of Capitalism in Japan," *Pacific Affairs*, 22, 2 (June 1949), 185–90.

*Kirby, R. J., trans., "Food and Wealth. An Essay by Dazai Jun," *TASJ*, 35, 2 (1908), 113-190.

*Knox, G. W., trans., "'Hyō-chū-ori-taku-shiba-no-ki,' Autobiography of Arai Hakuseki, a Scholar, Poet, Historian, Economist, Moralist, and Statesman of the End of the 17th and Beginning of the 18th Century A.D.," *TASJ*, 30, 2 (1902), 1–11, 89–238.

Mitsui, Takafusa, "Chōnin's Life under Feudalism," *Cultural Nippon*, 8, 2 (June 1940), 65–96.

Norman, E. Herbert, "Andō Shōeki and the Anatomy of Japanese Feudalism," *TASJ*, 3rd Series II (Dec. 1949), 340 pp.

Royds, W. M., "Japanese Patent Medicines," *TASJ*, XXXV, Part I (Aug. 1907), 1–14.

*Sano Zensaku and Sentaro Iura, "Commodity Exchanges in Japan," *Annals of the American Academy of Social and Political Science*, 155 (May 1931), 223–233.

Sawada, Sho, "Financial Difficulties of the Edo Bakufu," (Trans. by Hugh Borton), *Harvard Journal of Asiatic Studies*, I, 3–4 (1936), 308–26.

Sheldon, Charles David, "Some Economic Reasons for the Marked Contrast in Japanese and Chinese Modernization, as Seen in Examples from 'Pre-modern' Shipping and Trading by Water," *KUER*, XXIII, 2 (Oct. 1953), 30–60.

*Simmons, D.B., and Wigmore, John H., Notes on Land Tenure and Local Institutions in Old Japan," *TASJ*, XIX (1891), 37–270.

*Smith, Neil Skene, "An Introduction to Some Japanese Economic Writings of the 18th Century," *TASJ*, XI (2nd Series), 1934, 32–165.

Smith, Neil Skene, ed., "Materials on Japanese Social and Economic History: Tokugawa Japan," *TASJ*, XIV (2nd Series), 1937, 1–175.

Smith, Thomas C., "The Introduction of Western Industry to Japan during the Last Years of the Tokugawa Period," *Harvard Journal of Asiatic Studies*, II, 1–2 (June, 1948), 130–152.

Smith, Thomas C., "The Japanese Village in the Seventeenth Century," "Journal of Economic History, XII, 1 (Winter, 1952), 1–20.

Spurr, William A., "Business Cycles in Japan before 1853," *Journal of Political Economy*, XLVI, 5 (Oct. 1938), 653–87.

Wigmore, John Henry, ed., "Materials for the Study of Private Law in Old Japan," *TASJ*, XX (1892), Supplement I, Introduction, 1–203.

Wittfogel, Karl, "The Foundations and Stages of Chinese Economic History," *Zeitschrift fur Sozialforschung*, IV (1935), 26–60.

*Zachert, Herbert, "Social Changes During the Tokugawa Period, *TASJ*, 2nd Series, 17 (1938), 238–54.

III. General Works.

Honjo, Eijiro, *The Social and Economic History of Japan*. Kyoto: Institute for Research in Economic History of Japan, 1935. 410 pp.

Murdoch, James, *A History of Japan*. London: Kegan Paul, 1926. 3 Vols.

Sansom, George B., *Japan, a Short Cultural History*. New York: D. Appleton-Century Co., Revised Edition, 1943. 554 pp.

Sansom, George B., *The Western World and Japan*. New York: Knopf, 1950. 504. pp.

Takekoshi, Yosoburo (sic), *The Economic Aspects of the History of the Civilization of Japan*. London: Allen and Unwin, Ltd., 1930. 3 Vols.

Takekoshi Yosaburō 竹越與三郎, *Nihon Keizai Shi* 日本經濟史 [Economic History of Japan]. Tokyo: Heibonsha, 3rd ed., 1936. 12 Vols.

IV. Japanese Bibliographical and Reference works.

Honjō Eijirō, ed., *Nihon Keizai Shi Bunken* 日本經濟史文献 [A Bibliography of Japanese Economic History]. Tokyo, Nihon Hyōronsha, 1933-1953. 3 Vols.

Honjō, ed., *Nihon Keizai Shi Jiten* 日本經濟史辭典 [A Dictionary of Japanese Economic History]. Tokyo: Nihon Hyōronsha, 1940. 3 Vols., or 6 fascicles, with continuous pagination.

INDEX

Abacus (*soroban*), 69

Abortion, 100

Actors, 94

Advertising: lack of effective medium, 48; "singing commercial," ftnte., p. 48; immoral to stimulate demand for commercial goods, 141

Agricultural productivity; increase in early period, 4; only small gains after Genroku, 100; improvement of, ftnte., pp. 141–142; crop encouragement, 148

Ainu, 70, 150

Aizu, 46, 148, 157

Akita, 162

Alienation of land, 27, 75

Andō Shōeki, ftnte., p. 143

Anonymous combinations for plural ownership of enterprises, 51–52

Apprentice system, 52–53; ftnte., p. 66; 91, 112

Arai Hakuseki, ftntes., pp. 67 and 112

Artisans (*shokunin*): rationale of social status, 26; treatment as a class by the *Bakufu*, 30–31; outproduced by peasants, 150

Artisan-merchants (*shoku-akindo*), 26

Ashikaga period, 12, 22, 45, 165

"Back-to-Ieyasu" movement, 104

"Back-room renters," ftnte., p. 118

Bakufu, 4, 8, 9, 12, 13, 17, 18, 20, 22, 33–37, 41, 42, 46, 49, 50, 51, 58, 65, 66, 68, 71, 73, 76, 77, 86, 87, 99, 102–108, 110–120, 122–125, 127–130, 136–138, 141–143, 145, 149, 150, 162–163, 165, 166, 168

Banishment, ftntes., pp. 103, 119 and 129

Bansen system, 59, 61, 62, 73

Bantō (chief apprentices), 52, 53; ftnte., p. 66

Barriers (*sekisho*), 12–13, 15, 24

Barter economy, 144

Bekke (separate merchant's or artisan's establishment), 52

Bills of exchange (*tegata*), 43, 56, 65, 70, 149

Birth control, 100

Biwako (Lake Biwa), 32

Black-listing by *nakama*, 56

"Blind money," 77

Bodhisattva, 92, 139

Bon (Buddhist festival for the dead), 52; ftnte., p. 68

Bottomry (*nagegane*), 19

Brass guild, ftnte., p. 50; 115–116

Bridge building, 15

Bribery. See Gifts and bribes.

Buddhist organizations: formidable enemies of Nobunaga; 7; Shin sect, 9, 138; temple warehouses, 10; protecting merchants, 12; temple "manors" (*shōen*), 13; money lending by temples, 75; keeping prostitutes, ftnte., p. 115

Bugyō (magistrate), ftnte., p. 33

Bunka-Bunsei eras, 102, 124

Bushidō (code of the warriors), 96

Buying on margin, 56, 57

By-passing and breaking of city monopolies by provincial merchants, 160–161, 164

Canal building, 68

Cancellation of debts (*kien*), 122 and ftnte.; 123, 127–128, 130, 166; (*tokusei*), 166

Candle guild (*rōsoku-za*) of Kaga, 156–158, 164

194

APPENDIX

'PRE-MODERN' MERCHANTS AND
MODERNIZATION IN JAPAN[1]

THE problem of the degree of economic development which took place in the Tokugawa period (1600–1868) and its effects on the modernization of Japan .has given rise to considerable controversy. This is in part due to Marxist efforts to fit this development into Marxian categories, and to see in it elements of class struggle. These efforts have met stiff opposition from historians who have shown fairly persuasively how inapplicable these concepts are to the period. The trouble goes much further than this, however. Any kind of statistical measurement of the degree of economic development before 1868 is vastly complicated by the scarcity and by the notorious inaccuracy of Tokugawa statistical records, both public and private. Then, there is the inherent difficulty of discovering exactly how important a role the merchant class, for example, played in the downfall of the Tokugawa Shogunate, in the demise of feudalism, and in the modernization of Japan which followed. The general lines of the story of the merchant class before 1868, whose 'rise' was chiefly economic and cultural, rather than political, are fairly well known among students of Japan. They have been outlined, for example, in this writer's book on the subject. But a number of points of interpretation remain to be made, even drawing largely from material in that book. Here, after sketching in the background, we would like to push the interpretation of the role of the merchants a bit further, taking into consideration more recent scholarship on the subject.

A hundred years ago, the Japanese were on the threshold of the dynamic transformation which has resulted in what we can now call a modernized, industrialized nation. In fact, Japan has become the third most important industrial nation in the world, after the USA and the USSR. When Commodore Perry arrived to force open the

[1]Reprinted from *Modern Asian Studies,* 5, 3 (1971), Cambridge University Press

door a crack, Japan was still a largely feudal state, with roughly 75 per cent of its population engaged in agriculture. For more than two hundred years, Japan had been largely isolated from the rest of the world. The nationalism which supplied the motive force for the effort to modernize got out of hand in the 1930s and 1940s, with unfortunate results. But Japan's economic achievement, largely a bootstrap operation, sets Japan aside as the only Asian nation to modernize successfully. Little help came from outside; some loans were resorted to, mainly for railway construction, but these were quickly repaid due to fears, largely unjustified, of economic dependence leading to a further loss of sovereignty. Students were sent abroad, and for a time foreign technicians, advisers and educators were employed. Japan's achievement becomes all the more impressive when one remembers the poverty of the bulk of the population, already more than thirty million in 1868, the poverty in natural resources, and the fact that Japan's efforts were somewhat hampered by the unequal treaties (complete tariff autonomy was obtained only in 1911). Given this seemingly unpromising beginning, how do we account for this successful response, which contrasts so strikingly with China's, to the threat posed by the intrusion of the Western powers?

Western observers, seeing the Japanese quickly adapting Western ideas, techniques and institutions to their own use, interpreted it as a kind of miracle of energetic pragmatism, a rather gratifying proof of the superiority of Western European or American ways, and of their applicability to non-European societies. They assumed that underdeveloped (they would have said 'backward') countries, given sufficiently clear-sighted and energetic leadership, could easily do likewise. But as more recent experience with the economic and political troubles of modernization has shown, energetic and clear-sighted leadership, as in India, cannot alone assure success in modernization.

Clearly, a political and economic system that changed so rapidly had to have already existing within it a very great potential for change. To begin with, Japan had been undergoing a long period of feudalism, during which contractual relationships and a more impersonal, bureaucratic rule of law were beginning to emerge. The obvious analogy here is not to Asia, but to Europe, where capitalism grew out of similar feudal systems. In looking more closely at Japan's history before 1868, historians have found the Tokugawa period not nearly so static as earlier scholars had assumed. The Japanese involved in the modernizing process, who themselves were the beneficiaries of changes which had occurred during the Tokugawa period, viewed it as dull, static and stultifying, in contrast to the colour, excitement and relative freedom of modernizing Japan. But this is no doubt because, as Marius Jansen has put it, 'They were so glad to be out of it that they had nothing good to say for it.'[2] Historians have nevertheless discovered in the Tokugawa period many elements which combined to furnish an important set of preconditions essential to modernization. These included, in 1868, the consciousness of the nation as the principal object of loyalty, and the existence of a literate population estimated at about 35 per cent, capable of translating national goals into reality at the local as well as the national level. The majority of the population proved willing to accept, even to welcome, radical changes, towards which some steps had already been taken before 1868.

The very considerable growth, within the Tokugawa feudal system, of a money economy, domestic trade on a national scale, and incipient capitalism in agriculture as well as in handicraft industry, spread throughout much of Japan the profit motive and the substitution of a 'cash nexus' for feudal or traditional social relations. This played a crucial part in creating a more rational, pragmatic approach to problems, and an openness to change. Here we will confine ourselves to a short outline of the economic changes in which the merchant was the foremost agent. He was also the unknowing agent of economic forces which, although they did not bring down the feudal system, did much to weaken the position of the Tokugawa regime.

In 1467, when armed struggles broke out which led to more than a century of sporadic civil wars, feudal localism had reached the point where neither the Shogun nor the Emperor had any real national power or influence. Important institutional changes took place during the wars among local barons (daimyō), until a gradual consolidation of domains took place with the appearance of able military leaders who made use of new methods of warfare, including firearms, and more effective political organization, to achieve the unification of Japan. It was left to the Tokugawa Shoguns, who completed this process, to transform their military organization into a peacetime governing bureaucracy (or rather, as the military organization was retained, to change its functions to deal with peacetime problems). Merchants,

---

[2] 'Tokugawa and Modern Japan' in Jansen and Hall, eds., *Studies in the Institutional History of Early Modern Japan* (Princeton: 1968), 318–19. Also in this collection, E. S. Crawcour, in 'Changes in Japanese Commerce in the Tokugawa Period', 189–212, ably and rightly stresses the regional, functional, and chronological diversity of the Tokugawa merchants, but in presenting the study as a revision of previous work, criticizes it in a somewhat uncharitable and inaccurate manner. (See my review in *Pacific Affairs*, Winter 1969–70, 528–9.)

some of them living in self-governing commercial towns, who had risen to prominence as purveyors of goods needed in the wars, or who had prospered in the foreign trade, lost their immediate importance and influence with the feudal lords and Shoguns when the wars ended and most foreign trade was cut off. They had to be content with developing domestic commerce and banking, which they did with energy.

Although no longer having a political role to play, townsmen were given new economic advantages. The feudal rulers competed among themselves to welcome merchants and artisans to their fast-growing castle towns and cities, offering them free business sites and excusing them from the payment of property taxes, in order to provide for the economic services they needed. The military men began to settle down to enjoy the peace they had achieved, served by the lesser members of the society. Neo-Confucian ideas were utilized in stabilizing the society, and an ancient Chinese theory of social class was seized upon in an effort to prevent the recurrence of what was seen as the social chaos of the preceding years. *Shinōkōshō*, in its Japanese pronunciation, was a physiocratic theory classifying people into four major functional categories. In order of importance, they were: (*shi*) the *samurai*, a small educated ruling class; (*nō*) peasants, the only real producers, and the bulk of the population; (*kō*) artisans, who changed the form of things, and were therefore useful, and (*shō*) merchants, who merely moved things around and held them available for purchase, and were accordingly the least important of all. This theory was taken seriously only in the late 16th century and integrated into an effort to avoid the unsettling social mobility of the civil wars which had finally been brought to an end. It was applied to a degree and in a way never imagined in China.

A legal monopoly of function (including weapons for the *samurai*) and a particularistic criminal code were fixed according to class. Movement between classes was prohibited, and status was hereditary. 'The offspring of a toad is a toad; of a merchant, a merchant!' 'Know your station in life!' These were popular sayings of the time.

The *samurai* were thus both morally and legally placed above matters of commerce and money-making, and the merchants, at the bottom of the social scale, were given a monopoly of these functions.[3] Merchants lost little time in taking advantage of this, elaborating an extremely complex financial and distribution system, and forging a new class consciousness and solidarity within the feudal system. They built the

[3] It should be remembered that in the agrarian society of the late sixteenth century, these functions were still not very important.

great storehouses in Osaka and other centres used for the excess tax commodities (mostly rice) sent by the feudal rulers to the central markets, for which they collected a modest standard commission for storing and selling, totalling from 2 per cent to 4 per cent of market value. These privileged rice merchants were given stipends and permitted by the feudal lords to use surnames and to wear the two swords, otherwise the privilege of the *samurai*. But the bulk of their incomes came from loans. They made advances to the feudal lords and *samurai* on the security of crops not yet harvested, because members of the ruling class, whose spending tended to run far ahead of income, needed money throughout the year. The merchants collected usually from 15 per cent to 20 per cent per annum on these loans. Fifteen per cent was the legal maximum during most of the Tokugawa period, but lenders often made additional charges. The privileged rice merchants also prospered on the money and commodity exchanges, and became expert at waiting for higher prices before marketing goods.

The Shogunal institution which contributed most to the development of the money economy and to the prosperity of the merchants was the *sankin kōtai*. This was the system of alternate attendance on the Shogun. The feudal lords, who economically were virtually independent in their domains and paid no taxes to the Shogun, were required to travel with their retinues to Edo, the Shogun's capital, and remain for regular intervals, usually a year, spending the alternate year in their own domains. As their families were required to live permanently in Edo, they had to build and maintain residences there, and their wives and children became hostages to guarantee the loyalty of the lords during their absences from the capital. Roughly half the expenditures from the treasuries of the feudal lords were connected with the *sankin kōtai*. In addition, these expenditures had to be made outside their own domains in money which they had no legal right to coin (although many obtained the right to issue paper money for use within their own domains). This made it necessary for them to send off to national markets like Osaka and Edo maximum amounts of commodities collected as taxes, in order to convert them into cash. The entire operation was managed by merchants who, of course, handled non-official goods as well. Villages began to abandon their traditional self-sufficient economies, and itinerant merchants began to appear, selling fertilizers, tools, and other needs of the peasants, including increasing amounts of consumer goods. By the late 17th century, the money economy had penetrated into the agricultural villages. The Osaka novelist Ihara Saikaku (1642–93) was surprised to find money in use in the most remote villages, where as he wrote, 'they think dried sea-bream grow on trees, and where no one knows how to use an umbrella'.[4]

The next logical step was for merchants to make arrangements for the villages to produce the goods which were in demand in the cities and towns. Farmers devoted more acres to cash crops, and engaged in cottage handicrafts when not occupied in the fields. Putting-out systems were in operation in the late 17th century, and a factory system, without power-driven machinery, which had begun earlier in such industries as *sake* brewing, extended to textiles and other handicraft industries in the 18th and 19th centuries. Many small establishments were operated by well-to-do peasants in the villages.

There were several factors stimulating this development of investment in productive enterprises: to begin with, there was inflation. The price of rice rose by three and a half times in the 17th century, and by the middle of the 19th century it had reached eleven times the price in 1616. The attraction of usury was still strong, but inflation operated in favour of investment in productive enterprises, as one could expect that in the future goods produced would be sold at higher prices, while the money paid back by debtors would have less value. There is more to it than this, of course, and it raises the question of why interest on loans in Japan remained so low compared to India and China. The feudal rulers had a way of arbitrarily confiscating merchants' wealth when their profiteering exceeded what was thought proper, so fear of retribution had something to do with it. But strong desires for social esteem in a society whose ideals called for the sacrifice of individual to group interests were perhaps more important. Also the merchants' monopoly of commercial and financial functions offered little motivation for profiteering in order to buy oneself or one's descendants into a higher social class, illegal in any case, but occasionally done. The merchant code called for honesty, moderate profits, frugality, and the establishment of good reputation and credit. The family enterprise head's primary responsibility was to the family, of whom ancestors and descendants were equal members. As the enterprise had been built up by the ancestors, it was essential, indeed something akin to a religious duty, to preserve it, expand it, and assure a better future for the heirs-to-come, and this encouraged a long-run view of business profits.

There is little doubt that by the end of the 17th century, prosperity was more widespread than at any earlier time in Japanese history. The observant German physician at the small Dutch trading post in

⁴ Howard S. Hibbett, 'Saikaku as a Realist', *Harvard Journal of Asiatic Studies*, 15, 3-4 (December 1952), 411.

Nagasaki, Engelbert Kaempfer, who had a rare opportunity to travel to the 'three great cities', Osaka, Kyoto (the Imperial city), and (Y)edo, wrote, in 1691, 'The city of Jedo is a nursery of artists, handicraftsmen, merchants and tradesmen, and yet everything is sold dearer than anywhere else in the Empire, by reason of the great concourse of people, and the number of idle monks and courtiers, as also the difficult importing of provisions and other commodities. . . .' Of Kyoto, he said, 'There are but few houses in all the chief streets, where there is not something to be sold, and for my part, I could not help admiring, whence they can have customers enough for such an immense quantity of goods.' In another passage, he observes, 'It is scarce credible, how much trade and commerce is carried on between the several provinces and parts of the Empire! how full their ports of ships! how many rich and flourishing towns up and down the Country! There are such multitudes of people along the coasts, and near the sea-ports, such a noise of oars and sails . . . that one would be apt to imagine the whole nation had settled there, and all the inland parts of the Country were left quite desart and empty.'[5] The population of Osaka was roughly 350,000, Kyoto 450,000 and Edo 800,000 at the time. Sir George Sansom has well described the Genroku period (1688–1703) as the 'zenith of Tokugawa prosperity, and perhaps even the justification of feudal rule, for here was peace and plenty and a great flourishing of the arts—a happy society as human societies go'.[6]

But even by 1703 there were signs that the economic expansion was slowing to a halt. The great period of building after the destructive civil wars, of castles, temples, castle towns and cities, including the imposing residences in Edo of the feudal lords and their retainers, was at an end, and peasants coming into the cities and towns looking for work found little. By the middle of the 18th century it was clear that there was a widening gap between rich and poor, in the villages as well as in the cities and towns. Japan had entered what later historians came to call the 'Tokugawa plateau', a period in which there was little further expansion and little further increase in population. There was much evidence of endemic depression with terrible famines, increasingly frequent local peasant uprisings and, finally, riots and looting in the cities directed mainly at merchants who were thought, often correctly, to be hoarding foodstuffs in periods of scarcity, waiting for even higher prices. The feudal authorities found no permanent solutions.

[5] *History of Japan, 1690–1692* (New York: 1906, English translation of 1727), III, 76, 316–17.
[6] *The Western World and Japan* (New York: 1950), 197.

This is perhaps understandable in a period when Malthusian controls were operating in a largely isolated country unable to import needed foodstuffs in emergencies, and where even to move foodstuffs over feudal boundaries within the country was almost impossible. Debasement of the coinage, forced loans and confiscations levied against the merchants, who were blamed, because of their 'greed', for the high prices and the general economic dislocation, and inept efforts at price control, only caused even greater price fluctuations. The feudal rulers and *samurai*, despite reforms including retrenchment and frugality measures, remained deeply in debt to merchant lenders, and peasants who had failed to adjust to the money economy and whose tax burden was increased, were in the depths of poverty made all the harder to bear by the obvious prosperity of well-to-do peasants in the villages who were flourishing in commerce, usury, and often in industry as well.

Most Japanese writers on Tokugawa economic history see the rise of the money economy controlled by the merchants, the spread of commercialism in the agricultural villages, and the beginnings of capitalistic organization of production, as 'inevitably contradictory' to the feudal system based on land tenure. It is hard to agree, for several reasons:

(1) During the first hundred years of the Tokugawa period, the unification of the country and peace brought an unprecedented expansion of towns and cities, a steady increase in agricultural production greater than the population increase (from about 18 million in 1600 to about 26 million in 1700), economic expansion, higher standards of living and increasing prosperity which affected even the villages. During this time there was quite clearly a rather happy coexistence between the commercial and money economy operated by prosperous merchants, who were thought of as commercial retainers and furnishers of money and loans to the feudal lords and *samurai*, and the feudal system under which the military ruling class collected taxes in kind from the land.

(2) It would appear that throughout the period, the vast majority of Tokugawa merchants were fairly well satisfied with the *status quo*, and one looks in vain for revolutionaries among them. There was a modest attempt by scholarly writers, including merchant writers, to justify trade and reasonable profits, as contributing to the general welfare. But any expectation that merchant scholars would have striven for the enhancement of commerce is not fulfilled. They made no attempt to glorify trade or to claim a more realistic (*i.e.*, higher) place in society for the merchant class. Rather, they tried to harmonize commerce and the merchants within the feudal system, and to make the merchants

satisfied with the social structure as it was. The acceptance by merchant scholars of a subordinate role for merchants was no doubt based in part on the recognition of the close interdependence of the merchants and the *samurai*, their principal customers and protectors of the privileged rice merchants, financial agents and purveyors who were the élite members of the class. The merchants, who enjoyed no legal security of person or property, had reason to fear a sometimes aroused tyranny, and the more cautious, established merchants were obviously aware of the force of the popular adage that the protruding nail will be hit on the head. This general attitude was also strongly influenced by powerful social pressures for the sacrifice of individual, family or small group interests to the larger group, ultimately, to the interests of the society as a whole.

(3) In the event, Tokugawa merchants played a largely passive role in the Restoration movement. It is true that merchants provided funds, on occasion, for the Imperial armies during the struggle against the pro-Tokugawa forces. But these contributions can hardly have been called voluntary. They took the form of forced loans from merchants in Osaka when the city had been taken by the Imperial armies, and additional 'contributions' from prominent merchant bankers like the Mitsui who continued, through necessity, to supply funds to the other side. Also, some sons of merchants joined the militia units organized, for example, in Chōshū, the most consistently anti-Tokugawa feudal domain, when Chōshū was preparing to defend itself both against foreigners and Shogunal punitive forces. But these were chiefly sons who were not inheriting the family enterprise, and this was, hopefully, a means of rising socially from the lowest to the highest position.

(4) Finally, the Restoration movement, which in the period 1853–68 brought down the old Tokugawa regime and substituted a more centralized political control under the Emperor, was not led by advocates of a modern, capitalist economy, which was in any case little understood at the time. The two feudal domains whose semi-modernized military forces forced the resignation of the Shogun were perhaps the most feudal in organization and outlook in Japan. At the same time, they were convinced of the effectiveness of Western arms and tactics, and had made excellent use of surplus American rifles secretly purchased after the American Civil War. The *samurai* leaders from these two fiefs did not mean to replace the feudal system, but only to replace the Tokugawa semi-centralized political system by one which would exclude the Tokugawa and create a much more effectively centralized system under the Emperor which would put their own domains, and themselves, formerly largely excluded from national political life, into control. The

old régime, clearly unable to deal effectively with either financial problems or troublesome foreign powers, was seen as a liability to the nation. There was a pressing need for a truly national government which could deal effectively with the double menace: the domestic crisis and the foreign threat.

It was only later that the new leaders, now in control of an imperial government, and aided by others with greater knowledge of the West, began to realize that the West was not simply a threat, but a challenge and an opportunity as well. Old solutions had proved wanting, and with the slogan, 'A prosperous nation, a strong military', they began an ambitious program of political and economic reform, to catch up with the West. The *samurai* were the natural political leaders in this effort, and played a conspicuous part, especially in the first years, in leading the economic modernization.

To go back for a moment to the problem of the 'Tokugawa plateau', one can find many reasons for it. Some have already been suggested. One could add here the point that the *sankin kōtai* system, which did so much to stimulate the economic expansion of the 17th century, acted as a drag after that time. Financial difficulties, retrenchment, cutting of *samurai*'s stipends, and exhortations to frugality affected not only general spending but the scale of the *sankin kōtai* system as well: the numbers of retainers brought along to Edo, and the style of life of the feudal lords and their retainers. Also, there was a continued trend towards a retreat by the feudal lords from freer trade, and mercantilistic efforts to ship goods out, prohibit certain imports, and bring money into the various feudal domains ultimately became self-defeating and inhibited the further expansion of commerce.

Among peasants, the switch, gradual but far-reaching, from basic food crops to cash crops complicated the task of the feudal authorities in collecting increased taxes in commodities to provide sufficient income for the increasing *samurai* population, which reached about two million, including families, by 1868, while still leaving enough food for the peasants in years when crops were bad. Socially, the earlier cooperative self-sufficient organization of the villages had been to some degree replaced, especially in areas near the cities and towns, by small individual families dependent upon their very small holdings and unstable markets and no longer enjoying the security of the larger group.[7]

[7] See Thomas C. Smith, *The Agrarian Origins of Modern Japan* (Stanford: 1959). In the Tokugawa period, people can be classified either by actual function or by social class, and this can cause some confusion. Smith's peasant usurers, traders and capitalists and my 'provincial merchants' are roughly identical.

Although capitalistic farming had brought potential advantages, it also brought much insecurity and economic dislocation. Unable to pay debts, many smallholders absconded, sometimes leaving the land untilled, and peasant rebellions from time to time also decreased the yield of the land.

Among all classes, the 'cash nexus' had begun to replace traditional relationships, and the *samurai*, pressed for money, dismissed retainers, who were expected to fight with them, or hired them for short periods. As war seemed to have been permanently abolished, they did not keep up martial exercises (some were too busy staving off poverty with cottage industries in their homes). Many even sold or pawned their weapons and armour. These trends were much stronger in the areas of Japan which had developed first, where exploitation of agriculture and commerce had been most efficient, that is, in the central areas, where most of the domains of the Tokugawa family and its hereditary followers were concentrated.

The least economically troubled areas included the parts of western and southern Japan where there had been much more potential for agricultural improvements and expansion, and in this area were the two 'outer' fiefs, Chōshū and Satsuma, which combined ultimately to bring down the Tokugawa regime. Chōshū and Satsuma had been notably successful in keeping commercialism both at a minimum and under control, and in preserving feudal loyalties and fighting spirit. In this way it can be said that the money economy controlled by the merchants, who without doubt were quite unaware of any responsibility, contributed to the fall of the Shoguns. But the money economy was by no means the sole cause of the Shoguns' troubles. Basically, the population was simply too large, given the isolation of Japan, the limitations of the political structure, and the stage of technological development of agriculture and industry. Things were quite otherwise after Japan abandoned its isolation and its outdated political structure, and began the great effort, ultimately successful, for change and technological improvement.

In its economic reforms of the Meiji period (1868–1912), the new government, seizing upon the Western example, instituted financial policies and institutional reforms essential to Japan's economic modernization. It also took the initiative in establishing modern capitalist enterprises, model factories, etc., later mostly sold to private entrepreneurs. The building of a modern economy was considered a patriotic duty, giving commerce, industry and finance a new respectability. Patriotism provided a heaven-sent justification for the participation of *samurai* (deprived of their traditional prerogatives and given government bonds in place of stipends) and affluent former 'peasants' as well in the otherwise defiling business of making money. Seldom have self gain and national gain been so closely identified. In Natsume Sōseki's novel, *Sore Kara* (Since Then), the son of a successful Meiji capitalist says, 'Father . . . told me that from the age of eighteen until today he has gone on serving the country to the best of his ability. . . . If you can make as much money as father has by serving the nation, I wouldn't mind serving it myself.'[8]

The principal economic planners and instigators in government were without doubt former *samurai*, although some moved between government and industry, and some were of very recent *samurai* status. Shibusawa Ei'ichi, who began the first large modern cotton spinning mill, is a good example of this type. Until recently, the generally accepted view was that the chief entrepreneurs were ex-*samurai* who had the initial advantages of close associations within the government and superior education, sometimes including foreign travel and study. They lacked the extreme conservatism and caution which had become typical of the established merchants, were willing to take risks, and thought less of personal, or family, gain than of the national good. This represented a natural Meiji period adaptation of the *samurai* ethic of loyalty and service under which business leaders could fight on an economic battlefield to raise Japan from shameful inferiority to the position of a great power, and a prosperous one. This type of enterpriser, considered unique and representative, has been called 'the community-centered entrepreneur'.[9]

But recent scholarship asks just how important class lines were, whether the *samurai* entrepreneur was truly representative, and, perhaps most important, questions whether the *samurai* ethic of selfless devotion to the nation furnished the real motive of Meiji businessmen. First, the picture was modified by Father Hirschmeier in the most substantial contribution thus far to the study of Meiji entrepreneurs. He has shown the class lines blurring, brave new *samurai* enterprises meeting early and untimely deaths, and men of essentially merchant origins (many coming from the villages, where commercial activities had been less

[8] Quoted in Maruyama Masao, *Thought and Behaviour in Modern Japanese Politics* (London: 1963), 7. The effort to create a respectable image for the entrepreneur is most interestingly treated in Johannes Hirschmeier, *The Origins of Entrepreneurship in Meiji Japan* (Harvard: 1964), 162–75. Also see B. K. Marshall, *Capitalism and Nationalism in Prewar Japan, The Ideology of the Business Elite, 1868–1941* (Stanford: 1967).

[9] See G. Ranis, 'The Community-centered Entrepreneur in Japanese Development', *Explorations in Entrepreneurial History* 2 (December 1955), 80–97.

shackled by tradition and conservatism), coming to the fore as business leaders. Established merchants tended to hold back, waiting to see where the best new opportunities lay. Sometimes forced to change by new competition, both foreign and domestic, many finally joined in the effort which was to bring the economy up to date and create 'a prosperous nation and a strong military', but only when it was clearly profitable to do so. On the difficult problem of motives, Hirschmeier on the whole tends to take Meiji businessmen at their word as putting the good of the nation before their own interests. His examples of the reckless pursuit of unpromising projects give substance to this view. Hirschmeier's typical captains of industry are romantic, not always rational operators who may have begun out of love of profits and power, but, leaving the past behind, achieved 'a vision of a new order and a new ideal', and became 'industrial pioneers with a sense of mission for the country and its economy'.[10]

More recently, Yamamura Kozo, who has done good work on the *zaibatsu*, the leading commercial–industrial–financial combines, and on the lives of Meiji business leaders, apparently views the 'community-centered' entrepreneur as rather too flattering a concept. He assigns greater importance to commercial origins and motives, concentrating on examples of profit-making and seeing expressions of high-minded patriotism as little more than the erection of pious, conventional façades. Yasuda Zenjirō, the founder of the famous banking-centred *zaibatsu*, as described by Yamamura, was a self-made man of humble provincial origins, a remarkable example of the rational, far-sighted, single-minded profit maximizer who fits closely the Western, especially the American, image of the business tycoon.[11] *Samurai* in banking, after some early failures, provided capital rather than management for banking enterprises; merchant money exchangers and bankers dominated the field after 1876, when the new banking law made banking profitable.[12] It is perhaps understandable that experienced merchant

---

[10] *The Origins of Entrepreneurship* . . ., 244. See also, in W. W. Lockwood, ed., *The State and Economic Enterprise in Japan* (Princeton: 1965), two important contributions which pursue this general line: Horie Yasuzō, 'Modern Entrepreneurship in Meiji Japan', 183–208, and Hirschmeier, 'Shibusawa Eiichi: Industrial Pioneer', 209–47, a somewhat laudatory account of perhaps the outstanding Meiji entrepreneur.

[11] 'A Re-examination of Entrepreneurship in Meiji Japan (1868–1912)', *Economic History Review*, 2nd Ser. 21 (April 1968), 144–58.

[12] 'The Role of the Samurai in the Development of Modern Banking in Japan', *Journal of Economic History* XXVII (1967), 198–220. Hugh T. Patrick, in R. Cameron, ed., *Banking in the Early Stages of Industrialization* (New York: 1967), 'Japan, 1868–1914', 239–89, gives support to Yamamura's interpretation of the profit motive in banking, which played such a crucial role in Japan's industrialization.

bankers, putting profits first, would come to control the complex world of banking and finance, but Yamamura imputes the same motives to at least one major '*samurai*' enterprise. The founder of the Mitsubishi *zaibatsu*, Iwasaki Yatarō, whose family had purchased low grade country *samurai* status in Tosa, made a point of employing former *samurai* as managers and enjoyed advantageous personal connexions with government officials. Yamamura's evidence classifies him too as ruthlessly bent on profits before all else.[13]

In the vast Tokugawa merchant houses, Mitsui and Sumitomo, which became the greatest of the modern *zaibatsu*, as well as in most lesser ones, the managers were virtually all merchants, mostly provincial ones, in early training and outlook, if not always in formal classification. They embodied the chief ideals of the Tokugawa merchant code: hard work, frugality, and close calculation which preferred steady and sure profits, even if only moderate, over short-term speculation and which placed great emphasis on saving for investment and reinvestment. In modern as in pre-modern business, the Japanese revealed qualities of enterprise, ingenuity and flexibility. In Meiji times there occurred, rapidly and incompletely, a fusion of merchant and *samurai* values, but much detailed work is required before we can generalize with confidence about the nature of this fusion. In any case, whether their real desires were for personal advantage or national gain and prestige, the energetic activities of the business pioneers did much to profit the nation and the people at large.

The nationwide economy which the 'pre-modern' merchants made into a reality, despite the limitations of technology and of the economic autonomy of the feudal domains, did much to create a general consciousness of the nation as the ultimate object of allegiance. Also, the experience of the Tokugawa merchants, and the profit motive which they had been instrumental in spreading throughout the nation, were essential preconditions to Japan's modernization.

[13] 'The founding of Mitsubishi: A Case Study in Japanese Business History', *Business History Review* XLI (1967), 141–60.